THE MANUAL OF SEED SAVING

THE MANUAL OF SEED SAVING

Harvesting,
Storing,
and Sowing
Techniques
for Vegetables,
Herbs, and Fruits

Andrea Heistinger
In association with
Arche Noah
Pro Specie Rara
translated by **Ian Miller**

Timber Press Portland | London

Frontispiece: Lukas Heilingsetzer's polyculture garden, Austria.
Polycultures help crops outcompete weeds and are in and of
themselves more stable ecosystems.

Copyright © 2003, 2010 by Loewenzahn.
Andrea Heistinger/Beate Koller/Pro Specie Rara: *Handbuch
Samengärtnerei. Sorten erhalten. Vielfalt vermehren. Gemüse geniessen.*
© Loewenzahn Verlag in der Studienverlag Ges.m.b.H.,
Innsbruck-Wien 2004.

Published in 2013 by Timber Press, Inc.

The Haseltine Building
133 S.W. Second Avenue, Suite 450
Portland, Oregon 97204-3527
timberpress.com

2 The Quadrant
135 Salusbury Road
London NW6 6RJ
timberpress.co.uk

Book design by Susan Applegate
Printed in China

Library of Congress Cataloging-in-Publication Data

Heistinger, Andrea.
    [Handbuch Samengärtnerei. English]
    The manual of seed saving: harvesting, storing, and sowing techniques for
vegetables, herbs, and fruits/Andrea Heistinger; Arche Noah, Pro Specie Rara;
translated by Ian Miller.—English-language ed.
        p. cm.
    Translation of: Handbuch Samengärtnerei. Sorten erhalten. Vielfalt vermehren.
Gemüse geniessen.
    Includes bibliographical references and index.
    ISBN 978-1-60469-382-9
    1. Vegetables—Seeds. 2. Vegetables—Propagation. 3. Vegetables—Varieties.
4. Vegetable gardening. I. Arche Noah. II. Pro Specie Rara (Foundation) III. Title.
    SB324.75.H4513 2013
    635—dc23   2012050582

A catalog record for this book is also available from the British Library.

CONTENTS

Radicchio page 74

Kohlrabi page 104

Carrots page 140

Mallow page 161

Pole beans page 186

Malabar spinach page 214

Poppyseed page 245

Fig-leaf gourd page 288

Tomatoes page 302

Tomatillo page 317

ACKNOWLEDGMENTS

THANKS TO

—contributors to the entire book: Beate Koller and Peter Zipser (Arche Noah); Kurt Eichenberger (Pro Specie Rara)

—contributors to individual chapters: Peter Lassnig and Penny Lichtenecker (Arche Noah); Bernd Horneburg, Ludwig Watschong, Quirin Wember, Reinhard Ehrentraut, Friedmunt Sonnemann, and Gerald Krebs (Dreschflegel); Andreas Emmerling-Skala and Ursula Reinhard (VEN)

—Pat and Markus Meier, who made the publishing of this book possible

—Loewenzahn Verlag, and especially Eva Simeaner, for their dedicated support

—all those who have done so much to document crop diversity and promote seed propagation, especially Nancy Arrowsmith and Bernward Geier

—Peter Zipser, who, as head of Arche Noah's preservation gardens, has gained vast knowledge of the cultivation of innumerable species and varieties, which represented an important basis for this book

—Sativa (Amadeus Tschunke), ReinSaat (Reinhild Frech-Emmelmann), Rebekka Herzog, and Lukas Heilingsetzer, for all the beautiful photos they allowed us to take in their gardens

—Thomas Gladis, for consulting on scientific names and pollination

—Robert Holenweger, gardener at Schlossgarten Wildegg, for his tireless efforts in advising us on the photographs contained in this book

—Stefan Emmelmann and Markus Zuber, for making portraits of plants with camera and pencil

—gardeners all, who over millennia helped develop the crop diversity described in this volume

FOREWORD

IT HAS NOW BEEN FIVE YEARS since the first edition of *The Seed Saver's Handbook* was published, and we look back with pride on what has happened since. The Deutsche Gesellschaft für Gartenbau (the German equivalent of the UK's Royal Horticultural Society) named the *Handbook* its Book of the Year in 2005; over 10,000 copies have been sold; it has been released in paperback, a Swedish translation is underway, and other translations are being planned. This is a huge success for a nonfiction book, and it goes to show the renewed enthusiasm for a topic even now occasionally dismissed as "antiquated": propagating your own garden seed.

For Arche Noah (Noah's Ark) and Pro Specie Rara (literally, "for rare species"), this nearly lost knowledge is a precious treasure; and both nonprofits (Austrian and Swiss, respectively) view the continued development of crop plants as being in grave danger without it. We would like to empower all farmers and gardeners, to help them see themselves, once more, as those who create the nutritious foods of our future—as people who, literally and figuratively, take seed back into their own hands.

Up until a few decades ago, gardeners did not think twice about propagating their own seed. Every pea that you hold in your hand is the end link of a chain of food, propagation, and breeding that stretches back many millennia. Professional plant breeding broke this chain, through hybridizing, genetic modification, and other highly specialized breeding methods. It is impossible under normal conditions to develop new varieties from plants bred in these ways. Thus, gardeners have slowly been dispossessed of a common good and basic raw material.

It is our hope that this book continues to help ensure our reconnection with heirloom varieties and that once again, farmers and gardeners confidently take responsibility for propagating the plants that nourish us all. So have fun experimenting! And don't forget: the only thing more wonderful than propagating your own seed is passing it on to others!

BEATE KOLLER, Arche Noah
BÉLA BARTHA, Pro Specie Rara

FOREWORD to the first edition

WE HAVE WRITTEN this book to give you clear, practical instructions on how to grow vegetables for seed. And because we would like both beginning and experienced gardeners to benefit from it, we have included not only the relevant "rules" but also the exceptions that inevitably come up when dealing with living things. It is a practice-oriented approach, based upon long, combined years of experience at Arche Noah and Pro Specie Rara. Chapters on individual crops were supplemented with knowledge gained by VEN (the Verein zur Erhaltung der Nutzpflanzenvielfalt/Association for the Maintenance of Crop Diversity) and Dreschflegel (a German organization similar to Arche Noah and Pro Specie Rara).

The book is not meant to be an encyclopedic tome that discusses every possible topic concerning seed propagation; such a volume would at best be an historical inventory of vegetable seed production. Nor is it an attempt to summarize documented knowledge of the subject: methods of propagation are as diverse as

gardeners themselves and the regions in which they grow food.

We are confident that, besides the techniques we describe here, there are many more that will also work. We encourage you to take the "recipes" we give and change them as needed to make them work for you and your garden. One approach to seed propagation is to maintain the traits that keep the plant true-to-type; another is to allow plants to express their inner dynamism and, in time, develop new varieties.

One of the last German-language books about growing vegetables for seed was Karl Reichelt's *Der Gemüsesamenbau im landwirtschaftlichen Betrieb* (Growing vegetables for seed on the farm). In the years following its publication in 1946, seed propagation ceased to be interesting to the book market; general information about selecting and propagating vegetables was the exclusive province of a few plant breeders, whose specialized methods were trade secrets and not the stuff of books.

Ingeborg Haensel is one of the most important trailblazers in maintaining and breeding vegetable varieties in the German-speaking world. She is self-taught, having ordered Karl Reichelt's book in 1974 to learn the basics of seed propagation. The publisher sent her the book with the following letter: "Dear Ms. Haensel, Thank you very much for your card dated 11 August 1974. We are sending you gratis our last copy (the so-called shelf warmer) of *Der Gemüsesamenbau*. Sincerely, C. V. Engelhard & Co." For years after, copy-machine copies of that shelf warmer made the rounds of amateur seed growers.

Now, nearly three decades later, we place before you this new *Seed Saver's Handbook*. The times have certainly changed. With Loewenzahn, we have found a committed publisher that has enthusiastically embraced the topic. Many people who tend their own garden want not just vegetables but also seed; and they do not want designer varieties that have been bred to work satisfactorily in any garden. Rather, they want their own heirloom varieties, those which thrive in their specific growing conditions. Maintaining varieties, propagating diversity, and enjoying vegetables: these are the subjects and the goals of this new handbook of seed propagation. We hope it finds the many passionate gardeners who yearn for the knowledge contained herein and that it will be reprinted and revised for years to come. We wish you joy in the cultivation and celebration of diversity in your garden!

Arche Noah
Pro Specie Rara
Andrea Heistinger
Schiltern and Aarau
September 2003

The delicate golden umbels of fennel blossoms, a favorite destination of hoverflies

Why propagate your own vegetable seed?

THIS QUESTION may occur to someone perusing the latest colorful catalog from a seed company. It does not, however, occur to the many gardeners who have been propagating their own seed for years. Such gardeners proudly tell stories of "their" varieties, of caring for an unusually beautiful plant to ensure that it produces seed, of an especially bountiful seed harvest, or of techniques they have developed to improve seed yield in some way. Many old and rare varieties, which must be propagated and passed along by home gardeners in order to be maintained, are not even available from seed companies. The life cycle of a plant begins and ends with the seed. Those who grow plants and select and harvest their seed experience the complete life cycle of those plants.

Up until a few decades ago, it was common practice to grow heirloom varieties that were passed down, along with the house, garden, and fields. These varieties were practically family members and were perfectly adapted, through generations of selection, to the growing conditions and culinary preferences found locally. The knowledge of propagating these plants was deeply connected with the plants themselves and to the place they were cultivated. The more a variety is adapted to its growing site, the easier it is to grow it.

A plant sleeps in every seed

Each plant produces seeds typical of its species; shape, size, and color are all distinguishing features of the seed. Everyone recognizes beans, whether ripe or unripe, or even pepper and pumpkin seeds. Seed growers carefully set aside some fruits, clean and dry them, and spread their seed the following year. Often you will find the seeds of individual species, whose propagation we describe, pictured in this book.

Crop diversity is organic

With this book, we want to inspire you to give seed propagation and selective breeding in your own garden a try. There is no such thing as a "finished" variety; varieties are constantly evolving. From this point of view, there are no heirlooms, no "old varieties," but rather only varieties of the present—as long as they continue to be grown and used. To propagate seed is to breed seed. One learns to closely observe plants and perceive their various traits. Do the fruits from each pepper plant in my garden taste the same? Is there a squash plant in my garden that yields higher than the others? Do any of the carrots I harvested taste particularly sweet? Are some of the celery plants more vigorous than others? Which of the lettuce plants makes the best-looking head? Are the plants that came from a good-looking plant that I selected last year just as good-looking as the mother plant? He or she who selects plants that will be grown for seed does this with their own ideas of the "ideal" version of the variety. Do the rounded or the longer beets look better? Which do I like more, the tastier ones or the smoother ones? In consumer society, we seldom have such a living relationship with the things we consume and use. To not merely consume what is on offer but to have a say in how it is produced—this is what propagating seed is all about: on the one hand maintaining ancient wisdom, on the other being creative. Those who start propagating their own vegetable seeds quickly become hooked and often just as quickly find that their gardens have become too small. Through growing and propagating seed, we give crop plants a chance to continue to develop together with us. No longer are they mere objects in a museum.

An abundance of seed

Those who have propagated crop seed know that each plant typically produces much more than you can use the following year. Plants produce seeds galore in an effort to secure the future of their respective species. What this means for us as seed growers is that for many of the vegetables we grow, we will have not only enough for next year but also the year after that (and the year after that)—and still enough to trade with our neighbors and give away to our friends.

Diversity is a question of time

The development of the immense crop diversity we now know was a long time coming. Many crops have been cultivated for several millennia. Selection and propagation of these crops have been in the hands of farmers and gardeners since the beginning of agriculture. Today's crop diversity came to be over the course of countless generations and is often based on a lifelong connection between people and individual varieties. Until about 150 years ago, no distinction was made between gardener and breeder; the timespan of the professional plant breeder is relatively short.

The disappearance of cultivars

Over the last few decades, hundreds of cultivated varieties (cultivars) have disappeared from seed catalogs and gardens. Seed catalogs from the early 1900s offered a plethora of useful and interesting varieties that are now completely unknown. The variety of shapes and colors alone (violet potatoes, white and yellow tomatoes, blue-podded peas) makes some seed catalogs look dull. Individual varieties were often available only regionally and were different from valley to valley, county to county.

Before the beginning of the industrialization of agriculture and the differentiation of organic and conventional agriculture, crop diversity was far more vast. For example, over 400 different grain varieties that were still being grown in the 1920s and '30s in the western valleys of the Austrian Alps are now being stored in the former regional office for plant breeding and seed testing in the Austrian province of Tyrol. These heirloom varieties manifest much more genetic variability than modern varieties; only a handful are being grown today.

Although a diverse array of cultivars is seemingly available today, it pales in comparison to what was on offer less than a century ago. Just consider apples or tomatoes, where a handful of varieties dominate the market. Modern, professionally bred varieties often hardly differentiate themselves from one another, whether in appearance or flavor. Home gardeners often have to search far and wide for varieties that have not been specifically bred for mass production (because this is where the money is for plant breeders). Traits that make sense for mass production—extremely high yields, machine harvestability, transportability, shelf life—are often irrelevant (or worse!) for the home gardener compared to traits like long harvest period, good flavor, appropriateness to growing conditions, vigor, and resistance to diseases and pests.

Cultivating varieties that are well adapted to growing conditions is important in market gardening and large-scale production, reducing the amount of pesticides and fertilizer needed. But most seed today is produced in countries where labor is cheap, which tend to also be countries that have ideal growing conditions. The result is that domestic seed producers cannot compete with large-scale enterprises. Newer seed companies that specialize in organic seed are the exception; however, until they offer more varieties that are ideal for organic production, they will have to compete with the comparatively homogeneous spectrum of seeds offered by large conventional seed companies.

Restrictive laws in the world of seed production have also contributed to a reduction in crop diversity. In Europe, only the seed of cultivars that pass a governmental licensing procedure are allowed to be sold at all, which has led in the last few decades to the disappearance of hundreds of interesting varieties in favor of high-performance and hybrid varieties. In addition, the licensing procedure is very expensive, which dooms many small breeders. A law that was intended to protect consumers and breeders has led to an increasing monopolization of the seed production sector, heavily favoring the large players.

Varieties are maintained and new diversity is created

The gardeners of Arche Noah in Austria, Pro Specie Rara in Switzerland, and like-minded organizations in Germany and beyond propagate and maintain endangered varieties that have not found a home in the professional seed breeding world. The home gardens and fields of these organizations' members constitute "ecological niches," as it were, for crop diversity that exist outside the pressures of market production. By maintaining cultivars in numerous scattered gardens, new diversity can also arise, as these cultivars acclimate themselves to their respective location. Gardeners influence the appearance of these varieties over time and slowly develop their own strains. Traits like flavor, suitability for cooking, attractiveness, and adaptation to local conditions tend to be paramount here, as opposed to what is valued in mass production, where yield, transportability, synchronous ripening, or the ability to be processed by machine are the sought-after traits.

Promoting amateur plant breeding

The knowledge of seed propagation is extremely important to Arche Noah and Pro Specie Rara. Indeed, it is the foundation for maintaining a given variety. Unlike paintings, books, and other cultural possessions, crop plants are a living inheritance that constantly changes and evolves. If you want to maintain a variety with all of its true-to-type characteristics, a bit of technical knowledge is necessary, which is what we aim to get across, in a clear and succinct way, with this book. It picks up, then, where home garden propagation leaves off and can be used as a guide book for increasing crop diversity.

It is an open framework that you can fill with your own experiences.

Breeding requires time

We recommend starting by growing one or two varieties for seed (say, lettuce and carrots) and paying close attention to them. What traits would you like the carrots to have? Which traits have been passed on to the next generation and which can be traced to your cultivation techniques? How can you overwinter the carrots with the means at your disposal? How do you plant out the carrot roots you selected in the spring? Do all the lettuce plants bolt at the same time, or do some maintain their shape and flavor for longer? These questions refine observational skills and inevitably, slowly but surely, we start to see our gardens in a whole new light.

How this book works

Each crop plant is covered in its own entry, and these are bundled into sections by botanical family. The introduction to each section summarizes the traits and characteristics that are typical of the respective family; specifics on how to grow each crop plant for seed and harvest are found in the individual entries, which generally include, among other topics, notes on pollination biology, distinguishing characteristics and selection criteria, diseases and pests, and cultivation history. For some species, additional information like stories of individual varieties, interesting cultivation techniques, or regional recipes using the plant are included.

Beforehand you will find a crash course in Seed Gardening 101. This chapter summarizes general seed propagation knowledge and techniques.

All botanical terminology is from Zander's 1993 *Handwörterbuch der Pflanzennamen* (Handheld dictionary of plant names) and *Mansfeld's World Database of Agricultural and Horticultural Crops.*

Arche Noah display garden, Schiltern, Austria

On crop diversity

THE DIVERSITY of crop plants came to be through the efforts of farmers and gardeners over many millennia. One example that beautifully illustrates the power of selective breeding is *Brassica oleracea*: cabbage, kohlrabi, broccoli, cauliflower, Brussels sprouts, and kale can all be traced to this same wild species. Through different use and selection of different parts of the plant—leaf, stem, bud—these cole crops, as they are also known, developed in different locations into the forms and varieties we know today; and always in the context of farming and gardening.

Propagation is cultivation

Traditionally in farming and gardening, growing for food and growing for seed are not separate but closely interconnected tasks that influence each other: with this understanding, all who grow, care for, eat, and harvest seed from plants are plant breeders. The understanding that farmers and gardeners breed crop plants is found in many Austrian-German dialects in the word *Zigeln*, which is used to refer to the simple growing of vegetables but is based on the word *Züchten* ("breeding"), i.e., "She breeds zucchini in her garden," not "She grows zucchini in her garden." Since the late 1800s, however, breeders and growers have been seen as two separate things, an attitude Carl Fruwirth, one of the first professional plant breeders, betrayed in 1896: "Farmers are often heard saying that they 'breed' hops, or they might describe themselves as flax 'breeders.' In reality, though, they merely grow these crops."

Local varieties steeped in their garden habitats . . .

Crops are grown in fields and gardens and their seeds ripen there as well, thus producing a new generation of seed. This is how heirloom varieties are propagated and maintained. Thirty years is a typical time for a cultivar to fully adapt to local conditions, but varieties can also change and develop new traits in much shorter time frames. Whatever the timespan, the

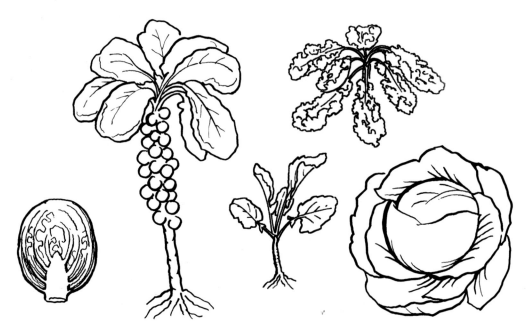

Diversity in form as developed through amateur breeding: various cabbages, Brussels sprouts, and kale can all be traced back to the same wild ancestor (middle).

plant's environment does the selecting through variables such as length of growing season; type and frequency of precipitation, drought, and cold periods; and intensity of light, to name but a few. At the same time, the people who grow these plants are selecting for traits by choosing which plants to allow to go to seed based on their own criteria, in order to meet their own needs for income, food, and/or flavor.

. . . and methods of cultivation

Heirloom varieties always exist in the context of the cultivation system they are raised in, which is why they typically do very well with minimal fertilizer. They arise from agricultural systems that used manure and compost, with no imported fertilizers. Such pastoral breeding, where all crops grown were also grown for seed, is where crop diversity comes from.

Biocommunication

An important aspect of pastoral breeding is that plants that have long been grown and propagated in the same general location slowly adjust to the diseases and pests that are found there. Biocommunication is a young branch of chemical ecology. It is already known, however, that plants can develop certain defense mechanisms against pests and can even summon beneficial insects to their defense via pheromones. Grain breeder Peter Kunz describes these mechanisms as "sustainable resistance," based on the principle of "live and let live." In this kind of resistance, a harmful fungus, for example,

may indeed be present, but the plants are so robust that the fungus has little or no effect on yield. Co-evolution between plants and pests requires field cultivation, something that cannot be replicated in the laboratory, but plant breeder Raoul A. Robinson has worked to promote collaborations between breeders and farmers in so-called plant breeding clubs.

Taking back our crops

In recent years, professional plant breeders have succeeded in gradually restricting the rights to cultivated varieties. Through plant variety rights protection, patent protection, or (in the case of hybrid varieties) biological patents, many cultivars in Europe are no longer common goods that farmers, gardeners, and home breeders can use for their own ends. Yet crop diversity

Breeding means selecting the best plants of the garden plot every year.

Comparison of important characteristics
of amateur (farmer/gardener) and professional plant breeding

	AMATEUR PLANT BREEDING	PROFESSIONAL PLANT BREEDING
OBJECT UNDER CONSIDERATION	The plant and the environment that influences it (phenotype)	Gene as "smallest unit" of life (genotype)
CAPABILITY OF REPRODUCTION	High Open-pollinated varieties are never "done" and anyone can always continue breeding them	Low or eliminated (hybrids, terminator genes) Varieties are one-time products
PURPOSE OF BREEDING	Adaptation to local conditions Security of harvest	Yield maximization Uniformity Novelty
KNOWLEDGE AND METHODS	Knowledge is received and/or self-acquired No generally applicable rules, only "basic recipes" Improvising and trial-and-error play an important role	Scientific knowledge Generally applicable rules and procedures Methods are constantly being updated
BASIC ECONOMIC CONDITIONS	Embedded in the economics of formal and informal agricultural cooperatives	Complies with market forces
RIGHTS OF DISPOSAL	Seed is seen as a common good that can be traded and passed on	Seed is seen as private property, with both legal (plant variety protection, patents) and biological (hybridization, terminator genes) protections New development: open source breeding
MAJOR PLAYERS	Farmers and gardeners (breeders and farmers/gardeners are one and the same)	Professionals International conglomerates
ORIENTATION	Breeding and cultivation are one and the same Direct connection to kitchen and food Flavor and particular processing qualities play an important role	Components that can be isolated, measured, and known Flavor is subordinate to qualities valued by conventional agriculture (mechanization, transportability, suitability for storage, specific resistances)
TIME	Varieties have no beginning or end point Breeding period therefore plays a subordinate role	Time is an economic factor ("time is money") Shortening of the breeding period is therefore a goal

After Heistinger 2001

came to be through this free availability of seed. Seed traveled with people to new places with new growing conditions, was selected using new considerations and, through these various influences, ultimately altered itself. Farmers of the global South know more than anyone about what it means for seed to no longer be a common good, for seed to be armed with patent protection, to be turned into a lifeless commodity. Many people in developing countries have reacted in anger to seed patents, privatization of the commons, and terminator genes.

A manifesto on the future of seeds

All over the world, people have begun defending themselves against the privatization of crop plants. In India, women formed plant exchanges to maintain and preserve agricultural life for their village communities, successfully ridding themselves of multinational seed companies in their regions. In Mexico, farmers protested the patenting of traditional corn (maize) varieties by U.S. conglomerates. In Mali, the farmers' assembly resolved to allow no genetically modified plants to enter the country and to protect domestic crop plants as a basis for preserving their food sovereignty. In Europe, there are an increasing number of initiatives for the reclamation of "old" heirloom varieties, and farmers are calling for a reinstatement of their ancient right to sow and trade seeds they harvest themselves.

Indian activist and winner of the Alternative Nobel Prize Vandana Shiva has been working for over three decades for the rights of small farmers. With the help of countless dedicated individuals, she founded, together with former president of the Tuscan regional government Claudio Martini, the International Commission on the Future of Food and Agriculture. In 2007, this commission presented the "Manifesto on the Future of Seeds," a call for the free exchange of seed between farmers:

> Seeds are a gift of nature, of past generations and diverse cultures. As such it is our inherent duty and responsibility to protect them and to pass them on to future generations. Seeds are the first link in the food chain, and the embodiment of biological and cultural diversity, and the repository of life's future evolution. Since the onset of the Neolithic Revolution

Vandana Shiva and Peter Zipser, chairman of Arche Noah, present the "Manifesto on the Future of Seeds." For more, visit navdanya.org and futurefood.org.

some 10,000 years ago, farmers and communities have worked to improve yield, taste, nutritional and other qualities of seeds. They have expanded and passed on knowledge about health impacts and healing properties of plants as well as about the peculiar growing habits of plants and interaction with other plants and animals, soil and water. Rare initial events of hybridization have boosted larger scale cultivation of certain crops in their Centres of Origin (such as wheat in Mesopotamia, rice in Indochina and India, maize and potato in Central America), which have since spread around the globe.

The free exchange of seed among farmers has been the basis to maintaining biodiversity as well as food security. This exchange is based on cooperation and reciprocity, where farmers generally exchange equal quantities of seed. This freedom goes beyond the mere exchange of seed: it also involves the sharing and exchange of ideas and knowledge, of culture and heritage. This tradition and accumulation of knowledge and know-how on working the seed is gained by farmers actually watching the seed grow in each other's fields. The cultural and religious significance of the plant, its gastronomic values, drought, disease and pest resistance properties, and other values shape the knowledge that the community accords to the seed and the plant it produces. [...]

The freedom of seed and freedom of farmers are threatened by new property rights and new technologies which are transforming seed from a commons shared by farmers to a commodity under the central monopoly of corporations. Similarly, the rapid extinction of diverse crops and crop varieties and the development of non-renewable seeds such as property hybrids and sterile seeds based on the terminator technology, threaten the very future of seed, and with it the future of farmers and food security. [...]

Systems of rights and responsibilities must be put in place which recognize both the collective rights of local communities as well as the right of seed sovereignty of farmers, and the mutual interdependence between diverse cultures and countries.

Open-pollinated varieties of tomatoes—
an overflow of diversity

Seed
Gardening
101

Propagation

There are two ways to propagate plants: by seed or by division or cuttings. Propagating by seed is also called generative or sexual propagation. Propagating by division or cuttings is also called vegetative or asexual propagation. With vegetative propagation, one uses roots, stems, or both; runners or stolons; or underground tubers or bulbs to grow new plants and rejuvenate old ones. For some plants, vegetative propagation is easier than seed propagation; for plants that produce no seeds at all (Chinese artichoke, for example), vegetative propagation is the only choice.

Vegetables that are predominantly or exclusively propagated vegetatively:

- potato, Chinese artichoke (tuber)
- garlic, topsetting onion (bulbil)
- chives, many herbaceous perennials (dividing plant)
- horseradish (root cutting)
- mints (runners)
- asparagus (rhizome)
- shallots (offsets)

In vegetative propagation, one plant produces many plants which are genetically identical to the mother plant, the only difference being that the new plants are younger.

This is not the case, however, with propagation by seed. One seed comes to be by the union of male genetic material (found in pollen) and female genetic material (found in the ovule). Through this union, genetic material of both parents is mixed together (recombined), which is why the plant that grows from a seed is similar, but not identical, to both parents. Offspring differentiate themselves from one another in this way; for out-crossing plants, seeds from one plant can be fertilized by pollen from many different father plants.

Open-pollinated varieties

Plants can be reliably bred true-to-type only with open-pollinated varieties, which pass their traits on over and over, from generation to generation. Progeny are similar to the parent plants, and traits change gradually, not abruptly. All this is not the case with hybrid seed (see sidebar).

The technique used to breed a given seed is not visually evident on the seed itself, so it is therefore impossible to tell just by looking if a given seed is from a hybrid variety or from an open-pollinated variety. The following kinds of varieties are essentially always open-pollinated and can be propagated and bred at home:

Heirloom varieties
These are varieties that have been grown and propagated on the same farm or in the same garden over a long period of time. Many do not even have names; they are simply "beans" or "lettuce." Such varieties are typically easiest to grow in the same general area in which they have traditionally been grown.

Old commercial varieties
These are varieties that our grandparents would likely recognize. Many carry the name of the place they were bred, hence 'Stuttgarter Filderkraut' (Stuttgart field

cabbage) or 'Erfurter Schwarzkopf' (Erfurt black head) cabbage. Others have artful names, such as 'Maikönig' (May king) lettuce or the pole bean 'Ohne Gleichen' (one-of-a-kind). And who would doubt the leaf size and hardiness of 'Riesen-Eskimo' (giant Eskimo) spinach?

New varieties from organic breeding

Organic and especially biodynamic breeders work with open-pollinated varieties. Biodynamic agriculture strives for a closed-loop system. In the case of crop breeding, that means working with plants that maintain their natural reproductive agency and high vitality, such that they can produce more seed and adjust to their surroundings. Open-pollinated varieties have always been and still are the basis for crop diversity.

Pollination and true-to-type propagation

Why is it important to understand the pollination relationships of a given variety? The type of pollination determines whether different varieties of the same species can cross with each other or not. This knowledge can also help you get an

Hybrid seed (= F1 seed)

Hybrid varieties are "one-time" things. The seed they produce will either be infertile or will yield wildly varying plants that are not true-to-type: the variety in and of itself is not permanent, not even in the short term, and hybrid seed must therefore be purchased new every year. This is, of course, an advantage for seed companies: one could say hybrid seed has a built-in "copyright." Because hybrid seed is always first-generation (F1) seed from crossing two different varieties, it cannot change or adapt to its location and cannot as such serve as a basis for crop diversity.

Currently, many open-pollinated varieties are being removed from the EU's common catalog of agricultural plants, and the contingent of hybrid varieties is rising drastically. For tomatoes, peppers, and Chinese cabbage, the percentage of hybrids listed is up to 80%.

Hybrid seed is the end of a long, complicated reproductive cycle. First inbred strains of the varieties involved are established by self-pollinating individual plants. Since most vegetable species are outcrossers, self-pollination is accomplished by human intervention, sometimes minimally, sometimes via biotechnology.

Through the breeding of hybrids, a vicious circle of dependency is entered upon between plant breeding and seed production on the one hand, and agricultural production on the other. Large-scale growing of homogeneous hybrid varieties can lead to ecological problems, such as increased pest and disease pressure.

idea of the probability of cross-pollination and what to pay attention to for a successful seed harvest. The hallmark traits of a given variety are lost through cross-pollination; and, in extreme cases, traits of the vegetable itself can disappear.

For example, since many squash varieties cross with each other, cucurbitacin (a bitter-tasting cytotoxin found in ornamental squashes and gourds) can find its way into edible squash; or the typical shape or color of a given variety might disappear. Cultivated carrots can cross with wild carrots (Queen Anne's lace), as seen in carrot seed that bolts in the first year and develops pale, tough, small roots. In the case of Swiss chard crossing with beets, the useful traits of both crops disappear.

Those who grow vegetables in their garden and harvest their seed expect that next year's crop will look the same as this year's (unless the intent is to breed something new). To confidently expect the same, you need to know the biological basis for propagating seed.

The flower

Flowers catch the eye with their colorful, often conspicuous displays, attracting and delighting both people and insects. The important reproductive parts are hidden in their inner parts: the ovary with its ovules (literally, "small eggs") and the stamens, which generate that carrier of male genetic material, pollen. A flower can take

Women in Küttigen, Switzerland, harvesting 'Küttiger Rüebli', an heirloom carrot that is typical of the region and clearly differentiated from other carrot varieties

on many different shapes and forms, but the way it is put together is always according to the pattern typical of the family it belongs to. All brassicas, for example, have flowers with four petals arranged in the shape of a cross, and all mints produce flowers with lip-shaped petals. Yet despite all this diversity of form, the inner configuration of the flower always follows one of the following three schemes:

Perfect

The flower contains both male and female reproductive organs. A few examples:

- brassicas (Brassicaceae)—cabbage, radish, mustard
- legumes (Fabaceae)—beans, peas, lentils
- umbellifers (Apiaceae)—carrot, parsnip, fennel
- composites (Asteraceae)—lettuce, scorzonera, sunflower
- alliums (Amaryllidaceae)—onion, leek, chives

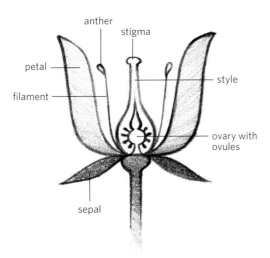

The parts of a perfect flower

- nightshades (Solanaceae)—tomato, pepper, eggplant

Monoecious

Each plant produces separate male and female flowers. For these plants, individual flowers are either purely male or purely female. One of the more striking examples is squash. Inside its long-stemmed male flower, the pollen-releasing anthers are clearly visible. Most female flowers develop later; the pronounced ovary is clearly visible and already has the shape of the squash fruit-to-be, though not yet nearly as large. The inner architecture

The perfect flowers of alliums have male and female reproductive organs.

Inner architecture of monoecious squash flowers: left female, right male

of the female flower is clearly different from the male flower: the stigma is ring-shaped and bulges out. Some other examples:

- cucumber, melon
- corn (maize)

Dioecious

When individual plants produce either only male or only female flowers, they are called dioecious. In this case there are, so to speak, male and female plants. Some examples:

- spinach
- asparagus

Dioecious: the small flowers of a male asparagus plant (top) and the spherical fruits of the female plant (above)

The ovary

The extension of the ovary is the style, at the tip of which is the stigma, which can take on many shapes and receives pollen. Ovary, style, and stigma together form the pistil of the flower. Inside the ovary, its store of ovules (literally, "little eggs") is found. The number of ovules found in the ovary differs vastly from species to species: a poppy flower ovary holds ca. 2,000 ovules, whereas that of a spinach flower holds only one, the ovary of a parsley flower, two.

Pollen and pollination

Grains of pollen develop in the anther and are released when they are sufficiently mature to effect pollination; they are microscopically small and contain paternal genetic material.

Pollination occurs when male pollen grains reach the stigma of a flower. This can happen in many ways, the major distinction being between self-pollination and cross-pollination. As is often the case in nature, it is a fine line between the two, and for many plants, both kinds of pollination can occur. Self-pollination and cross-pollination lead to very different genetic effects. Outcrossers (those plants that rely on cross-pollination) are much more variable than selfers; they produce more diverse offspring, thus making selection easier.

SELF-POLLINATION

This is when a flower's own pollen reaches its own stigma, resulting in the plant fertilizing itself. For some species, this takes place in the flower bud before it even opens (cleistogamy), for example in lettuce, peas, bush beans, pole beans, soybeans, and tomatoes.

Those species that can self-pollinate and do this under conditions of isolation (greenhouse, isolation cage) can be considered potential self-pollinators. When grown in the field, however, these crops (poppy, pepper, fava bean, eggplant) will often be cross-pollinated by insects. Some self-pollinators, or selfers, require insects or the wind to "trip" the flower or flower bud so that pollen can fall on the stigma; for example, hothouse tomatoes may develop no fruit at all (or at least fewer than when grown outdoors) without extra measures to trip the flowers. Market gardeners typically introduce bumblebees.

Species that always self-pollinate essentially do not exist, but the degree to which cross-pollination plays a role depends upon the circumstances—for instance, the presence of pollinator insects, or of flowers with which to cross at all.

CROSS-POLLINATION

In this case, the pollen from another plant reaches a flower's stigma and fertilizes an ovule. Since plants are, of course, not nearly as mobile as people and other animals, they require the services of one helper or another—myriad insects, the wind, even raindrops—and tend to adapt themselves to them.

It is crucial that you closely observe those crops which you intend to grow for seed. Are insects attracted to the blossoms or not? If so, which ones? Insects play an important role in growing vegetables for seed. Honeybees are particularly effective pollinators and can make a big difference in seed yield. Some species produce no seed at all, or, at best, small, weak seed, when insects have no access to their blossoms. The ideal garden for growing vegetables for seed is one that, through a great diversity of flowers, attracts as many insects as possible.

Insect-pollinated species

Many species have, in the course of their evolution, developed symbiotic relationships with insects that do the work of transporting pollen grains. They attract insects with sweet nectar and conspicuous floral displays. The most important pollinating insects are wild bees, honeybees, hoverflies, bumblebees, and wasps, though beetles, butterflies, and other insects can also contribute to pollination. Some insect-pollinated vegetables: cabbage, radish, squash, runner bean.

The adaptation of plants and insects to each other is often very specific. When people take a crop plant out of its original habitat, it can turn from an outcrosser into a predominantly self-pollinating plant simply because of the absence of adapted pollinator insects. Co-evolution continues, however, and insects local to the new habitat can become pollinators. Take the pepper plant: originally from South America, the pepper is considered to be a selfer in central Europe; but in Hungary, where the pepper has long been grown on a large scale, it is treated as an outcrosser.

Wind-pollinated species

The pollen of some species is so fine-grained that it can be transported by the wind. Plants that depend on the wind for pollination do not develop conspicuous flowers or produce nectar. Some examples: beets, Swiss chard, corn (maize), and amaranth.

Self-infertile species (obligate crossers)

Some plants have a genetically built-in barrier to self-pollination. For these so-called obligate crossers, the stigma must be pollinated with pollen from another plant in order for fertilization to occur. It is all but impossible to induce fertilization with pollen from another flower of the same plant (= selfing). This phenomenon is a protective mechanism against inbreeding and natural way to ensure genetic diversity. Self-infertility is common for brassicas. Squashes are sometimes self-infertile: they do not set fruit at all, or fruits that result from self-pollination develop no seeds. This is why one lone zucchini plant in the garden produces no or poorly developed fruits, while several plants in the same garden, pollinating each other via insects, yield abundantly.

Germination and fertilization

When a grain of pollen has reached the waiting stigma, it is then stimulated to germinate. A pollen tube grows out of the pollen grain, down the style, and into the ovary, where the male sex cell exits the pollen tube and conjoins with the ovule. This conjunction is called fertilization. At the time of flowering, ovules are still microscopically small, invisible to the naked eye. After successful fertilization, cell division begins and the ovary swells.

A seed contains not just a seedling but also endosperm, nutritive tissue which the embryo needs for its development as well as for germination.

Selfers vs outcrossers

Growing self-pollinating species for seed is relatively simple: when multiple varieties of the same species are grown near each other, crossing is seldom an issue. Such is not the case with outcrossers—in this case different varieties of the same species that are not grown in isolation can and often do pollinate each other.

For this reason, it is important to know which crops are selfers and which are outcrossers. Furthermore, it is important to know the botanical or scientific name of the plant you intend to grow for seed (in this book, it is found at the beginning of individual entries, under the common name).

Two parts make up a botanical name, sort of like a first and last name: the genus name and the species name. Here are two examples:

Squash

The gourd family (Cucurbitaceae) is composed of several genera, one being the genus for squash (*Cucurbita*) and its species, including *C. maxima*, *C. pepo*, and *C. moschata*. Cultivars belonging to the same species can pollinate one another; that is, they can cross-pollinate. Cultivars belonging to different species cannot, for the most part, cross with one another.

Brassicas

Several brassicas belong to a single botanical species, *Brassica oleracea*: cabbage, cauliflower, broccoli, and kohlrabi, among others. All vegetables of this species can cross with each other—for example, kohlrabi with cabbage. The progeny of this crossing will be wildly varied, all exhibiting traits of each parent plant to varying degrees, though many will develop neither a juicy, swollen stem like kohlrabi nor a compact head of leaves like cabbage.

Checklist for maintaining trueness-to-type

1. Do multiple varieties being grown for seed belong to the same botanical species?
   ☐ NO: no risk of crossing*
   ☐ YES: potential for crossing

2. Are the plants selfers or outcrossers?
   ☐ SELFER: little or no risk of crossing
   ☐ OUTCROSSER: potential for crossing

3. If outcrosser: are plants insect- or wind-pollinated?
   ☐ WIND: provide sufficient spatial isolation or cover well with row cover
   ☐ INSECT: provide sufficient spatial isolation or use isolation cages

4. In isolation cages: are plants able to self-pollinate?
   ☐ YES: pollinating insects are not necessary
   ☐ NO: pollinating insects are necessary

*There are some rare exceptions, which are discussed in individual entries.

Isolation

In order to prevent multiple varieties of the same species from crossing with each other, plants being grown from seed can be isolated from each other in one way or another.

Spatial isolation

The principle here is that multiple varieties blossom so far away from each other that there is no chance for them to exchange pollen. For insect-pollinated plants, this involves growing the second variety outside the pollinator's typical range of motion. For wind-pollinated plants, the distance needed is that over which pollen grains can no longer travel by wind. Spatial isolation can often not be accomplished in the home garden, as the distance required is larger than the space available. Minimum isolation distances are also difficult to accurately calculate because they are dependent on a multitude of variable local conditions:

- **Landscape form:** Is there a hedge or taller plants growing between varieties of the same species that might interfere with pollen transmission? Are there other physical barriers like a house or tool shed?

- **Population size:** The more plants of two different varieties grown at the same time, the larger the isolation distance required.

- **Flower diversity:** In gardens with high flower diversity, pollinators are constantly "distracted," and the likelihood that an insect would fly directly from the flower of one vegetable variety to another variety of the same vegetable decreases. But when, for example, two runner bean varieties are in bloom in the garden and nothing else, not even 650 ft. (200 m) will suffice to prevent cross-pollination.

- **Attractiveness of the flowers to insects:** Size, color, and nectar production all play a role in attracting insects.
- **Prevailing wind direction:** For all out-crossers, isolation distance must be greater for varieties grown in alignment with the prevailing wind direction than when grown in a line perpendicular to it.

For large-scale commercial seed propagation, isolation distances of 1.5 miles (2.5 km) are used to minimize the possibility of cross-pollination. Much smaller isolation distances can safely be used in home gardens, however. In gardens that are optimally designed for seed propagation, the following isolation distances can be observed for garden plots of up to 50 ft.[2] (5 m²):

- Insect-pollinated plants: 300–500 ft. (100–150 m)
- Wind-pollinated plants: 1000 ft. (300 m)

You will likely have to experiment a bit to come up with appropriate isolation distances for your home garden. Remember to consider what is being grown in neighboring gardens, as garden fences are notoriously poor at stopping bees or the wind.

Temporal isolation

Temporal isolation can be a simple way to avoid the danger of cross-pollination.

It is for the most part only realistic to use this method with plants that have a short growing season in climates that have a long growing season, thus allowing for two or three sowings in the same season. Staggered sowings of different varieties lead to different flowering times, thus eliminating the risk of cross-pollination (unless a wild variety of the same species grows in your area). At Arche Noah in zone 6, we have had positive experiences with corn salad and spinach.

Simpler than temporal isolation within a growing season is the temporal isolation of simply growing one variety per growing season. For example, one year growing an ornamental corn, the next flint corn, the next popcorn. Or with brassicas: first year kohlrabi, second year cabbage, third year collard greens.

Mechanical isolation

Mechanical isolation can also be practiced in small home gardens, though it takes time to build the structures required.

When grown in cages or tunnels, plants are separated from wild insects. In this way, a large number of varieties of the same species can be grown for seed at the same time without risk of crossing with each other. The addition of pollinating insects is, however, necessary, unless the plant in question can potentially self-pollinate (see earlier, "Pollen and Pollination"). A simple technique that has worked well for us is to stretch non-woven polypropylene fabric over pieces of heavy wire bent into a semi-circle to make a tunnel. This row cover is held down with ground staples, so outside pollinators are unable to get inside it to interfere with pollination.

Wind-pollinated plants cannot be grown for seed in such cages, since row cover or insect netting is no barrier for fine-grained windblown pollen. In this case, densely woven polyester fabric is needed (and pollinating insects are not). Be aware that fungal diseases and pests often thrive in such an isolation cage and that vegetables grown in them will likely require extra attention. Some plants that can be grown for seed in this way: Swiss chard, beets, amaranth.

Pollinating insects

Do not use honeybees as a pollinator in isolation cages. They are social creatures that desire only to return to their colony and will not visit flowers and spread pollen. Some appropriate pollinating insects:

- **Blowflies or carrion flies** (Calliphoridae spp.): These are available in fishing stores as grubs for bait. It takes about three weeks at room temperature for grubs to pupate and hatch. Time your purchase such that the flies are ready when plants blossom.
- **Mason bees** (*Osmia rufa*): The mason bee is a solitary bee (it lives alone and not in a colony). They can be bred in captivity with relative ease and used in isolation cages. Other wild solitary bees can be used for pollinating in isolation cages as well.
- **European hoverflies or drone flies** (*Eristalis tenax*): This large hoverfly lays its eggs in the liquid portion of manure

Out-crossing vegetable plants being grown in isolation tunnels at Arche Noah. Smaller isolation tunnels for individual cultures in home gardens can be easily constructed.

piles. Its larvae then develop in the manure pile, and the simplest way to acquire them is to collect them there, as captive breeding is laborious. Pupation can also take several weeks.

- **Buff-tailed bumblebees** (*Bombus terrestris*): Small, queen-less colonies can be purchased by mail in Europe for use in isolation cages and, unlike honeybees, are not so married to one particular place. They adjust quickly to new conditions and are good pollinators of any flower that suits them, shape- and size-wise. Never use bumblebees that you have caught yourself in spring and early summer, as these are almost certainly queen bumblebees. Every captured queen dooms an entire bumblebee colony.

Hand pollination

For some crop species, hand pollination can be more efficient and cheaper than mechanical isolation. Hand pollinating perfect flowers is laborious and is generally done in commercial breeding only to intentionally cross specific varieties with one another. But hand pollinating imperfect flowers is practical in home gardens;

Hoverfly on a radish flower

the methods involved are described in detail in the entries for corn and squash.

Population size

The number of plants of a variety you grow in your garden is often a question of space (most people find their gardens to be too small to begin with), your personal preferences, and needs. In general, the larger the population size of the variety you are growing for seed, the better it is for preserving the variety's genetic diversity. Furthermore, the larger the population size grown for produce, the easier it is to select plants to let go to seed. (The number of plants we consider the minimum population size is given in individual entries, under "What You'll Need.")

Crop plants are exposed to changing conditions every year. One summer may be hot and dry; the next, cool and rainy. The last frost could come early or late. Soil conditions, nutrient availability, and pest and disease pressure can shift annually. Over the course of one growing season, we see how some plants of a given variety thrive and others struggle with local conditions in that year. The more genetic variability present in the seed stock, the greater the likelihood that at least some plants will thrive every year, regardless of environmental trends. This flexibility and adaptability is an elementary hallmark of all living things.

Hybrid varieties are relatively uniform and exhibit no polymorphism (diversity in form) from which selections can be made. Because their traits compartmentalize themselves in individual plants in the next generation (i.e., offspring are highly varied), propagating seed from hybrid varieties is not particularly worthwhile. Hybrid varieties exist outside natural life cycles and can be thought of genetically as "one-time" entities that cannot adapt (see earlier sidebar on "Hybrid Seed").

Transformation and selection

The often high genetic diversity of out-crossing open-pollinated cultivars can lead to changes in the variety after a few reproductive cycles, even when selection for particular traits was not your intent. In this way, dense, tight cabbage heads may become looser and looser in time; heads of lettuce may become smaller from year to year; or orache or Florence fennel may slowly lose its resistance to bolting. Crop plants often display the tendency to revert back to their wild form and to lose those traits that people have selected them for. Or sometimes plants are bred that are not ideal for passing on desired traits. What happens when, for example, the first lettuce plant to bolt is always used for seed? The trait "early bolting" is selected for.

This ultimately means that gardeners who grow certain varieties for seed every year are not only gardeners but also plant breeders—whether intentionally or not! Even backyard gardeners need to be aware of basic plant breeding principles if the varieties they propagate are to maintain the form in which they were originally received. And of course we can, with a little experience and a trained eye, develop crops in new directions if we so choose: in color, size, or shape of fruits,

or in resistance to wetness, drought, or certain pests.

Humans have developed crop plants over centuries through selection, and some crops are now completely dependent on humans for their reproduction. Some lettuces, for example, develop heads that are so tight and compact that the stalk can no longer penetrate the leaves to flower; the grower has to slice an X in the head for it to be able to flower. Selection is all the more effective the larger the population size, where chances are increased of finding plants with all desired traits. Some varieties can be traced back to two or sometimes even one plant selected from a huge population. Such an extreme selection should not be done more than once, and only from a very large population size, however, to avoid inbreeding depression and the resultant loss of vitality.

Home gardeners are often happy to allow a certain range of diversity in their plots as long as their needs are being met. In fact, highly diverse crop stands often meet the needs of subsistence growers more than highly uniform varieties. Fruits ripening over a longer period of time is, for example, often useful in home gardening.

There are two basic styles of selection in horticultural practice, a negative and a positive: weak, fragile, leggier seedlings are removed (negative selection) and strong, vigorous plants are planted out in the field (positive selection). Those plants that will ultimately be allowed to go to seed are selected as the plant makes its way to eating ripeness:

- **Negative selection:** All plants are propagated except those that do not possess the desired traits (that is, they have undesirable leaf shape, stem color, fruit color, etc.) or are fragile or sick.
- **Positive selection:** Usually from a plot that is too large to have an overview of all plants. Only the best plants are propagated for seed.

In order to cultivate healthy, high-yielding plants for seed, one first has to grow healthy vegetables. Up to the point of ripeness for use as food, plants being grown for seed have the same needs as plants that are being grown to be eaten. Ideally plants grown for seed are grown in such a way that it is also possible to harvest food from them, thus allowing for a selection for traits like flavor and consistency. Gardeners who start their own plants from seed are involved in the selection process from the beginning. And those who, for example, start with seeds from the squash that overwintered longest in the root cellar are also selecting for long-storing squash fruits. On the other hand, for some plants, we need to take care that we do not eat the most beautiful plants but rather leave them in the garden and let them go to seed. This is not always easy, as we would often rather bring the best-looking lettuce to the salad bowl than leave it in the garden to bolt. At such times, think about the wonderful heads of lettuce that will be growing from the seed of that beauty next year.

Timing

For many species, the culture length when growing for seed can be very different from when growing that same vegetable for food.

Annual plants
These vegetables develop ripe vegetables and ripe seeds in one growing season. Some examples: beans, peas, tomatoes, peppers, squash, cucumber, melon, orache, garden cress, spinach.

Biennial plants
These vegetables develop ripe vegetables in the first year and seeds in the next. Some examples: onions, leeks, carrots, parsnip, celery, beets, Swiss chard, salsify, kohlrabi, cabbage. Biennial plants being grown for seed need to be overwintered somehow.

Annual/biennial plants
Depending on the variety, cultivation techniques, and season length, some plants that are otherwise typically grown for seed as a biennial can be grown for seed in one season. Some examples: endive, chicory, broccoli, cauliflower. Lettuce and radish produce ripe vegetables and ripe seeds in one growing season, whereas turnip, cabbage, and carrot need to go through one winter (vernalization period) before they bolt, flower, and produce seed.

Perennial plants
These vegetables produce seed every year, provided they survive the winter where they are growing. Some examples: chives,

garlic chives, sorrel, cardoon, sea kale, artichoke, Welsh onion, skirret, and many perennial herbs.

Cultivation

Here we have put together a few points and techniques that we find important in growing vegetables for seed.

Sun and warmth
Crop plants need more sunlight hours and higher average temperatures when growing for seed than when simply growing for food. So, while radishes and lettuce do fine shaded and in wet weather, they would not necessarily produce healthy, ripe seed in such conditions.

Nutrients
Plants being grown for seed need sufficient nutrients to develop high-quality seed. Extreme lack of nutrients can lead to fragile, less-viable seed. At the same time, seed-producing plants do not do well with too much nitrogen; this is especially the case for biennials. Taller plants take up a lot of water, which can contribute to the proliferation of fungal diseases and rot in storage over the winter. Biennials like carrots (and other root crops), kohlrabi, and celery use nutrients stored in their roots and stems from the previous year to help ensure sufficient nutrients to produce seed.

Water
When the flowering period comes to a close, irrigation should be drastically reduced, which allows seeds to ripen faster. (An exception to this are, of course, fruit-producing plants like tomatoes, squash, and peppers.) For vegetables destined for the root cellar, reduced watering in autumn leads to better winter storage. Do not bring wet vegetables (heads of cabbage, root vegetables, etc.) into storage. In areas with high amounts of autumn precipitation, protect plants to be overwintered indoors from the rain with a roof or tarp to reduce the amount of water they take up.

Support
Offer all long-stalked plants enough support to keep them from being knocked to the ground by wind, rain, etc. Individual seed-bearing branches can become quite heavy. Seedheads that have made contact with the ground are particularly susceptible to fungal diseases when it rains. For crops that develop large, heavy stalks (brassicas, beets), support each individual plant. Other species with denser

Second-year kale supported by stakes

Carrot stalks held up by string tightened around and between stakes at two different heights

vegetative growth (orache, lettuce) can be supported all at once with string or netting horizontally tightened on poles at the corners of the garden bed. Options for plant support are given throughout, but please do not feel limited by our suggestions. Use whatever creative method works for you and your plants.

Space

Seed stalks can take up a large amount of space. A large bush develops out of the otherwise tiny radish with cumbersome stalks growing in all directions. Low-lying lettuce plants grow seed stalks over a yard

Pictured in the foreground is typical pea and bean trellis netting, which can be tightened horizontally to support the stalks of bolting plants.

(1 m) long. All this extra growth makes sufficient plant spacing crucial. Having enough space simplifies selection, reduces the risk of fungal disease by enabling plants to dry out after rain (or simply from the morning dew), and contributes to faster ripening of seeds.

Rain protection

Some species are particularly sensitive when it comes to seed ripening. Stalks can become riddled with fungi, and seeds can be washed away by the rain. Artichokes, lettuce, and other aster family members in particular need to be protected from rain as their seeds ripen. Often a strong tarp stretched over metal arches or a wooden frame suffices as a portable roof. Large plastic panes on posts or leaned against each other to form an A-frame could also do the job. Do not water bolted plants from above but rather directly at the base, ideally with drip irrigation lines.

Root cellar

Ideal root cellars are frost proof, with a constant temperature of 33–40°F (1–5°C). For root vegetables, it should also be pitch black (as in a true root cellar or in an earthen mound or pit). For some leaf vegetables (some brassicas, leeks, etc.) and for overwintering young plants to grow for seed the next year, bright, frost-free sites (unheated winter garden, greenhouse) can also be useful. Overwinter only good-looking, healthy, non-injured vegetables; otherwise, one sick, rotting vegetable can spread its diseases to the rest of the plants in storage. After loading in plants, check on them every week and remove sick or rotting plants. Disinfect pruning wounds with bone char or ashes.

Planting out the second year

Allow plants to slowly acclimate themselves to sunlight and wind before planting them out the following year. Root vegetables can be taken out of the root cellar about a week before planting out to allow them to produce more chlorophyll in their leaves.

The ideal day for planting out overwintered plants is cloudy, mild, and somewhat rainy. Planting on a sunny day can lead to "sunburning" the plants. If there are no cloudy days in the forecast, set up some shading for the first few days.

Of utmost importance. Water all newly replanted plants very well, especially kohlrabi, beets, celeriac, and other root vegetables, until they have developed new root systems.

First in pots, then out in the field. If plants have begun to grow in the root cellar but the weather is not yet appropriate for them to be planted outdoors, plant them in pots. Grow them in a frost-proof, cool, and not-too-sunny spot, and slowly harden them off before planting them out in the field. This is time-consuming, but it is worth it. Pay attention to insect-pollinated species like brassicas; plants should not flower before bees and other insects are active (typically midspring).

Gauging ripeness

Seeds slowly expand as the embryo grows; during development, they become larger than they will be when ripe, due to their higher water content. Water facilitates the flow of nutrients out of the plant and into the seed. The so-called milk ripeness is the point when the germ is fully developed and stores of nutrients are full, but the water content is still very high. At this phase, the fruit (or pod, shell, or husk, as the case may be) is fully grown but still green. The seeds too are still green with a whitish skin, juicy, and firmly attached to the inside wall of the fruit. From this point, everything begins to dry out. Seeds give off excess water and shrink, becoming smaller and firmer. The outer skin becomes tougher and harder, turning into the seed coat.

For many plants (peas, beans, brassicas), the fruit also undergoes a drying process. This all continues until ripe seeds are surrounded by strawy, papery pods or husks that eventually (sometimes within a few days) open, allowing the seeds to spill forth. Seed harvested at this "dead ripeness" stage is the ideal seed. Unfortunately, it is not always possible to wait until this stage to harvest, because most of the seed already would have dropped to the ground. This is especially the case for plants whose seed does not all ripen at once but rather over a longer period of time, like brassicas. For these plants, cut seed-bearing stalks during the milk-ripe stage, when the pods are just beginning to turn color.

Harvesting times

Unlike sowing times, ideal harvesting times cannot be given so exactly because of variables like weather (hot or cold periods, rain, drought, frost danger), location of the garden (high or low humidity, sunny, shady, windy), and traits of the variety in question. Some crop varieties that are well adapted to local conditions will ripen even when autumn weather comes earlier than usual. Other varieties, which were perhaps developed in an area warmer than their current spot, only ripen with a little help, luck, or both. Varieties are only able to adapt to a specific site when they are successfully grown for seed there on a regular basis. This is the (often unconscious) breeding work that gardeners over the centuries have done to bring forth the crop diversity we know today. Opposite are some guidelines for timing the seed harvest.

Postharvest

Steps must be taken after harvest to ready seeds for storage. Two basic methods of seed processing are used, depending on the crop:

- Wet processing for vegetable fruits
- Dry processing for all other plants

WET PROCESSING
This is the method used for tomatoes, cucumbers, squash, and other fruits. Wet processing can be done with or without fermentation.

- With fermentation: tomatoes and cucumbers; the fermentation process is used to remove the germination-inhibiting sac that surrounds each seed in the fruit
- Without fermentation: all other vegetable fruits

• What you'll need: knife, spoon, glass jars, bucket, sieves, coffee filters

Wet processing with fermentation

Fermentation. Cut the tomato or cucumber in half. With a spoon, scrape the seeds into a glass jar and add a little water (do not use seeds from rotten fruits). Glass jars are used so that one can see when seeds sink to the bottom. Cover the jar loosely to prevent pressure from building up inside due to fermentation. If this is your first time fermenting seeds, proceed with care and observe the seeds closely. Once the germination-inhibiting layer is gone, the seeds then find themselves in

Determining the right moment for seed harvest

VEGETABLE FRUITS

Take seed only from fully ripened fruits.

Wait for fruits to change color:

Cucumbers
green → yellow

Tomatoes
green → yellow
green → red
green → orange

Peppers
green/yellow → red/orange
yellow → red
violet → orange/red

Eggplant (aubergine)
violet, green, or white → golden yellow

Asparagus
green → red

COMPOSITE FLOWER

Lettuce, salsify, and other aster family plants
Harvest just before seeds fall out on their own; discs where hundreds of flowers are clustered together should not be exposed to long periods of rain (may necessitate covering during ripening)

PODS

Peas, beans, and other legumes
Harvest when completely dry and brittle (exception: some bean varieties become tough instead of brittle)

PODS

Cabbage, radish, and other brassicas
Harvest when the first pods dry and the majority of pods are golden brown, but still soft

SPECIAL CASES

When ripening takes too long or when autumn frost comes early, it is possible to stimulate premature ripening: hang full plants, that have been either pulled out of the ground or cut at their bases, indoors to dry. This works only if the seeds have reached at least the milk-ripe stage. In a pinch, unripe umbellifers (e.g., Florence fennel) or brassicas (e.g., broccoli) can be transferred to containers in a frost-proof environment to ripen.

optimal conditions to germinate (warm and moist)—if the seed germinates now, it is essentially ruined. To guard against this, use a simple finger test: when the seeds no longer feel slippery, but rather rough instead (usually after a day or two), that means the gelatinous sac surrounding the seed is gone. Seed sinking to the bottom, with the pulp remaining at the surface, also indicates that the sac has dissolved.

A grayish white layer of mold may develop on the surface. Frequent stirring can prevent a dense layer of mold, which could potentially infect the seeds, from forming on the surface and also encourages consistent fermentation throughout the solution. If there is little pulp in the jar with the seed, add a pinch of sugar (as a replacement for the fructose contained in tomato pulp) to ensure vigorous fermentation and to suppress the formation of mold. Fermentation is not complete until seeds have separated from the pulp.

Ideal temperature range for fermentation: 73–86°F (23–30°C).

Cleaning. Add water to the fermented seed-pulp mixture and mix. When the seeds have sunk to the bottom, pour off the pulp and any dead seeds floating at the top. Repeat this process of adding water and pouring off pulp until the water is clear. Clean further under a powerful stream of water in a sieve if needed. This is typically all the cleaning that is needed.

Drying. At this point it is important that the seeds be dried as quickly as possible. We place the seed in coffee filters, which quickly wick away moisture. Warning: do not press water out of the seeds, which may cause the seeds to clump together such that they cannot be separated without damaging them. Place up to one teaspoon of seeds in each coffee filter. Seeds can also be dried on a plate. Set out in a warm, but not hot, place (73–86°F [23–30°C]) with good air circulation and

Wet processing tomato seeds with fermentation. Cut tomatoes in half, scoop the seeds out into a glass jar or, as pictured here, a petri dish. Ferment together with tomato pulp. A thin yeast or mold layer may develop on the surface. When the gelatinous sacs around the seeds have dissolved (finger test), add water, stir, then pour off the pulp. Repeat until the seed-containing water is clear. Clean further in a sieve under running water, if necessary. Allow to dry thoroughly on filter paper or in a coffee filter.

label. Seeds should be dry in two days at the most. If needed, seeds can be further cleaned in sieves after drying.

Wet processing without fermentation

In wet processing without fermentation, seed is simply removed from the fruit and then washed in a sieve under running water. This is done with, for example, melon, eggplant, and groundcherry. If the seed does not separate from the fruit by this method, soak the fruit for 12 to 24 hours (keep cool; the point is not to ferment but rather to soften the tissue of the fruit). Dry seed well afterward.

DRY PROCESSING

There are three steps in the dry processing of seed: drying (of the entire plant or seed), threshing, and winnowing.

Drying

Drying seed on the plant. The seeds of beans, peas, chicory, cereal grains, poppy, and some pepper varieties dry fairly well while still inside the fruit. Beware of long, wet periods just before harvest, however, as seeds are immediately capable of germinating and may germinate instead of drying!

Drying seed indoors. Another practice is to pull or cut entire plants with the seeds still contained in capsules, pods, etc., for further ripening and drying. This is typically done for brassicas, corn salad, miner's lettuce, and arugula. Some Arche Noah members have reported that hanging entire plants with the roots makes for better seed ripening. In this case, bag the roots, so that the soil that clings to them does not get mixed in with the seed.

Premature ripening indoors. In a year with a shortened growing season or a wet autumn, seed-bearing plants can be cut at their bases and hung upside down indoors, stimulating a premature ripening of the plants' seeds. Pole beans being grown at

high elevations may require this technique to ripen, for example.

For other plants, plants can be transferred to containers to finish their life cycle in a frost-free environment. Late broccoli varieties, Florence fennel, and peppers may require this technique. Take special care to not damage the roots while transplanting.

Drying harvested seeds. Dry cleaned seeds for at least a week. Make sure the temperature at which the seeds are drying does not exceed 95°F (35°C) for long, as this could damage the seeds' germ. Some places that are potentially appropriate for seed drying: an attic, near an oven, a boiler room, or an incubator. If there is no appropriate space available, seed can be dried using silica gel, which is available as tiny balls from many suppliers. Place equal amounts of silica gel and seed in an open jar or cloth bag and dry for a

week. Do not allow seed and silica to be in direct contact with one another!

Threshing

Most people are familiar with the concept of threshing from grain harvesting, but many vegetable varieties undergo the process as well. Threshing is the process of removing seed from its containing organ (pod, husk, etc.). For small amounts of seed, this is most easily accomplished by hand, as when peas or beans are shelled from their dried, brittle pods. For larger seed amounts, other methods are easier and faster:

For seeds found in leaf axils or in fragile seed capsules (beets, flax, spinach). Place seed stalks in an old pillowcase or other cloth bag and strike against a wall. The seeds separate from the plant and collect at the bottom of the bag.

For seeds in tough seed capsules (chicory, endive, radish, poppy, artichoke). Place seed stalks in a cloth bag on a relatively firm underlay and strike with a flail or stomp with your feet.

For seeds that are easily threshed but would be damaged by being struck hard (beans, peas, lettuce, brassicas). Thresh in a bag on a soft underlay or carefully stomp with your feet.

For still larger amounts, there are special hand-threshing machines, but owning your own machine is really necessary only if you are growing large amounts of seed every year. The following items will serve the seed-cleaning needs of the average home garden:

At Arche Noah, we dry seeds in coffee filters. Write the variety name on the filter in waterproof ink. Here, many different seeds are hung from a laundry drying rack, away from direct sunlight, in the shade.

- old floor, mattress, futon, or tarp as underlay
- flail (e.g., an old spade or ax handle)
- old sheets or other bed linen (patch holes if necessary)
- funnels and paper bags
- bowls, basins, and buckets

Winnowing

It is especially important to winnow fine-grained seed prior to storage, as soil particles and pieces of plant material can carry diseases with them. Seed from plants that have struggled with disease should be especially well cleaned. Use sieves and the wind to winnow seed after threshing. It is often necessary to repeat the same process many times and/or use a combination of methods to clean seed thoroughly. We recommend the following methods for winnowing seed:

By hand. Small amounts of seed can simply be cleaned by hand.

By screening. Screening is a simple and fast method for cleaning seed. A mesh size larger than the seed size allows seed to pass through, while holding back anything larger. A mesh size smaller than the seed allows debris smaller than the seed to pass through, while holding seed and anything larger back.

By swinging, rocking, shaking, and circling. This method is extremely efficient but difficult to master. Fine-meshed, large sieves are ideal, allowing heavier and lighter seeds to separate based on their relative density. Swing the sieve in circles and slightly tilted.

This can also be done in bowls. Plant debris tends to come to the surface, where it can be removed. A stem here or there that remains with the seed is not a problem.

With the wind. Move the sieve quickly toward the ground to simulate it falling. Fine plant debris falls slower and "rises" relative to everything else in the sieve. When the sieve is then quickly jerked to the side, this fine plant debris falls to the ground, while the rest stays in the sieve. This too takes practice. Use a finely meshed sieve and spread an old sheet underneath to catch any seeds that accidentally fall.

An alternative method is to pour the seed from one container into another. Lighter debris blows away in the wind, heavier seeds fall into the receiving container. This is especially effective for larger seeds like cereal grains or beans.

By blowing. When small, light impurities remain in the seed, these can be blown away with the breath if the seed is first transferred to a plate or flat bowl. To clean larger amounts in this way, use a hair dryer with the heat turned off.

With water. After dry processing, some seeds can then be separated in water: heavy, viable seed sinks to the bottom, plant debris and dead seed swim at the top. Seeds must then be dried immediately (coffee filter or paper plate).

Sieves

Sieves are available in a wide variety of mesh sizes and can also be made out of

Threshing and winnowing lettuce seed at Arche Noah.
Wrap ripe and dry lettuce seed stalks in a towel and
pound with an old spade handle.

Next, winnow with a sieve. Seed and small debris fall
through the first sieve, leaving the stalks behind; seed
is further separated from debris with a slotted sieve.

Nonviable seed is lighter than viable seed. When
winnowing with the wind, light plant debris and
nonviable seeds "rise" from the sieve; when the sieve

is then quickly moved to one side, the heavy viable
seeds stay in the sieve while the rest falls to the ground.
Practice makes perfect!

Do all this over bed linen to ensure nothing gets lost
by mistake.

Complete cleaning by swirling the seed in a bowl and
blowing off the light plant debris that "floats" on the
heavier seed. Dry processing is accomplished, and the
lettuce seed is now ready for storage.

hardware cloth. Mesh size—the crucial element of a sieve—typically ranges from 0.5 in. (1 cm), through which all but the largest beans would fall, down to ¹⁄₆₄ in. (0.4 mm), through which only the smallest amaranth seeds would pass. We recommend having two different sizes each for fine seed (amaranth, brassicas), midsized seed (peppers, melons), and large seed (squash, fava beans), in addition to a slotted sieve with ¹⁄₃₂–³⁄₆₄ in. (0.8–1.2 mm) perforations. The greater the variety of seed you have to clean, the more sieves you'll need to get seed cleaned in a reasonable amount of time. They can be purchased or made yourself.

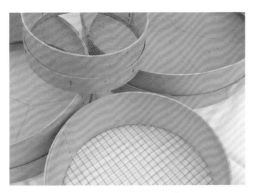

Seed-cleaning sieves with various mesh sizes

A slotted sieve—particularly handy for lettuce seed

Seed storage

Whether dry or wet processed, cleaned seed should be checked prior to storage for crossing (visible in first-generation seed for some species) or fungal infection; it is helpful to have some of the original seed, for comparison. Pay attention to color (true-to-type), size (remove runts and nonviable seed), smell (musty seed may be moldy; fresh seed often has the typical smell of the species), and moisture level (if seed feels damp, dry longer). Other important points for success:

Dry, cool, and dark

The combination of moisture and warmth not only can end the seed's dormancy but can also encourage the growth of damaging fungi and bacteria. The drier the seed, the better it maintains its viability. Seed that feels clammy should never go into storage: it will likely become moldy.

Optimal temperatures are 32–50°F (0–10°C). It is also important that the temperature remains constant and does not shift quickly. Seed can only be stored in the deep freezer if it has been very well dried (the germ can be destroyed by the expansion of freezing water). Use silica gel to dry, and store in metal-lined, heat-sealed packets. At −1°F (−18°C), seed can be stored for at least 10 years and some highly viable seeds can be stored for 20 or many more years. Keep seed in a dark room or in opaque containers in a box.

Airtight containers

The less air contact the seed has in storage, the less it "breathes," meaning that it stays in the same condition longer.

Choose containers that can be tightly closed, like jam jars, glass bottles with airtight caps, and mason jars with rubber gaskets. We have found glass jars with latched lids to be especially useful. Save space by storing several (labeled!) sacks of seed in one jar.

Safe from pests

Protect your seeds from insects (moths, bean weevils, and others) and rodents (mice and rats), to name the most important storage pests. Wooden crates, nylon/plastic bags, and cardboard bags or cartons are not suited for storing seed, as they provide no protection from pests (or moisture).

Labeling

Label your seed packets and jars, and label them well. Put the following information on a seed packet label:

- name of crop
- variety name
- harvest date (or, at least, year)

You may also want to note any distinctive features of the seed—for example: "carrot, 'Syrische Violette' 2013, well-ripened seed." Many gardeners keep a journal in which they take notes on the growing season such as:

- basic description of the variety (to track any changes in the variety over time)
- source of the seed being grown (to make comparisons and to avoid mixing up seed from different sources)
- the amount of seed harvested
- any pests or diseases the parent plants experienced

Seed viability

The germination rate of stored seed declines with time, with the seed of some species deteriorating faster than others. Under ideal storage conditions the seeds of some species can last for decades, whereas others last only a year or two. Actual performance in storage depends upon the ripeness of the seed (fully ripened seed lasts longer in storage than seed that did not fully develop) and the storage conditions. Despite their static appearance, seeds are alive, and life processes, however starkly reduced in speed, continue on the inside.

Even when a seed is still viable and will germinate, it may deteriorate in storage to the point that the plant that grows from it shows reduced vigor, higher disease susceptibility, and ultimately lower yield. The time needed for the seed to germinate may also increase. In the period of time between germination and development of

Tip

Never sow all the seed you have of a given variety, and it is an especially good idea to keep a sample of the original seed stock. This will help you identify the variety in case of a mix-up or crossing. Keeping older seed is also a hedge against crop failure and can prevent the loss of a variety.

Storage life expectancy of vegetable seeds

Very sensitive seed: These seeds must be sown right away or within a few months of harvesting (storage in a deep freezer can help lengthen storage life expectancy).

Short life expectancy: These seeds can maintain reasonable germination rates for two to three years.

Middle life expectancy: These seeds can maintain reasonable germination rates for four to five years.

Long life expectancy: These seeds can maintain reasonable germination rates for over five years.

bean	middle life expectancy
carrot	short life expectancy
celery	short to middle life expectancy
chives	very sensitive
cole (*Brassica oleracea*) crops (cabbage, kohlrabi, etc.)	long life expectancy
corn (maize), sweet corn	short to middle life expectancy
corn salad	middle life expectancy
cucumber	long life expectancy
eggplant (aubergine)	long life expectancy
endive	middle life expectancy
Florence fennel	short life expectancy
garlic	very sensitive
leek	very sensitive
lettuce	middle life expectancy

melon	long life expectancy
onion family (except chives)	very sensitive to short life expectancy
orache	long life expectancy
parsnip	very sensitive
pea	middle life expectancy
pepper	middle to long life expectancy
radish	middle life expectancy
scorzonera	very sensitive
spinach, New Zealand spinach	short to middle life expectancy
squash, pumpkin	long life expectancy
Swiss chard, beets	middle to long life expectancy
tomato	long life expectancy
turnip-rooted chervil	very sensitive

the cotyledons and the first roots, seedlings are especially vulnerable to pathogens that may be present in the soil or growing medium. The faster the seed germinates the better, in terms of avoiding infection. Fully ripened, well-stored seeds tend to germinate and grow more vigorously and with higher vitality. For home gardeners growing their own produce, it is important to use seed with a germination rate of at least 70%, though market gardeners may demand 90% or higher germination rates to ensure a good crop.

If you come across old seed of a variety that is no longer offered by seed companies, see if you can still manage to get some seed to germinate. Many such varieties have been saved by finding the few seeds that are still viable in a packet of old seed. And if you happen to come across an old unmarked packet of seeds in an old box somewhere, turn to a seed-saving organization like Arche Noah, Pro Specie Rara, Seed Savers Exchange, or others, which have years of experience in germinating seed in optimal conditions. You may well have saved a variety that would otherwise have been lost, and if the seed is still viable, you will receive freshly propagated seed in return.

In the preceding table, we have divided seed into four categories of life expectancy in storage. Since this depends on a multitude of factors, seeds cannot be considered as having a set "expiration date."

Germination testing

Germination tests should be performed on old seed and on seed that was harvested in less-than-ideal conditions or that was unripe when harvested. Perform germination tests regularly to ensure viability of your seed.

Lay 100 seeds (or fewer if limited by seed supply, but at least 20) on a moistened paper towel such that they are not in contact with one another (to help prevent any fungus that may be present from spreading to other seeds). Roll this "germination packet" up and place in a plastic bag with air holes. Store at a constant temperature between 68°F (20°C) and 77°F (25°C)—e.g., under a 40-watt light bulb. Use a thermometer to ensure a correct and consistent temperature. Caution: some species require high temperatures to

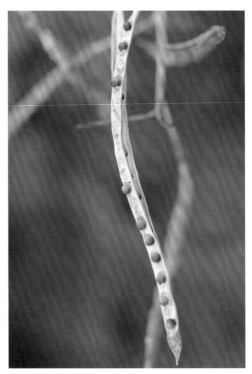

Fully ripened seeds germinate at a higher rate and with more vigor.

germinate, and others germinate at lower temperatures (see table).

When performing multiple germination tests, be sure to label each test with crop type, variety name, and date. Depending on the crop, seeds will have germinated in days or weeks. Seeds have germinated when radicles (embryonic roots), shoots, or even cotyledons are visible. Since seeds never germinate at exactly the same time, inspect the germination packet several times, and keep moist with a spray bottle if necessary.

When you have the impression that everything that is going to germinate has germinated (rules of thumb for germination times: legumes one week, peppers and tomatoes one to two weeks, umbellifers three to four weeks), wait another few days, then count the number of germinated and ungerminated seeds. Count again a few days later, to be sure germination is at an end. Divide the number of germinated seeds by the total number of seeds tested to find the germination rate (50 germinated seeds divided by 100 tested seeds means a germination rate of 50%).

Seed health and quality

Healthy seed is an important part of growing and harvesting healthy vegetables. One basic requirement for healthy plants is growing them organically. Crop vitality is reflected in its "willingness to reproduce," that is, its seed yield. The most important prerequisite for growing and propagating vegetables is a healthy, humus-rich soil. A basic principle of organic gardening is the development and

Germination temperatures of selected vegetable seeds

CROP	MINIMUM TEMP. IN °F (°C)	OPTIMAL TEMP. IN °F (°C)
bean (bush, pole)	46 (7.7)	77 (25)
beet	36 (2.1)	68 (20)
cabbage	35 (1.9)	68 (20)
carrot	34 (1.3)	72 (22)
celery	40 (4.6)	68 (20)
chicory	42 (5.3)	59–64 (15–18)
corn salad	32 (0)	68 (20)
cucumber	55 (12.7)	77–82 (25–28)
eggplant (aubergine)	54 (12.1)	77–82 (25–28)
endive	36 (2.2)	68 (20)
fava bean	33 (0.4)	68 (20)
garden cress	34 (1)	68 (20)
leek	35 (1.7)	68–77 (20–25)
lettuce	38 (3.5)	59–64 (15–18)
melon	54 (12.1)	77–82 (25–28)
onion	35 (1.4)	59–68 (15–20)
parsley	32 (0)	77 (25)
pea	35 (1.6)	68 (20)
pepper	44 (6.7)	77–82 (25–28)
purslane	52 (11)	68 (20)
radish	34 (1.2)	68 (20)
scorzonera	36 (2)	68 (20)
spinach	32 (0.1)	59–68 (15–20)
tomato	48 (8.7)	68–77 (20–25)

After Fritz and Stolze 1989

maintenance of organic matter in the soil. Good soil structure and crop rotation are effective in maintaining high soil fertility and reducing soil-borne disease pressure.

Plant disease

Plant diseases and pests must always be reckoned with in gardening, but the richer the soil is in organic matter and the better the plants are adapted to local conditions, the fewer problems you will have with them. Although pests (with the exception of some storage pests) are not seed-borne (that is, are not spread directly through the seed), many diseases are.

The most important plant diseases are discussed in the text with the individual crops. If you are unable to identify certain diseases, and you are uncertain if they might potentially affect the seed yield, consult a more experienced gardener or your extension office. Affected plant parts or seed that is suspected of infection can also be professionally examined.

In general, deal with plant diseases carefully and thoughtfully to avoid as much as possible the disease spreading to other plants. Often aphids and other sucking insects are important disease vectors, that is, they contribute to the spreading of diseases. But simply performing day-to-day tasks in the garden can spread disease. The spores of many fungi can be transported by wind and rain, and many lurk in the soil, waiting for the right host plant to afflict. Soil-borne fungal diseases can also be spread via shoes. Because of all this, pay special attention to the cleanliness of your gardening tools; wash them after use and occasionally disinfect them.

Warning: the tobacco mosaic virus can be spread from the fingers of smokers to those plants that are sensitive to this disease, so-called solanaceous crops (plants of the nightshade family: tomatoes, peppers, eggplants). Smokers should wash their hands thoroughly before working in the garden.

None of the known plant diseases affect humans, so humans are at no risk of infection by consuming affected vegetables, though consumption of plants with residues of plant protection

Some tips for identifying plant diseases

Fungal diseases tend to affect germinating seeds and seedlings ("damping off") or older plant parts and often lead to the swift death of an infected plant.

Bacterial diseases typically spread within an infected plant through its circulatory system, leading to blockages and, ultimately, the death of the plant. Bacterial diseases of vegetable plants can appear as a wet or soft rot, wilt, or as spots on stems and fruits.

Viral diseases are especially visible on the young leaves of young plants as a discoloration or crimped, crumpled growth. Viruses require living cells to reproduce and cause plants to develop poorly, sometimes to the point of being unusable, but they rarely kill plants quickly.

products like pesticides can be detrimental to one's health.

Hot water treatment

There are chemical, physical, and biological methods for treating seeds for seed-borne diseases. In conventional agriculture, several disinfecting methods involve chemicals that are not allowed in organic agriculture. There is, however, a time-tested organically allowed method for seed disinfection: the hot water treatment.

The crucial aspect of the hot water treatment is maintaining an exact temperature for the entire prescribed duration, which requires a very accurate thermometer and a heat source that provides a constant, controllable temperature (the only thing that truly guarantees that the temperature does not change rapidly is using a very large pot filled with water). The hot water treatment is only suitable for seed that is very vital and fresh. Older, less viable seed can be killed by the hot water treatment, so start with a small amount of seed and then test its germination rate. The seeds of

Course and efficacy of hot water treatment against certain diseases

CROP	WATER TEMPERATURE	TIME	DISEASE	EFFICACY
cabbage	122°F (50°C)	30 minutes	Alternaria brassicicola	98–100 percent
			Phoma lingam	84–100 percent
carrot	122°F (50°C)	30 minutes	Alternaria dauci	94–100 percent
			Alternaria radicina	64–100 percent
			Xanthomonas campestris pv. carotae	97–99 percent
celery	127°F (53°C)	10 minutes	Septoria apiicola	68–84 percent
			Phoma apiicola	83–87 percent
corn salad	122°F (50°C)	30 minutes	Phoma valerianellae	74–98 percent
parsley	122°F (50°C)	30 minutes	Septoria petroselini	68–91 percent
			Alternaria radicina	91–94 percent

Jahn 2003

different crops have their own individual heat and time requirements (see previous table). A hot water treatment of 122°F (50°C) for 30 minutes is effective or highly effective against all the disease pathogens we have reviewed, without reducing seed viability. In fact, after receiving a hot water treatment, seeds germinate faster,

---

Checklist for growing for seed

1. Seed propagation or vegetative propagation?
2. To what species does the crop belong and what other vegetables can it cross with?
3. Selfer or outcrosser? Wind- or insect-pollinated?
4. Is isolation necessary? If so, what kind?
5. What is the ideal time to sow seed?
6. What is the minimum population size?
7. Annual or biennial?
8. What is the overwintering strategy for biennial plants?
9. What are the important selection criteria?
10. What are the important diseases and pests?
11. What are the signs of ripeness and when is the right time to harvest seed?

---

fewer diseases appear, and yields increase. No seed should be heated to over 127°F (53°C), as this would kill the seed.

Genetic engineering

One particular breeding technology has taken over agricultural fields in recent decades: genetic engineering. No other breeding technology has ever spread so quickly—and this despite the fact that most people reject genetically modified seed and genetically modified food. In 1953, James D. Watson and Francis Crick laid the foundation for genetic engineering by establishing the structure of genetic material, thus making direct intervention possible. Genetic engineering is the technology whereby DNA sequences from one species are transferred to another. For the most part, such a transfer would not be possible through natural processes. The smallest unit of breeding is no longer primarily the organism as a whole, but rather that being split into its genes and its genetic effects. Twenty years later, in 1973, genetic engineering was already being applied practically. The first genetically modified plants were planted out in 1986, and currently an inconceivable 222 million acres (90 million hectares) of genetically modified organisms (GMOs) are grown annually, the most common being the cash crops soybeans (soya beans), corn (maize), oilseed rape (including canola), and cotton. Ninety percent of this activity is concentrated in five non-EU countries: USA, Canada, Argentina, Brazil, and China. In the EU, some genetically modified varieties of corn and oilseed rape are approved for growing by farmers; Austria has banned growing these varieties, although from the perspective of the World Trade Organization (WTO), national bans conflict with international trade rules.

GM plants in Europe

Following the numerous scientific trials of genetically modified varieties, from apples to sugar beets, and with the eventual introduction of GM crop plants, the state of breeding and maintaining varieties has radically changed. In order to establish a course of action in this situation, Arche Noah and Pro Specie Rara along with other similar organizations and professional plant breeding companies have founded the GMO-free Seed Syndicate (IG Saatgut). The syndicate finds itself confronted with one problem above all others: plant breeding organizations that do not use genetic engineering need to be able to guarantee that they are truly free of genetically modified organisms. But when non-GMO plants and GMO plants are grown near each other, they inevitably cross-pollinate, which means that not only do GMO plants need to be grown in strict isolation, but so do plants that are to be protected from genetic pollution from GMOs. Organizations like Arche Noah and organic plant breeders now have to bear the burden and costs of a technology that they themselves do not use and in fact reject.

We fear that large and in some cases irreversible damage has been done to old crop varieties through genetic pollution from GMOs, which affects crop diversity.

One strategy for dealing with this which is currently popular politically is the so-called coexistence of GMO and non-GMO agriculture. But in a country like Austria, with relatively small-scale agriculture, such a coexistence is physically impossible: particularly for out-crossing plants like corn and oilseed rape, cross-pollination is unavoidable in small-scale agriculture. Because of this, many regions have declared themselves GMO-free zones. Ten regions in Europe petitioned the EU Commission in 2003 to allow them to practice GMO-free agriculture that is not encumbered by over-regulation; the network, founded in the provinces of Tuscany (Italy) and Upper Austria, now numbers over 35 regions, including Brittany (France) and the Basque Country (Spain).

GMOs in gene banks

Several years ago it was learned that the largest collection of corn in the world, held in Mexico at the International Maize and Wheat Improvement Center (CIMMYT), was contaminated by GMOs. Even heirloom varieties, tended by subsistence farmers on *milpa* fields, have crossed with GM corn imported from the USA. And the gene bank IPK in Gatersleben, Germany, has come under fire from critics because of their practice of growing GM varieties in fields next to preservation grow-outs of older varieties in their collection. Gene banks have, especially in central Europe, long played an important role in maintaining old vegetable varieties. Collecting, maintaining, comparing, describing, and passing along seed from the almost unimaginable number of existing varieties are the most important tasks of gene banks. In growing GM crops directly next to non-GM crops in fields and greenhouses, the IPK gene bank is choosing to ignore its own most basic mission: the maintenance of non-GM crop diversity. In particular, IPK's wheat collection is highly threatened by contamination from GMOs. For over a decade now, the focus of research at IPK has been on molecular genetics, which has led to the practice of growing GMOs right next to heirloom varieties, despite massive protests. International demonstrations to establish a GMO-free zone, to shed light on the danger the IPK collection was facing ("Save the Gatersleben gene bank!"), and to demand a ban on GMO cultivation and research in public gene banks were held in 2007.

Consequences of GMOs

The myriad potential consequences of GM plants for ecosystems are for the most part still unknown, and the impact of the mechanisms through which plant and animal genetic material is changed is still unclear. Unexpected traits appear in GM plants time and again. Researchers have not yet explained the long-term consequences of eating foods based on GMOs; no experiments have been performed, except the civilization-wide test that is currently underway. Particularly alarming is the resistance to antibiotics that has been built into GM plants. This trait could potentially be transferred to bacteria, which could then reproduce. No one wants to take responsibility for the potential damages involved—not the industry that produces the GMOs, not the farmers who grow them, and not the insurance industry.

Hybrid seed—a GMO loophole?

Arche Noah and Pro Specie Rara oppose the use of hybrid seed. Not only because they do not fit in with the basic principles of organic farming and respect for natural cycles. Not only because of how the triumph in recent years of hybrid varieties has led to a decrease in the diversity of open-pollinated varieties. But mainly because biotechnological breeding methods are being increasingly used in hybrid seed production, making it next to impossible for organic farmers to completely eliminate GMOs from what they do.

Somatic fusion is more and more a part of professional plant breeding. This technique has yet to be banned by the International Federation of Organic Agriculture Movements (IFOAM), although the German Federal Association of Plant Breeders has categorized this practice as genetic engineering.

Myth: "GMOs are needed to feed the world"

Many proponents of genetic engineering argue that GM plants have higher yields and that we need these higher yields to feed the world. The non-governmental Food First Network has this reply: "Hunger is no myth, but myths distract us from ending hunger." They go on to compare the promises of the genetic engineering industry with those of the Green Revolution, a decades-long campaign to solve the problem of hunger with capital, pesticides, and chemical fertilizers. It did not succeed. Food scarcity remains a problem of distribution, not of quantities or technology. Despite population growth, 15% more food is available than 20 years ago. The higher yields have not made their way to starving people. Currently, nearly half of plant food grown (mostly corn and soy) is fed to livestock.

Genetically modified plants and animals are protected by patents. Their development and licensing require massive amounts of capital. The consequence: GM seeds and GM food products are more expensive and, in developing countries, are only affordable for those with foreign currency reserves. Farmers find themselves in almost complete subordination to seed companies.

Diversity tastes best fresh from the garden.

The
Plants

Amaranth
AMARANTHACEAE

In this family, *Amaranthus* is the genus that is most important to gardeners. Grain amaranth, leaf amaranth, and ornamental amaranths are found within it; there are dozens of species of amaranths from all over the world. Amaranth seeds and leaves have been used for over 5,000 years. Grain amaranth is considered a pseudocereal because botanically speaking it is not a cereal grain but is used like one and has similar nutritional properties. It was grown by the Incas, Aztecs, and many other peoples of Central and South America until, with the Spanish conquest, it, like so many other indigenous crops, all but disappeared. Lately there has been a renaissance of grain amaranth in the USA and in Europe, thanks to the "discovery" of its high protein content and favorable configuration of amino acids. Leaf amaranth is, by contrast, an important vegetable crop in southeast Asia.

⬤ ⬤

Amaranth, terminal flower head

BOTANICAL CHARACTERISTICS Most members of the amaranth family are herbaceous annuals or perennials. Leaves are simple, alternate and opposite. Amaranths mostly develop terminal, branching, clumping blossoms. The German name for the family, "foxtail," comes from the long, bushy, bent flower heads that do indeed look like the tail of a fox. Plants are monoecious, with inconspicuous flowers. Male flowers are at the base of the flower head, female at the tip. Whereas cultivated varieties of cereal grains have been selected for ever larger seeds, cultivars of amaranth have come to be through selecting for higher numbers of the small seeds they produce.

AMARANTH
Amaranthus spp.

Amaranths are divided into three main categories by use: grain, leaf vegetable, and ornamental. Grain amaranths are ancient crop plants that came into being mainly in the Andes. They are an increasingly important component of global nutrition. Grain amaranth seeds can be cooked like rice, steamed, roasted, or ground for soups. In Europe, puffed amaranth is a popular ingredient in granola bars and crackers. *Amaranthus hypochondriacus* and a subspecies of *A. caudatus* are among the grain amaranths; the latter, known to the Incas as *quihuicha* (kee-wee-cha), was one of the most important foods to South American Indians.

Many amaranths develop large ornamental masses of soft, fine leaves, colored green to red, with many uses, including medicinal. Leaves and shoots can be used for soups and stirfry. In India, young shoots and peeled side growth on older plants are used like asparagus. Dark red varieties of *Amaranthus cruentus* are used in India as well as other parts of the world as dye plants.

Amaranth seeds

Overview of *Amaranthus* species

SPECIES	COMMON NAME	USE
A. lividus	amaranth, wild amaranth, pigweed, purple amaranth	leaf vegetable, ornamental
A. tricolor	amaranth, red amaranth, Chinese spinach, Joseph's coat	leaf vegetable, ornamental
A. cruentus	amaranth, blood amaranth, red amaranth, purple amaranth, African spinach, Indian spinach	grain, leaf vegetable, ornamental
A. hypochondriacus	amaranth, prince's feather	grain, ornamental
A. hybridus	smooth amaranth, smooth pigweed, red amaranth	grain, leaf vegetable, medicinal
A. caudatus ssp. caudatus	love-lies-bleeding, pendant amaranth, tassel flower, velvet flower, foxtail amaranth	ornamental
A. caudatus ssp. mantegazzianus	Inca wheat	grain

Grain amaranth flower heads in a range of colors

WHAT YOU'LL NEED
- 10 to 15 healthy plants
- non-woven cloth bags

POLLINATION NOTES Amaranths are wind-pollinated outcrossers, but according to specialist literature from India, bees will visit amaranths with colorful flower heads. Several varieties can be unambiguously identified as belonging to one or another species only by the most experienced taxonomists, as there is minimal differentiation between them. If you are uncertain about the species of a given amaranth and you would like to propagate more than one variety, observe a spatial isolation distance of at least 650 ft. (200 m). Alternatively you could cover two or three flower heads of each variety with a cloth bag. Ask your neighbors if they are growing amaranth, perhaps as an ornamental; flower heads of ornamental amaranths are very long and sometimes hang all the way down to the ground. For most varieties, a hulled seed develops.

GROWING FOR SEED When starting indoors, time it such that seedlings can be planted out when they have two or three leaves to avoid stunting growth. Otherwise, direct seed outdoors around last frost; amaranth will then germinate when the ground is warm enough. To encourage tall, vigorous plants, thin (or plant out) to 8 in. (20 cm) within the row. Grain amaranth is drought resistant and can be grown in nutrient-poor soils. Vegetable amaranth, on the other hand, does better with plenty of water and rich soil and also needs warm conditions; its leaves can be harvested 20 to 30 days after sowing. Amaranth produces seeds prolifically; expect volunteer amaranth the following year, which can be harvested for its leaves.

HARVEST If a cloth bag has been used, it can be removed after flowering is over. Seeds ripen quickly, so check often to see if they have begun to fall out (tap seedheads with your hand). Harvest entire seedheads and dry on an underlay for several days in a warm, dry place. Thresh in a bag and winnow with the wind and a fine sieve.

SELECTION CHARACTERISTICS Strains and heirloom varieties of amaranth differentiate themselves in flavor, form, and other traits, coming as they do from various countries of origin. Many grain amaranths have flower heads with colors ranging from white to yellow to red, though they all develop seeds of the same color. Possible selection criteria for grain amaranth:

- early ripening
- synchronous ripening
- seed that holds to the plant well
- uniformity in growth, form
- stability

Possible selection criteria for vegetable amaranth:

- healthy, juicy leaves
- long harvesting period before flowering

DISEASES AND PESTS No problems have been observed at Arche Noah. In climates with a shorter growing season, it can be a challenge to get amaranth seed to ripen completely; try using short-season varieties.

CULTIVATION HISTORY The various species have cultivation histories as varied as their places of origins and eras of domestication. Amaranths from the Andes were domesticated thousands of years ago, and for many indigenous peoples, amaranth was the most important grain crop. Because of its high concentration of the essential amino acid lysine, amaranth is the ideal complement to corn (maize). Invading Spaniards were astonished by the vigor of aboriginal Central and South Americans; they learned that the natives ate of a fruit that was "no larger than a pinhead." In order to break the Indians once and for all, they sought to rid the world of this "devilish plant." And so it came to be that corn, beans, and potatoes all found their way into the Western diet—but amaranth was all but forgotten.

Amaranth is one of the most important vegetables in southeast Asia and has been grown in China for thousands of years. In Europe, the classic amaranth, *Amaranthus lividus*, has also been cultivated for millennia; the Greek botanist Theophrast reported the vegetable being grown in the 3rd century BC. Another species with a long tradition in Europe is *A. tricolor*, which was still a popular crop plant in many European countries at the end of the 19th century. Amaranth was also on the list of plants grown on Charlemagne's estates.

Artichoke and relatives

ASTERACEAE

Asteraceae is the largest and most diverse family, with members found all over the world. Its ranks of ornamentals alone are legion—everything from A for aster to Z for zinnia; the genera to which our crop plants belong are few in comparison. Still, it's hard to imagine a vegetable garden without lettuce, while others in the family, like burdock, are hardly thought of as crops at all. Most aster family plants have an aromatic scent and tangy flavor. Many store inulin (not to be confused with insulin) in their roots instead of starch; inulin is a sugar that diabetics can consume. An occasional family characteristic is production of a milky white or cream-colored fluid.

• •

BOTANICAL CHARACTERISTICS Individual flowers stand upon spherical or hemispherical, recessed "baskets." The previous name of the family, Compositae, and the derived common name "composite" (which is still used colloquially) refer to this floral arrangement. What we call the flower is, botanically speaking, a basket-shaped flowering head composed of numerous individual sessile flowers, each of which produces one seed when fertilized. Another common characteristic is the pappus, the feathery bristles that help the seeds be carried by the wind.

GENERAL PROPAGATION CHARACTERISTICS Aster family plants have perfect flowers. Most members are self-fertile outcrossers, running the gamut from strict self-pollination to principally cross-pollination; lettuce is a typical selfer that rarely cross-pollinates. The individual flowers of a flower head can sometimes pollinate each

The individual flowers of aster family plants occur in a basket-shaped flowering head.

other. For sunflower, salsify, or scorzonera, out-crossing is the rule, but self-pollination can occur. Artichoke, cardoon, and others pollinate only through insects.

Overview of the aster family

COMMON NAME	GENUS	SPECIES
lettuce	*Lactuca*	*sativa*
endive	*Cichorium*	*endivia*
chicory	*Cichorium*	*intybus*
artichoke	*Cynara*	*scolymus*
cardoon	*Cynara*	*cardunculus*
scorzonera	*Scorzonera*	*hispanica*
salsify	*Tragopogon*	*porrifolius*
burdock	*Arctium*	*lappa*
garland chrysanthemum	*Chrysanthemum*	*coronarium*
Jerusalem artichoke	*Helianthus*	*tuberosus*
sunflower	*Helianthus*	*annuus*

LETTUCE
Lactuca sativa

WHAT YOU'LL NEED
- 10 healthy heads of lettuce
- rods or horizontally stretched netting

POLLINATION NOTES Lettuce self-pollinates, with cross-pollination (usually by hoverflies) occurring only rarely (2% of the time). Ten or so feet (a few meters) of separation between beds of lettuce suffice. Plants that are not true-to-type in the next generation can simply be eaten and not further propagated, though if some of these suit your fancy, allow them to go to seed. The variety 'Maikönig' (May king) came to be in 1913 in this way, after being found in a plot of another variety.

GROWING FOR SEED Find the best-looking heads of lettuce in your plot and place a stick or something similar in the ground next to them to mark them. Never use the first heads of lettuce to bolt for seed; this selects for early bolting—a trait that no gardener known to us finds desirable.

If you are planting a bed specifically for growing lettuce for seed, plan on each flowering plant requiring about twice as much space in every direction as plants being grown for food.

When growing for seed, it is important to plant out as early as possible. All lettuce varieties (even those that would normally be grown later) should be started in late winter to early spring. Seeds need to then ripen in the driest period of the growing season. The exception here is winter lettuce, which should be grown and selected in late summer.

Bolting heads of lettuce (especially iceberg lettuce) often need help with getting their flowering stalks through the tight head of leaves. To this end, cut an X in the leaves with a sharp knife, taking care not to cut so deep as to injure the stalk. Once

Lettuce seeds can be, depending on the variety, white, black, or yellowish brown.

plants bolt, check leaves at the base of the stalk often for signs of rot and remove as necessary to ensure the health and stability of the stalk. Flowering lettuce needs additional support; they can be tied to, for example, the sticks you used to mark them in the first place. For larger plots, stretch wide-meshed netting horizontally over poles at each corner, through which the seed stalks of the lettuce plants can grow and be supported.

Take special care during the final phase of seed ripening, as seeds can be knocked free by rain or the entire plant could succumb to fungal disease in wet weather. Build a simple roof over flowering lettuce or grow in containers indoors.

Use the tendency of lettuce plants to self-sow to your advantage by planting these seedlings in their own bed for a late summer crop or by harvesting baby salad greens.

Overview of *Lactuca sativa* crops

COMMON NAME	BOTANICAL VARIETY	CENTERS OF CULTIVATION
romaine (cos)	var. *longifolia*	Mediterranean
butterhead	var. *capitata nidus jaggeri*	Europe, USA
iceberg (crisphead)	var. *capitata nidus tenerrima*	Europe, USA
loose leaf	var. *crispa*	Europe
celtus (asparagus lettuce)	var. *angustana*	Asia
deer tongue	unsettled	Mediterranean, North Africa, South America
oil types (cow lettuce)	unsettled	southern Egypt

HARVEST Seeds are ready for harvest 12 to 24 days after flowering. Each seed ripens at its own pace. Test by carefully rubbing seed capsules between your thumb and index fingers; seeds are ripe when the capsule crumbles, and the seed easily falls out. If this does not happen and the capsule still feels "doughy," allow more time to ripen. The best seeds are those from flowers along the main stalk.

There are many ways to harvest lettuce seeds; here's the one we use at Arche Noah: the first stage of harvesting consists of plucking ripe seeds from well-formed stalks. At this stage, shaking or striking as a method of separating seed from plant is not an option, as too few seeds on the plant are ripe. The second (or third, etc.) time through, seeds are rubbed or tapped into a container by carefully bending the stalks over a bucket (or sieve). This is more easily done with two people, with one person holding the container and the other carefully moving the stalks

The first seeds are ready for plucking.

By late summer, lettuce has self-sown from this lettuce plant. These seedlings can be placed in their own bed and harvested until winter.

into position and rubbing the seeds free between flattened hands. (Caution: different varieties have varying degrees of pliability; take care not to break stalks.)

Hang harvested seeds in a cloth bag in a room with good air circulation to dry. Most of the material in the bag will be plant debris and nonviable seed.

When wet weather threatens while seeds are ripening, harvest entire plants, roots and all, and hang them to dry in a rain-protected spot (clean soil from roots or place roots in a cloth bag to avoid soil getting mixed up with seed, which is difficult to clean). Place a towel or sheet underneath to catch seed that falls and thresh remaining seed from stalks when ripe.

Winnowing begins after a thorough threshing. Harvested materials should be very dry. Then comes winnowing with sieves, which requires some skill and

Stalks of the loose leaf lettuce 'Lollo Rossa'

improves with experience. Many find lettuce seed to be the vegetable seed that is the most difficult to clean. First, sieve out coarser plant debris like parts of stalks. Then use a slotted sieve, ideally with $\frac{1}{32}$–$\frac{3}{64}$ in. (0.8–1.2 mm) perforations, to separate seeds from remaining chaff. Use the wind to perform a final winnowing of small portions of seeds. The most effective cleaning step will depend on the variety, the harvest method (plucking or threshing), weather conditions during harvest, etc.

SELECTION CHARACTERISTICS Propagating lettuce in a greenhouse, though often convenient, risks unintentional selection for traits that are not useful for growing in outdoor gardens. Potential selection criteria:

- robust plants
- typical or special leaf shape and size
- size and firmness of head
- health and disease resistance
- flavor
- color scheme of leaves
- anthocyanin content (the source of red color in leaves)
- drought, cold, or heat tolerance
- resistance to downy mildew and other diseases
- late bolting
- soft leaves for butterhead lettuce, crispy leaves for iceberg lettuce
- "self-closing" romaine lettuce heads
- hardiness of winter lettuce

DISEASES AND PESTS The same diseases are of concern for lettuce whether growing for food or seed. Mosaic virus, evidenced by light to dark green spotted leaves, is usually spread by aphids or is seed-borne. Do not save seed from infected plants! Covering lettuce with fine-meshed netting can protect plants from aphids. White mold (*Sclerotinia sclerotiorum*) is treacherous when it infects seed stalks. Prevention: healthy soil, crop rotation. Treatment: soil can be treated with Contans WG, an organic biofungicide.

CULTIVATION HISTORY A direct ancestor of cultivated lettuce has never been satisfactorily identified. It was long assumed that prickly lettuce (*Lactuca serriola*) was the species from which cultivated lettuce was domesticated; now it is thought that *L. sativa* arose in cultivation and that, in addition to prickly lettuce, other lettuce species (such as wild lettuce, *L.*

Lettuce flowers

virosa, and willowleaf lettuce, *L. saligna*) were also involved. Lettuce is completely dependent on humans for reproduction and thus will not naturalize. The first breeding goals in the history of lettuce were likely the disappearance of the bristly thorns along the middle rib of the underside of the leaf and the reduction of the bitter milky fluid lactucarium. The delaying of bolting was and still is an important selection criterium, so a head rich in leaves that does not turn bitter has time to develop.

In Egypt, lettuces have been grown for over 4,000 years for oil (from lettuce seed), as a medicinal, and as food for humans and animals. Lettuce has been cultivated in Europe since around AD 800. The first description of butterhead lettuce was written in 1543 by Leonard Fuchs. Varieties that form a head presumably come from the combination of spontaneous mutations and selection by central European gardeners.

ENDIVE
Cichorium endivia

The three forms of endive—cultivated endive (var. *endivia*), curly endive (var. *crispum*), and escarole (var. *latifolia*)—differ from each other in shape, sowing and harvesting times, and use. Cultivated endive ("summer endive" in German, for that is the season of its use) quickly develops slender leaves but does not form a head. Curly endives often have finely slotted or curled leaves and can be used like an autumn lettuce. Escarole, with its smooth-bordered leaves, is a better storage endive.

WHAT YOU'LL NEED
- 10 to 15 well-formed and well-overwintered plants
- overwintering strategy
- trellis

POLLINATION NOTES Endives are insect-pollinated outcrossers. Multiple varieties can be cross-pollinated by insects, so in an ideally arranged home garden, use an isolation distance of 500 ft. (150 m) between different varieties (or grow only

Endive seed differentiates itself clearly from lettuce seed.

Endive and chicory flowers share the same brilliant blue color.

one variety per year). Since wild endive is not found wild in central Europe, crossing with it is not a danger there. Chicory varieties (*Cichorium intybus*) do not cross-pollinate endive (though endive can cross-pollinate chicory). When growing plants in isolation cages, mason bees, bumblebees, and some hoverfly species can be used. Flowers are open only in the morning. They wither at midday, and new flowers open the next day. Blossoming occurs over several weeks. Hand pollination is also a possibility: similar to what is done in hand pollinating squash, endive flower

Moderately curled escarole

Cultivated endive does not develop a head.

buds are shut with tape or covered with a non-woven cloth bag. Pollinate the next day with a brush and re-cover.

GROWING FOR SEED Endives are normally grown for seed as biennials. Some endive varieties (especially escaroles and cultivated endives) can flower in the first year but are unable to produce ripe seeds in a temperate climate. The exception that proves the rule: at Dreschflegel in Germany, a curly endive variety is sown early and seed is harvested the same year. When overwintering in a root cellar, the ideal time to start seeds is mid to late summer.

Where winters are frost-free and not too wet, endive can be overwintered in the ground outdoors. For overwintering in a root cellar, dig up plants in mid to late autumn, cut leaves back to about 2 in. (5 cm), and trim smaller and branched roots. Plants will store in sand or sandy soil for the winter at 32–39°F (0–4°C) and around 80% humidity for three to four months. Larger plants are more susceptible to rot than smaller ones; you may choose to overwinter only small plants for this reason. Curly endive doesn't store as well as other endives. For this reason, Arche Noah waits until early autumn to sow curly endive seed and then overwinters young plants in pots in a frost-free tunnel or cold frame. The best plants are selected the following spring once they have developed more leaves before flowering. The plants flower in early summer and grow to 24–48 in. (60–120 cm); the flower stalks are cumbersomely branched and have a light blue flower in each leaf axil.

HARVEST Plants often flower until late in autumn, which may give the impression that the harvest must wait until at least then. The best endive seeds, however, as with most crop plants, come from the first flowers to bloom, so pay close attention. Wait to harvest these early seeds, and you risk that finches and other birds get to them first, or that they'll be overcome by fungi. Better to harvest seeds as they ripen by plucking them from the plant, or cut whole stalks and hang them indoors to complete the ripening process. When plucking ripe seed, make sure you are actually getting seed and not empty pods, as storms can knock seeds free.

Seeds can be freed from pods with a rolling pin. Winnow with sieves and the wind.

SELECTION CHARACTERISTICS
- typical or exceptional leaf shape or size
- tight, well-developed rosette
- late bolting
- plants with lots of yellow (= low amounts of bitter compounds)

DISEASES AND PESTS We have observed hardly any diseases on plants being grown for seed, though endive rust (*Puccinia hieracii*), which can especially affect bolting endive plants, is described in the

Just-withered endive flower stalks

literature. Light spots appear all over the infected plant, including on petals.

CULTIVATION HISTORY The ancestor of cultivated endive is the wild endive (ssp. *pumilum*), native to the Mediterranean region; the family trees of the other two forms are not yet clear. The oldest verified accounts of endive cultivation are from Italy around the birth of Christ. In central Europe, endive is first given mention in Charlemagne's *Capitulare de Villis*. It was not until the 19th century, however, that endive was grown in larger quantities and bred into different varieties.

CHICORY
Cichorium intybus

Wild chicory (*Cichorium intybus* var. *intybus*), with its brilliant blue floral displays along paths and streets, is the ancestor of all cultivated varieties of chicory. This includes the red-white or yellowish green radicchio, which is mainly grown in Italy, especially in the Veneto; radicchio takes two forms: plants that develop into heads and plants that develop rosettes. A second type of chicory is sugarloaf, once called *Fleischkraut* (flesh cabbage) in German, which is typically grown as an autumn/winter salad crop. A third is Belgian endive (UK: chicory; despite its being called "endive" in the USA, this is, botanically speaking, a type of chicory); this type is mostly grown for the production of chicons (blanched chicory buds). All three types are considered leaf chicories (var. *foliosum*); root chicory is var. *sativum*.

All chicory cultivars contain the bitter compound lactucopicrin (intybin), which helps with digestion, although radicchio contains much more than Belgian endive.

WHAT YOU'LL NEED
- 15 well-developed and well-overwintered plants
- overwintering strategy
- support poles and string

POLLINATION NOTES What was said of endive applies here, for the most part, except that with chicory, you must be aware of your plants' potential for crossing with the wild form. Again, endive can cross-pollinate chicory (though not vice versa), so we advise growing only one chicory variety for seed per year. Alternatively, strictly observe a spatial isolation distance of at least 500 ft. (150 m) from all endive or chicory varieties (or use isolation cages).

GROWING FOR SEED Some varieties are sensitive to temperature; they bolt in the first

Red radicchio can have a rounded or a pointed shape. Heads are always enclosed in several surrounding loose leaves.

year when it starts to get cold. Do not save seed from early-bolting plants! Otherwise, all instructions for endive are valid for radicchio and leaf chicories.

Overwinter chicory roots with trimmed leaves in a root cellar. Select plants after they have begun to grow back in darkness in late winter and plant out, taking care to allow them to slowly adjust to sunlight to avoid "burning" leaves.

SELECTION CHARACTERISTICS
- typical or exceptional leaf shape, color, and size
- well-developed tight rosette
- late bolting
- vigorous taproot for Belgian endive
- large and especially tight chicons for Belgian endive
- large roots with consistent thickness for root chicory
- good aroma and sufficient level of bitter compounds for root chicory

CULTIVATION HISTORY Blanching of secondary growth from cut chicory plants was happened upon in 1850 in the Brussels Botanical Garden and further developed there. To produce chicons, roots of Belgian endives grown outdoors are cut and moved into dark rooms to keep the leaves white and prevent them from opening. Root chicory was grown on a large scale in Germany and Austria in the 19th century for the production of a chicory-based coffee substitute. Root chicory varieties with low contents of bitter compounds are grown in Italy and are found in winter vegetable markets as *soncino*.

ARTICHOKE
Cynara scolymus

Seen from a botanical point of view, the artichoke is a somewhat strange vegetable: the swollen flower receptacle of the bud (the "heart") and the swollen bud scales are what is eaten. Artichokes are known only in their cultivated form; they presumably derive from a wild form of cardoon (*Cynara cardunculus*).

WHAT YOU'LL NEED
- 10 to 15 healthy plants
- Mediterranean or maritime climate

POLLINATION NOTES What is colloquially called an artichoke flower is actually an entire inflorescence made up of dozens of small, individual flowers. These individual artichoke flowers are self-infertile: the anthers send their pollen out five days before the stigma is able to receive it. Individual flowers of the whole inflorescence of the plant can fertilize each other. Honeybees and bumblebees often visit artichoke flowers. Individual artichoke

Artichoke seeds

varieties can cross with each other and also with cardoon varieties, so they must be isolated from one another: 650–800 ft. (200–250 m) between varieties in a diversely planted garden. Hand pollination is also a possibility: bag the flowers of as many plants as possible with a paper or non-woven fabric bag. Pollinate each flower with a brush. In areas with a very mild climate, artichokes self-sow and can become a weed. Simply cut flowers if no seed is desired.

PROPAGATION Artichokes can be propagated sexually (by seed) or vegetatively (via basal side shoots). They can be grown for seed only in warm regions with long growing seasons; in central Europe, they are grown in sandy soils, which warm faster than heavier soils. Varieties that flower in the first year must be sown early (late winter/early spring) if the seeds are to ripen fully; many varieties do not bloom in the first year even when seed is sown early. Plants are not frost resistant, but in areas with mild winters, artichokes can be harvested for several years. Plants

Insects love the large violet flower heads of the artichoke.

produced by sexual propagation are often highly variable, requiring great care during selection. But propagation by seed is good for rejuvenation and to increase genetic diversity, which gives wider choice for selection; the best of these plants, produced sexually, can then be propagated vegetatively.

Artichokes can be overwintered outdoors by mulching heavily with leaves and soil. In areas with winter frosts, high precipitation, and rapidly changing temperatures, plants will likely not survive the winter. Water makes its way into the cut, hollow stems from the previous year, goes to the roots, freezes when cold enough, and quickly leads to rot. With the roots kept dry, plants are hardy to zone 6. Artichokes grown in hoop houses or high tunnels can survive the winter in even colder zones.

The following vegetative propagation method has been successful at Arche Noah: artichokes are dug up in mid to late autumn and overwintered in an unheated hoop house. (Overwintering in the root cellar was not successful.) They begin to grow again in late winter—that is, much too early for planting out. This new growth is much less hardy than the roots (and frozen shoots can lead to root death); therefore, it is important to dig up the artichokes from the hoop house when new growth starts to appear and place them in a frost-proof site. Remove the new shoots when they are 4–6 in. (10–15 cm) long with a sharp knife, taking care to leave a bit of the root attached; leave the two to four best shoots on the rootstock, which can then also be separated. Plant shoots in pots and place them in a cool, frost-proof environment. This way, you'll have many young plants that send up flower heads in their first year.

HARVEST Harvest artichoke heads as fuzz starts to develop in the open flower buds. Cut off entire flower heads and hang to dry. When the stems have dried, place flower heads one at a time in a cloth bag and break them open with a wide rubber mallet on a sturdy but pliable surface (e.g., an old futon or mattress). The relatively heavy seeds collect at the bottom of the bag. Remove these seeds before moving on to the next flower head to avoid damaging them.

SELECTION CHARACTERISTICS
• size of buds, wide shape of bud, "meatiness" of the heart or scales
• early ripeness
• uniform bud color
• vigorous growth
• resistance to frost and rot

DISEASES AND PESTS Artichoke flower heads and fruits are highly susceptible to fungal infections: their densely crowded pappus hairs hold water well and dry poorly, especially in late autumn.

CULTIVATION HISTORY The artichoke comes from the eastern Mediterranean, where it has been grown since ancient times. Introduced to Germany around 1650, it was even then an expensive delicacy. By the end of the 18th century, artichokes were a favored vegetable in Austria, so much so that gardeners were hardly able to meet demand and sold them at high prices. One was able to amass a small fortune by growing artichokes for the gentry; he dedicated his fine new Viennese house to the vegetable that had bestowed such wealth upon him: Zur goldenen Artischocke ("to the golden artichoke"). By the end of the 19th century, the Viennese artichoke craze had subsided.

CARDOON
Cynara cardunculus

Cardoon distinguishes itself from the artichoke with its much smaller and more numerous flower heads (that have no meaty "heart") and through its uses: the fleshy, blanched leaf stalks are used as a vegetable and its seeds are used for fermentation in goat cheese production. Cardoon, like the artichoke, contains cynarine, a bitter compound that aids digestion and stimulates bile activity. Plants take two forms, those with thorny,

The flower bud of the cardoon is very like an artichoke but does not develop swollen scales.

woolly-haired leaves (var. *ermis*) and those without (var. *inermis*).

WHAT YOU'LL NEED
- at least 10 (ideally 15) healthy plants
- leaf or straw mulch for winter

POLLINATION NOTES Cardoon can cross-pollinate with artichoke (which see). Isolation distance: 650–800 ft. (200–250 m).

GROWING FOR SEED Cardoon is a perennial plant that is grown as an annual for food, as a biennial for seed, and as a perennial when grown as an ornamental. It is always propagated sexually, by seed. In central Europe (zone 6), start seeds indoors in late winter. When sowing seed outdoors, place three or four seeds in a planting hole 2.5 in. (6 cm) deep every 3 ft. (1 m) in mid to late spring. After sprouting, keep the one most vigorous plant per hole. This is the standard cultivation method in France, Italy, and Spain, where cardoon is grown in fields. Plants flower in autumn, but since seeds can no longer ripen that late in the year (and a primary selection goal is good leaf stalk development), flower stalks should be removed at this point. Dig up plants, root ball and all, in mid to late autumn and store in a frost-free environment.

Cardoon is hardier than the artichoke. Plants usually survive the winter outdoors in central Europe. Cut back to heart leaves (4–6 in. [10–15 cm] above the ground) and mulch with leaves or straw. We recommend some kind of roofing, as wet leaves or straw quickly leads to rot. Seeds can be harvested the following year.

HARVEST As for artichokes.

SELECTION CHARACTERISTICS
- "meatiness" and minimal stringiness of leaf stalks
- minimal content of bitter compounds (taste blanched plants)
- resistance to frost (and rot)

Cardoon—a protected Swiss variety

Cardoon is part of the traditional Christmas meal in Geneva, Switzerland—not cooked but rather scalded, with boiling salt water and a bit of milk. The variety 'Cardon épineux Argenté de Plainpalais' recently received an AOC ("controlled designation of origin") certification and, when marketed as a traditional Swiss specialty, must be produced in the greater Geneva area. This variety came to be around 200 years ago and grows to be 5 ft. (1.5 m) tall; its fleshy leaf veins and stalks have prickles. Although difficult to grow and prepare, it is considered to be the best cultivar there is, culinarily speaking.

BLANCHING The blanched leaf stalks are what is eaten from cardoon plants. Blanching removes the fairly strong, bitter taste that cardoon naturally has. The blanching process is time-consuming, but the reward is a delicious winter vegetable. Starting in early autumn, plants are loosely tied together at numerous positions and covered with straw, ground cover, or cardboard. Be careful not to injure the leaf stalks. If needed, hill up soil around the plants to improve their stability. Depending on the temperature, blanched leaves can be harvested in two to four weeks. After around mid autumn blanching can no longer be done outdoors. Dig up plants with roots still encased in a ball of soil and continue to blanch from late autumn to late winter in a root cellar or other dark room.

CULTIVATION HISTORY Wild cardoon is recognizable by its extremely prickly leaves, stems, and flowers. It comes from the Mediterranean region, and the cultivated form presumably originated in Spain, whence it spread to southern France and eventually to central Europe. Cultivation in Germany began in the 17th century. Over and over again, cardoon was all but forgotten, only to be rediscovered. In western Switzerland, it is still grown on a large scale.

SCORZONERA, BLACK SALSIFY
Scorzonera hispanica

For the most part, only the long, soft taproots of scorzonera are eaten, but young shoots and flower buds can be cooked and eaten like asparagus. Young leaves cut in spring make for an excellent salad, with flower buds, sautéed in butter, sprinkled on top. Scorzonera, also called black salsify, is only black on the outside. The root is white on the inside with a milky "flesh"; the taste is reminiscent of asparagus for some, cauliflower for others, and still others are reminded of artichoke. If scorzonera is new to you, give it a try!

Cardoon overwintering in a root cellar in Switzerland: the enormous plants of the variety 'Cardon épineux Argenté de Plainpalais' are stood up in the cellar to blanch.

Scorzonera seeds

WHAT YOU'LL NEED
- 15 well-shaped plants

POLLINATION NOTES Scorzonera flowers are yellow, star-shaped basket flowers that smell like vanilla. They open early in the morning and close at midday. Multiple varieties grown together can be cross-pollinated by insects, so observe an isolation distance of 500 ft. (150 m) or isolate mechanically. Mason bees, bumblebees, and hoverflies are effective pollinators to use in cages.

GROWING FOR SEED Scorzonera is grown as a biennial for seed. The plants themselves are perennials, but do not produce seed until the second year. Sow seed as early as possible. Some varieties that have had little breeding work done on them bolt the first year. Do not collect seed from plants that bolt the first year. The roots overwinter well outdoors down to zone 4. Still, for selection purposes, dig up plants in autumn, cut back leaves, and store in moist sawdust (sawdust from freshly milled green wood) or sand at 32–39°F (0–4°C) and 90+% humidity. Plants should last at least four months when stored in these conditions. In early spring, select for size and shape, and plant these out. Do not harvest shoots from second-year scorzonera if you wish to harvest seed.

HARVEST Scorzonera seeds develop, like all aster family plants, on the flower receptacle. When the seed is ripe, it is easily released (e.g., by the slightest wind) from the receptacle and falls to the ground. We find it easiest to harvest seed stalks that are almost, but not quite, ripe. To determine the right time to harvest, watch for the terminal "fluff" to begin to open. Starting in midsummer, harvest

Scorzonera roots and flowers

Scorzonera flower

continually for several weeks. Leave seed in the shade for two to three days to dry. By rubbing and carefully threshing seed in a cloth bag, the seed is separated from the fluff and other plant debris. Nonviable seed easily bends or snaps. Seeds are dry enough for storage when they are no longer pliant.

SELECTION CHARACTERISTICS
- root: long, uniformly thick, unbranched, not hollow
- skin: beautiful black color and fine surface
- good flavor and no strings
- minimal susceptibility to powdery mildew

DISEASES AND PESTS Powdery mildew (*Erysiphe cichoracearum*) can appear in scorzonera patches. It typically appears after midsummer and does not affect root yield. Regular watering helps keep it at bay and encourages rapid growth of new leaves. What can be more problematic is a serious case of powdery mildew in the second year when growing for seed, which can affect flower and seed development. The fungus *Sclerotinia sclerotiorum* is a seed-borne mold. Upper parts of stems and flowers turn brown and flowers sometimes fall off the plant. Bean-shaped, black sclerotia (up to 0.5 in. [1 cm] compact mycelial masses) are found in the stems. This fungus can lead to rot, whether out in the field or in storage (treat soil with the biofungicide Contans WG). Several species of rust fungi (scorzonera rust, *Puccinia scorzonerae*, and white rust, *Albugo candida*) can cause problems; in the small plots of home gardens, however, the danger of infection is minimal.

Massive aphid infestations on flower stalks and buds and feeding damage from various caterpillars can reduce seed yields. For serious problems, use an organic plant protection product.

CULTIVATION HISTORY The cultivated version of this plant comes from southern Europe, where the wild form grows in dry fields and forest glades. Domestication presumably occurred in Spain, though the first written evidence of its cultivation comes from Italy (second half of 16th century). It was first used as a medicinal, and since 1600 in France as a vegetable. It has been grown in England since the late 17th century, which is around when it started to be grown in gardens in the German-speaking world.

SALSIFY
Tragopogon porrifolius

Common (or purple) salsify is a newly rediscovered crop plant. It is often compared to scorzonera, but it has a completely different flavor. Roots can become 6–12 in. (15–30 cm) long and 1–2 in. (2–5 cm) thick. Not only the root of salsify is edible: young leaves are fresh and tasty in salads or cooked like spinach. Buds and flowers enliven salads. Young shoots, a delicacy, can be eaten like asparagus. As fresh vegetables are few and far between in spring, the young shoots of many biennial plants, including salsify, have been traditionally used at this season.

WHAT YOU'LL NEED
- 15 well-formed plants
- rabbit-proof garden fence

POLLINATION NOTES Salsify is an outcrosser whose perfect flowers are pollinated by insects. Its extremely decorative purple basket flowers bloom from early to mid summer. To maintain varietal purity, observe isolation distances of 500 ft. (150 m), or mechanically isolate different varieties.

Old seed propagation literature claims that salsify will cross with meadow salsify aka Jack-go-to-bed-at-noon (*Tragopogon pratensis*), but we have never observed this at Arche Noah.

GROWING FOR SEED Salsify is grown for seed as a biennial. Do not save seed from plants that flower the first year (select instead for bolt resistance). In contrast to scorzonera, salsify becomes hard, woody, and inedible after flowering. It can be overwintered outdoors in zones 4 and above. Dig roots in the spring, select, then replant.

HARVEST As with all aster family plants, seeds develop on the flower receptacle and are ripe when they easily separate from it. Harvest seeds continually from midsummer to early autumn, as ripe seeds are easily carried away in the wind. Because the pappus "fuzz" and the seed often get wound up in a clump, harvest in the morning, when the pappus is still compact and can be easily twisted off the seed (see scorzonera).

SELECTION CHARACTERISTICS
- root: long, straight, thick, unbranched
- skin: smooth and fine

Salsify seeds

Salsify seeds ready for harvesting

The decorative flowers and beautifully shaped buds of salsify

- good flavor
- bolt resistance
- resistance to powdery mildew

DISEASES AND PESTS Like scorzonera, some varieties of salsify are susceptible to powdery mildew, in which case use farther planting distances to improve air circulation. Aphids, particularly blackflies, are known to infest flower stalks and flower buds especially; treat early to minimize damage. Rabbits like to eat buds and flowers in the spring. Mice and moles like to eat roots left in the ground over winter. Roots overwintered indoors are susceptible to rot or dark-winged fungus gnat infestation.

Salsify that has been selected for straight, unbranched roots for many generations

CULTIVATION HISTORY Salsify is a very old crop plant from southeastern Europe and northern Africa. It was apparently known and grown in ancient Greece; during the Renaissance it was mentioned in many plant books. Since then, however, it has been grown less and less in central Europe and has been all but forgotten. The roots of meadow salsify are also edible though much thinner.

BURDOCK
Arctium lappa

Edible burdock roots can grow to be up to 35 in. (90 cm) long and can be harvested in the first year of cultivation. In east Asia and in Australia, burdock is also grown by market gardeners. In professional cultivation they are often grown in raised beds for ease of harvest. Young shoots and the cores of young stalks from the second year make for delicious vegetables, usually cooked, fried, or boiled.

WHAT YOU'LL NEED
- 15 well-formed burdock roots
- strong poles to support seed stalks

POLLINATION NOTES Flowers self-pollinate, but multiple varieties can be cross-pollinated by insects. Because the plants are very conspicuous and are well liked by honeybees, plant multiple varieties at least 1000 ft. (300 m) apart. Cultivated burdock can cross with naturalized burdock growing in the wild.

GROWING FOR SEED Burdock is sown in late spring and harvested in autumn. If sown too early, the root will become hollow and too thick. Plants are biennial and tolerate intense heat and intense cold. Dig up roots in autumn for selection. In moist sand or in a mixture of wood shavings and cocopeat, roots can be overwintered in a root cellar just like carrots. Plant out in early spring at 30 by 40 in. (80 by 100 cm). Seed stalks can grow to be over 6 ft. (2 m) tall and require sturdy poles for support.

HARVEST Harvest fruits (burrs) when they become dry and brownish. Finches and other birds like to feed on burdock seed as well, so you may need to consider covering seed stalks with bird netting as seeds ripen. Only fully ripened fruits thresh well.

SELECTION CHARACTERISTICS The most important criterium is its workability in the kitchen: select for smooth and unbranched roots. The ideal size depends on what the root will be used for. Thicker, shorter roots are easier to pull from the ground in one piece.

DISEASES AND PESTS The fungal disease powdery mildew (*Erysiphe cichoracearum*) can affect the seed stalks of burdock.

Burdock seeds

The unusual flower of edible burdock

Leaf, fruits, and medium-sized roots of edible burdock

Although this is not technically a seed-borne disease, a case of powdery mildew infection can be so severe that spores cover the seeds. Greater plant separation (one plant per 10 ft.² [1 m²]) may help prevent outbreak. Massive aphid infestations on flowers and buds can reduce seed yield; treat early.

CULTIVATION HISTORY Cultivated burdock is native to Japan. In east Asia, it is widely grown as a vegetable, in the form of numerous small-leaved, large-rooted cultivars, such as 'Takinogawa'. Now naturalized all over the world, burdock is found in the wild in the meadows and forest glades of Europe, where it has long been used as a medicinal plant but is rarely eaten. Charlemagne recorded burdock in his *Capitulare de Villis* as "parduna."

GARLAND CHRYSANTHEMUM
Chrysanthemum coronarium

Garland chrysanthemum is related to colorful ornamentals we see each autumn. There are three types of garland chrysanthemum:

- with thin, finely separated, dark petals (from north China)
- with medium-sized petals (from Japan)
- with wide, bright green petals (from southwest China)

Wide-leaved varieties do best in warmer areas; in zone 6 central Europe, Japanese breeds do the best. Tender shoots and young leaves can be continuously harvested starting 30 days after sowing and continuing, in milder climates, throughout the winter. Commercial growers cut entire rosettes and sell them in bundles.

WHAT YOU'LL NEED
- 50 healthy plants

POLLINATION NOTES Garden chrysanthemums produce simple yellow composite flowers. These self-pollinate but can be cross-pollinated by insects. Observe an isolation distance of 1000 ft. (300 m) between multiple varieties. Alternatively, bag flowers or grow in an isolation cage (pollinator insects are not necessary).

Garland chrysanthemum seeds

Garland chrysanthemums are, thanks to their beautiful flowers, also frequently grown as ornamentals.

GROWING FOR SEED The garland chrysanthemum is an annual and grows to 8–15 in. (20–40 cm) tall. Sow midspring so that plants do not bolt so rapidly and can be selected for good leaf development, and seeds have ample time to ripen. When growing for edible leaves, sow from early spring to early autumn. For seed harvest and cleaning, proceed as for lettuce (*Lactuca sativa*).

DISEASES AND PESTS Under normal conditions, diseases and pests are rarely an issue with garland chrysanthemums. Occasionally, leaf spot disease (pathogens: *Gloeosporium chrysanthemi* or *Cercospora chrysanthemi*) can occur. Both fungi are seed-borne, so do not save seed from affected plants.

CULTIVATION HISTORY This chrysanthemum species comes from the Mediterranean region, presumably Portugal. It is widely cultivated in Japan and China as a vegetable and herb plant.

Ripe seeds of garland chrysanthemums can be plucked directly from the flower receptacles.

JERUSALEM ARTICHOKE
Helianthus tuberosus

The genus *Helianthus* contains 67 species, both annuals and perennials (e.g., *H. maximiliani*, Maximilian sunflower, which is grown for its thin but tasty root). Botanically speaking the Jerusalem artichoke is a tuber. Jerusalem artichokes come in practically every shape, size, and color: carrot-shaped with yellow tubers, white and red varieties with light-colored flesh, oblong and spherical and every imaginable combination thereof. In recent decades, this South American cousin of the sunflower has gained considerable popularity, thanks at least in part to its ability to produce vigorous vegetative growth year after year. At the same time, it is becoming more and more common to find it naturalized, especially along rivers, suppressing native species.

WHAT YOU'LL NEED
- 10 to 15 good-looking tubers
- lots of garden space or a rhizome barrier (well casing, used washing machine drum, culvert piece, etc.)

PROPAGATION Although some varieties will flower in temperate central Europe, none produce viable seed. For this reason, Jerusalem artichokes are propagated vegetatively via tubers, parts of tubers, or roots. Tubers overwinter well in the ground; when dug up, they begin to dry out within a few weeks. As long as mole damage is not a major risk, overwinter them in the ground where they were planted. Otherwise, pack them in moist

A name that tells a story

Or the other way around: the story of the Jerusalem artichoke is an exciting tale of how names are invented, whether or not they be accurate or appropriate. The Jerusalem artichoke was treasured for its edible tubers by the Hurons and Algonquins, native tribes of the North American Atlantic coast; yet somehow it became associated with the Tupinambá, a tribe native to Brazil, so that it is now known in French and German as *topinambour* and *Topinambur*, respectively. One explanation for the English common name Jerusalem artichoke is that the British mistook the Italian word *girasole* ("sunflower") for "Jerusalem." And "artichoke" was added, perhaps, because of the flavor and the relatedness of the two plants.

sand mixed with water-retaining fibers like cocopeat and store in a root cellar.

Since plants easily regrow even from root parts left behind after digging up tubers, do not plant Jerusalem artichokes in the middle of the garden; they can quickly take over, even after being dug up. If they are getting out of control, cut back shoots as often as possible to weaken the plants.

SELECTION CHARACTERISTICS For success, it is usually necessary to plant selected tubers at a new site, as even "fully harvested" Jerusalem artichokes often grow back from roots and parts of tubers left behind at the previous site.

- tuber shape: large, true-to-type, smooth (the smoother the tubers, the easier they are to clean)
- flavor: pleasantly mild, not bitter or soapy
- ease in harvesting: tubers close together in the soil, not spread over a wide area

DISEASES AND PESTS Jerusalem artichoke is one of the crops least susceptible to disease and is often unaffected by pests. The chief potential pest problem is herbivory from moles in the winter.

Large, smooth Jerusalem artichoke tubers are the most useful in the kitchen.

CULTIVATION HISTORY Jerusalem artichoke originated in eastern North America, where its tuber was used by indigenous Americans long before the arrival of Europeans. It first came to Europe in 1607, arriving in France and spreading over the course of the century to many other European regions, until, after about 1750, the potato became the tuber of choice. Many new varieties were created during intensive breeding work in Germany in the 1930s. In the Swiss canton of Jura, soil is hilled up to blanch the new shoots, which are cooked and eaten like asparagus and are delicious.

SUNFLOWER
Helianthus annuus

The sunflower is one of those plants that are found in nearly every garden, whether as an ornamental, for cut flowers, or to feed birds. Its name comes not only from its (usually) golden flowers but also from the tendency of its flower head(s) to follow the sun across the sky every day.

Sunflower seeds

Field-scale sunflower cultivation is for oil and seed production, with varieties bred for their oil content and seed size, respectively, being planted. Different varieties may have black, striped, mottled, spotted, white, or gray seeds, and some wild varieties have small, hairy seeds. Seeds can be eaten raw, sprouted, or roasted, and young flowers can be eaten as a vegetable. Tall-growing, highly branching varieties with colorful flowers are popular with home gardeners.

WHAT YOU'LL NEED
- 10 to 15 healthy plants
- bags big enough to contain flower heads, if more than one variety is being grown in a given season

POLLINATION NOTES Sunflowers are outcrossers and are visited by many insects. A large sunflower flower head can contain as many as 8,000 individual flowers, each of which is open for about two days. Anthers release pollen on the first day; on the second day, the stigma protrudes and is ready to receive pollen. All individual flowers open over the course of five to 19 days. A typical flower head has dried flowers along the outside edge, then a circle of flowers open for pollen reception, then a circle of flowers giving off pollen, then some unopened flowers. Some varieties are self-fertile, which means insects can simply carry pollen from one individual flower to another on the same flower head. Other varieties are self-infertile and are therefore obligate crossers. To prevent crossing in small-scale sunflower growing, an isolation distance of 1000 ft.

The individual flowers are clearly visible on large sunflower flower heads.

(300 m) is necessary. Large-scale growers use isolation distances of several miles. Another method is hand pollination. This is time-consuming but relatively easy to do: cover unopened flower heads with a bag or insect netting and close tightly. To pollinate, remove bags and rub flowers against each other daily. Beware of pollinator insects while doing this! To intentionally cross two varieties, simply grow them next to each other.

GROWING FOR SEED Except for measures to isolate multiple varieties, there is no difference in sunflower cultivation when growing for seed.

HARVEST After fertilization, seeds grow until the heads are full. Cut off seedheads as soon as the petals have fallen off, and dry with the seed side up. Make sure the drying site is free of birds; sometimes birds are so eager to eat the seeds, they will even fly into rooms to harvest them for themselves. Remove seeds from heads when they are completely dry. This can be done by hand for smaller quantities by rubbing seedheads together. For larger quantities, stretch hardware cloth with a mesh size larger than the sunflower seeds over an empty bucket or garbage can. Rub seedheads across the mesh until the seeds fall out and drop into the container.

Dryness test: try to bend the seeds. When they break, they are dry enough for storage. Lay seeds out flat in cardboard boxes in a warm, shady place safe from mice to dry.

SELECTION CHARACTERISTICS The many available cultivars differ from each other both in superficial traits (size and color of flowers, number and size of flower heads, etc.) and internal traits (oil content, fiber content, etc.). Home gardeners usually grow varieties with beautiful, conspicuous flowers. Select true-to-type plants for propagation. An important criterium for home gardeners as well as large-scale growers is plant stability.

DISEASES AND PESTS Diseases and pests are rarely an issue in the home garden. Birds can be a nuisance, picking sown seeds out of the ground and seeds from heads; cover with bird or insect netting, if necessary. Snails and slugs eat the seedlings. Powdery mildew can be a problem where sunflowers have been too densely sown and the air is calm.

CULTIVATION HISTORY Sunflowers, like Jerusalem artichokes, are an old American Indian crop and another of the few crop species that originate in North America. Archaeological finds of sunflowers date back 5,000 years. A research team in Tabasco, Mexico, found one (!) seed in 2001 at an archaeological dig, which has brought up the question of whether the sunflower was in fact originally domesticated in Central America. The sunflower appears to have arrived in Europe in 1510 with the Spaniards and was first grown as an ornamental. An Englishman discovered the sunflower's potential as an oil plant in 1716, but his patent arose no interest. Commercial sunflower oil production began in the Ukraine around 1835 and has since spread around the world. In the last several years, the EU has subsidized sunflower cultivation as a renewable resource. It is also being increasingly used as a green manure and bee forage plant. Seeds of recently bred varieties have an oil content of up to 50%. Hybrid varieties are being grown more and more.

Asparagus

ASPARAGACEAE

Asparagus (*Asparagus officinalis*) is a true delicacy among vegetables, often eaten steamed or raw in salads. It contains easily digestible carbohydrates and proteins, including the amino acid asparagine, which gives it its unique aroma. Asparagus acts as a diuretic and helps the body detoxify; it is often recommended for those with an ailing liver or kidneys. Saponins found in the shoots have been shown to prevent cancer. In our experience, older varieties are tastier than newer ones. Growing asparagus at home seems to have gone out of fashion, although it is fairly easy to grow and propagate. Asparagus shoots are naturally green (sometimes with hints of other colors) but can be grown blanched. German asparagus eaters swear by these last, while the French prefer green asparagus or the colorful violet varieties that have been bred there ('Jacq Ma Pourpre'). Green asparagus contains up to 2.5 times the amount of vitamin C as blanched asparagus.

● ●

WHAT YOU'LL NEED
- 10 to 20 plants for seed production
- five plants for vegetative propagation

POLLINATION NOTES Asparagus is a dioecious crop plant: plants produce either male flowers or female flowers exclusively. Insects deliver pollen from male plants to the flowers of female plants. Female plants produce fewer shoots than male plants, though those they do produce are thicker. Female plants also have a shorter life span than male plants. For these reasons, commercial growers tend to use male plants exclusively; these can often be recognized by their stereotypically macho names like 'Mars', 'Sieg' (victory), or 'Vulkan' (volcano). Nearly all commercial varieties of asparagus are purely male varieties, older varieties have both male and female plants.

PROPAGATION Plants are usually propagated vegetatively. We have been able to propagate asparagus by seed but not so that the results are varietally pure: plants from seed are usable but are not necessarily identical to the mother. Sow seeds in trays, transplant 2–3 in. (5–8 cm) seedlings to pots, and plant out in late spring (12 in. [30 cm] rows, 4 in. [10 cm] within row). Dig up the following year and plant in its final location, pruning rhizomes back to a uniform length of 4 in. (10 cm). Asparagus prefers light soils (which are also easier to harvest in). Planting for green asparagus: dig a furrow 4 in. (10 cm) deep and 12 in. (30 cm) wide and set plants in flat, 10–12 in. (25–30 cm) apart. Planting for white asparagus: plant deeper or establish raised beds. Adding manure and compost is beneficial in asparagus cultivation, especially in the first two years. Asparagus can be harvested for the table

starting in the third year, with full yields starting in the fourth year. Plants can be harvested for edible shoots for 10 to 15 years. Harvesting blanched asparagus is very labor-intensive: shoots are cut once or twice a day, lest they grow to be so long that they see daylight and turn green, thus reducing the product's market value (though by no means harming the plant).

HARVEST Seeds are ready for harvest when the red berries that contain them begin to shrivel and seeds have turned black. Rub berries on a grater, then soak for 24 hours and separate seed from fruit. Next use a bucket of water to separate viable from nonviable seeds, as with onions. Dry immediately thereafter.

In the asparagus field: it is still impossible to tell whether the plant is male or female.

The spherical fruits of a female asparagus plant

SELECTION CHARACTERISTICS Select desired plants when they have sent up edible shoots and mark with a stick or pole. Do this with at least 10 asparagus plants, as half will likely be female (or better yet, figure out which plants are male and female the previous year). Potential selection criteria:

- vigorous growth, powerful shoots
- no hollow shoots
- tightly closed heads of shoots
- thin skin
- earliness
- high yield and harvestable over a long period
- minimal susceptibility to disease
- lack of sensitivity to low temperatures

DISEASES AND PESTS Asparagus rarely faces major problems in small-scale growing. As a preventative measure against the asparagus fly (*Platyparea poeciloptera*), cut back stalks in autumn and burn them. In some areas, the common asparagus beetle (*Crioceris asparagi*) is a problem, infesting plantings starting in late spring.

Symptoms: herbivory of above-ground plant parts. Plants can no longer assimilate and dry up. Light infestations do not affect yield. Asparagus rust (*Puccinia asparagi*) can affect the ends of asparagus shoots, especially of young plants, turning them a rusty red and killing them. Spraying with copper can be very effective. Destroy infected vegetation (though this will cause plants to be delayed in development).

CULTIVATION HISTORY Wild asparagus is found in Europe, the Middle East, western Siberia, and northern Africa. Cultivation of asparagus has been documented back to Roman times. In the Middle Ages it was grown mostly at monasteries as a medicinal and as a vegetable. Originally asparagus was grown for its green shoots, but then blanching shoots became popular in the Netherlands (17th century) and England (end of 18th century). Field-scale growing began in the 19th century when the first canning factories opened. In India, oil is extracted from rhizomes and used as a calmative.

Brassicas

BRASSICACEAE

The brassica or cabbage family contains 350 genera, many of them common in agriculture and ornamental gardening. The vegetables of the species *Brassica oleracea* are among the most important crops in the garden: cabbage, kohlrabi, cauliflower, Brussels sprouts, and broccoli, among others. The oil, vegetable, and fodder crops of the species *B. napus* and *B. rapa* belong to the cabbage family as well, as do radishes. Other brassicas cultivated for their tasty, pungent leaves include arugula, garden cress, watercress, and perennial wallrocket. Many brassicas cannot tolerate heat at all; they thrive in spring and autumn and like cool sites (north slopes, high altitudes).

Brassicas were formerly known as crucifers, a reference to the fact that the four petals of their flowers are in the shape of a cross. Brassica flowers are usually yellow (in some cases, white) and develop into fruits in the form of seedpods.

● ●

GENERAL PROPAGATION CHARACTERISTICS
Many brassicas are grown for seed as biennials, though some crops (arugula, radish, cauliflower, broccoli) will produce seed in the first year. All brassicas are outcrossers and most are self-infertile, meaning pollen from a flower on one plant cannot pollinate another flower of the same plant. This condition is a natural mechanism for promoting genetic diversity, though it also requires that brassicas be grown for seed in plots of at least 10 to 15 plants. If only

The petals of brassica flowers form the shape of a cross.

one plant is left to flower, it will not produce any usable seed.

Overview of brassicas (cabbage family)

COMMON NAME	GENUS	SPECIES
cole crops: cabbage, cauliflower, broccoli, savoy cabbage, kohlrabi, Brussels sprouts, kale, collard greens	*Brassica*	*oleracea*
turnip, Chinese cabbage, bok choy (pak choi), broccoli raab, mizuna	*Brassica*	*rapa*
rutabaga, oilseed rape	*Brassica*	*napus*
mustard	*Brassica*	*juncea*
white mustard	*Sinapis*	*alba*
radish, daikon radish	*Raphanus*	*sativus*
horseradish	*Armoracia*	*rusticana*
arugula (rocket)	*Eruca*	*sativa*
perennial wallrocket	*Diplotaxis*	*tenuifolia*
sea kale	*Crambe*	*maritima*
garden cress	*Lepidium*	*sativum*
bittercress	*Barbarea*	*vulgaris*
watercress	*Nasturtium*	*officinale*
scurvygrass	*Cochlearia*	*officinalis*

Hoverflies are good for pollinating brassicas.

Brassica oleracea

Several vegetable garden favorites (also known as cole crops) belong to this species, despite their having completely different looks. Each has its own peculiarities when growing for seed because each has its own unique shape, uses, and needs. We start here with a general overview of *Brassica oleracea* crops and handle the details of individual cole crops, as usual, in the pages to come.

Overview of *Brassica oleracea* (cole crops)

COMMON NAME	BOTANICAL VARIETY
white cabbage	convar. *capitata* var. *capitata alba*
red cabbage	convar. *capitata* var. *capitata rubra*
savoy cabbage	convar. *capitata* var. *sabauda*
kohlrabi	convar. *caulorapa* var. *gongylodes*
cauliflower	convar. *botrytis* var. *botrytis*
broccoli	convar. *botrytis* var. *italica*
Brussels sprouts	convar. *fruticosa* var. *gemmifera*
kale	convar. *acephala* var. *sabellica*
collard greens	convar. *acephala* var. *medullosa*

POLLINATION NOTES Cole crops are primarily pollinated by insects: honeybees, hoverflies, and houseflies visit their sulfur-yellow flowers. Multiple varieties of the same crop or multiple cole crops grown for seed in the same year must be isolated to avoid cross-pollination. Well-pollinated cole crops can, in a good year, yield many thousand seeds, so it is worth it to pay close attention to your crop for its entire life span. Seeds maintain reasonable viability for four to five years and individual (well-ripened, well-stored) seeds may last up to 10 years.

GROWING FOR SEED Plant out heads of cabbage, kohlrabi, or other cole crops that produce seed the second year in the spring when the soil is workable (early to mid spring). If it is too cold in spring to plant out but plants are beginning to come out of dormancy, plant out in containers in a well-lit but cool place. Harden off before planting out. When planting out, set plants deeper than they were in autumn when they were dug up. The "neck" of cabbage, for example, should be entirely underground, such that the head sits on the ground. This helps the plant develop new roots. Water plants well when planting out and as they develop new roots. Some varieties send up seed stalks as high as 6 ft. (2 m) and need plenty of space, optimally 24 by 24 in. (60 by 60 cm). Support each individual plant and, as they emerge, the seed stalks, as they can become too heavy for the plant to support once seeds have developed. The largest, most viable seed comes from the central stalk; be sure this stalk develops well, pruning weaker side growth if necessary, so the plant can concentrate its energy on developing good seeds on the central stalk.

HARVEST Seeds are ready for harvest when the pods turn golden brown, usually mid to late summer. If individual stalks ripen at different rates (which is often the case, especially if there are many side stalks present), harvest entire individual stalks as they become ripe to avoid older seed dropping to the ground when seedpods burst open while waiting for other pods to ripen. If all pods are ripe at the same time, cut all stalks from the plant at once. Hang harvested stalks in a cloth bag in a warm, dry room with good air circulation (such as an attic, not in direct sun) to dry. Pods are ready for threshing when they are easily breakable with your fingers and the seeds fall out. Thresh on a tarp or tightly woven fabric by rubbing pods between the hands or with a flail on a soft underlay. For larger quantities, walk on seedpods spread on a tarp. At Arche Noah, threshing in a cloth bag on a soft surface has been highly successful, especially with smaller quantities of seed, where it is crucial to prevent losing seed. Seeds that are not easily threshed are likely unripe and therefore of poor quality or not viable at all. Winnow seed in sieves and in the wind (separate out smaller, poorly developed seeds at this time as well). Dry seeds further after cleaning before putting into storage.

Exact labeling of harvested seed stalks and threshed seed is extremely important, as it is often impossible to tell seed from *Brassica oleracea*, *B. rapa*, and *B. napus* crops apart. There is one trick that may

When flowers have been well pollinated, seedpods grow to be fairly long and the outlines of seeds are clearly visible.

help, though, if seeds do get mixed up: when wet, *B. oleracea* seeds feel slimy, seeds of other brassica species do not.

DISEASES AND PESTS Cole crops are subject to a large number of diseases and pests. There are two phases of the reproductive cycle that are critical. First is overwintering, where numerous fungal infections can occur. The second is during flowering: in areas where oilseed rape (including canola) is grown, rapeseed pests thrive. Rapeseed is often just finishing up with flowering when cole crops being grown for seed are beginning to flower, which is a welcome treat for these pests. They include pollen beetles (*Meligethes aeneus*), the rape stem weevil (*Ceutorhynchus quadridens*), the brassica pod midge (*Dasineura brassicae*), and the green peach aphid (*Myzus persicae*), to name but the most prevalent. Growing cabbage for seed in areas where oilseed rape is not grown is no problem at all; but at Arche Noah, oilseed rape is grown in the surrounding areas, and it is no longer possible to grow cabbage for seed without isolation cages to keep pests out. These sucking and biting insects also lay eggs in the pods of brassicas and easily ruin an entire seed crop. Insect netting has been the only effective organic measure, though this sort of mechanical isolation requires the introduction of pollinator insects. Leaf beetles (*Phyllotreta* spp.) like to attack fresh seedlings or freshly planted plants and can cause great damage. These beetles are capable of jumping like fleas. They overwinter in the soil and immediately attack brassica plant-outs. Prevention: cover plants immediately after planting with leaf beetle–proof netting. Weed and water frequently when leaf beetles appear.

Phoma lingam is the cause of the seed-borne blackleg disease. This kills young plants but can also affect older plants. A head of cabbage carrying this disease can cause all other plants to rot in storage. This fungus causes black spots on stalks that quickly spread to other plants and can affect seed yield. The disease can live on and inside seeds. The disease spreads quickly during propagation by seed, meaning a small amount of infected seed can lead to a large amount of infected plants. Prevention: crop rotation, wide planting distances of second-year plants, disinfecting root cellar, hot water treatment (30 minutes at exactly 122°F [50°C]). With the same hot water treatment, the pathogen causing brassica dark leaf spot (*Alternaria brassicicola*) can also be mitigated. Symptoms: spots on the leaves of seedlings, black spots on shoots.

CULTIVATION HISTORY Cole crops are among the few to have originated in Europe. Wild cabbage is a relatively inconspicuous plant that grows on rocks and beaches; it is mainly found in the Mediterranean region, but also on the Atlantic coasts of England, Spain, France, and northern Germany. It is perennial and can live to be five to eight years old. Wild cabbage originally appeared in several different isolated locations, which, through spontaneous mutations and selection by humans, led to varied crop forms such as heading cabbage and the swollen-stemmed kohlrabi.

CABBAGE

Brassica oleracea convar. *capitata* var. *capitata*

WHAT YOU'LL NEED
- 10 to 15 healthy plants, selected from at least 30 plants
- overwintering strategy
- insect netting (or absence of cabbage pests)
- trellis or one support pole per flowering plant
- bed sheet or cloth bag

GROWING FOR SEED Cabbage is a two-year crop when grown for seed. The timing for sowing seed depends upon the method used for overwintering the plants and the local climate. For overwintering complete cabbage heads, sow seed late (late spring to early summer) so that the heads stay compact and small. Such heads overwinter far better than large, fully ripe heads. This late-sowing method is especially important for early cabbage varieties, whose heads ripen quickly.

Cabbage seeds

Cabbage plants grow their heads the first year, but do not send up stalks for flowering until the second year. Plants require a vernalization period, where temperatures stay below 50°F (10°C) for several weeks, before they begin to grow stalks that will later produce flowers. In the Mediterranean region and in southern England, some local cabbage varieties are started in late summer/autumn which in the following year produce ripe heads in early spring and ripe seed by summer. Young cabbage plants can be overwintered outdoors in areas with mild winters and in colder areas with the help of sufficient frost protection. Full cabbage heads, however, are fairly frost sensitive, handling temperatures as low as 23°F (−5°C) only briefly. Harvest plants to be overwintered at the same time as plants for eating. Dig them up with a spade or digging fork and remove outer leaves such that only a tight, compact head remains atop the plant. Shake and drip dry cabbage heads for storage that have gotten wet from the rain.

OVERWINTERING ENTIRE PLANTS Cabbage heads must then be guided through a sort of hibernation to ensure they survive the winter. This is often the most challenging phase of cultivation. Several different methods have been tested and developed by gardeners over the years, and their appropriateness depends upon the climate of your region (severity of winter, humidity, length of growing season) and the availability of overwintering facilities. For the three overwintering methods outlined here, we have also given the locations where they are practiced. Ultimately, however, the exact methods employed are up to you, based on your preferences and what you find most effective. When over-wintering indoors, whether in a root cellar, in an attic, or elsewhere, check plants on a regular basis. Gray mold (fungus: *Botrytis cinerea*) often appears on outer leaves in storage. Remove affected leaves and cut out deeper infections with a sharp knife. Disinfect resultant wounds with bone black or wood ash.

Toward the end of the winter, the first flower stalks begin to form in the leaf axils of the main stem. The largest (and most viable) seeds come from the primary stalks. These stalks often have

difficulty penetrating the tightly packed leaves of the head. To help them find their way through, cut an X into the leaves of the head in mid to late winter. In South Tyrol, Italy, this is traditionally performed on Candlemas, 2 February, but in other regions it is often not done until the cabbage is planted out in early spring. Take care to not injure the apical meristem, the growing tip of the stem, by adjusting the depth of the cut to the size and shape of the cabbage head, usually 1–2.5 in. (2.5–6 cm). Often the cut can be made just deep enough that the head, under pressure of its own tightly grown leaves, "bursts" open on its own. Varieties that send out stalks

At Wildegg Castle's display gardens in Switzerland, cabbage plants are dug up in midautumn and overwinter in a root cellar.

less vigorously can be further helped by breaking open the "quadrants" established by cutting the X. (Start shallow, remove deeper plant material thereafter as necessary.)

Overwintering entire plants in a dirt or gravel-floored root cellar. Ideal for much of northern North America and other regions with deep winter frosts yet relatively low humidity in the winter; in central Europe, this applies to southern Alpine regions and dry valleys of the inner Alps. Dig up full plants with stalk and roots. Bring into root cellar, stand up on the ground, and lean against the wall (head should not be in contact with the ground); individual plants should not touch each other. Plants can also be hung upside down, roots above head. Dirt or gravel-floored root cellars are more humid than cement-floored cellars, which helps prevent plant roots and stalks from drying out. Air the room out on days with an air temperature above freezing. Ideally, the outer leaves of the head will dry like parchment paper.

Overwintering entire plants in a frost-proof room. Ideal for regions with deep winter frosts and relatively high humidity in the winter, such as we experience at Arche Noah. Our dirt-floored root cellar is too humid for cabbage to overwinter without too many diseases, and the winter is too cold to overwinter plants

Overwintered cabbage heads being planted out in early spring. Over the course of the winter, several leaf layers were removed.

outdoors, even in a hoop house. The place that ultimately ended up working best was an attic. Temperatures should not fall below freezing for too long, though cabbage can briefly handle as low as 23°F (−5°C). Nor should temperatures climb above 41°F (5°C), as this could bring plants out of dormancy too early.

Overwintering entire plants outdoors.
Appropriate for regions with mild winters (temperature drops to around freezing at the lowest): southern, maritime, and Mediterranean regions. One method is frequently described in older seed propagation literature. Lay entire cabbage plants the long way in deep furrows, making sure that the plants do not touch each other. Cover with soil. If frost is expected, cover additionally with straw or leaves to insulate. Remove this layer in the spring. Plants bolt on their own in the spring and need not be dug up. In wet winters, plants may rot in the ground; if this is a concern, use one of the two aforementioned methods.

OVERWINTERING TRUNKS An alternative to overwintering entire heads of cabbage is to overwinter only the leafless but not-yet-bolted "trunks." This method is suitable when plants are grown in hoop houses and high tunnels. If you are interested in using this method, start your planning with the timing of seed sowing: cabbage overwintered in this way must be started as early as possible. In late summer, remove the entire fully developed head by making slanted cuts with a sharp knife. Ideally, this wound will heal

quickly with a few hot, dry days. Disinfect the wound with bone black or wood ash. The dried, healed wound can also be sealed with artificial bark to prevent entry by disease-causing agents. Overwinter the stalks in one of the three ways just described. The main advantage of this method is reduced maintenance over the winter. The main drawback is reduced seed yield.

OVERWINTERING YOUNG PLANTS This should be done as a last resort, as plants do not develop large heads with this method, thus eliminating the possibility of selecting for anything useful. Sow seeds

Cabbage in bloom

in late summer so that plants develop at least two leaves as big as the palm of a hand and overwinter them in this state. These young plants can handle temperatures as low as 19°F (−7°C). If the plants have yet to "fatten up" and are kept "dry" through minimal watering in autumn, they can handle even colder temperatures. If plants are too young (about the size of cabbage plant-outs) when winter starts, they will not flower the second year but rather form a head, as if it were the first season.

SELECTION CHARACTERISTICS Ideal cabbage plants for seed are medium-sized ones with tightly formed heads. Other selection criteria:

- heads that have not opened (e.g., after heavy rainfall in autumn)
- leaves that are not easily loosened from main stalk
- lack of bacterial or fungal disease
- short inner stalk (not necessarily noticeable from without; comes with experience)
- true-to-type head shape (flat, flat-round, round, flat-conical, pointy-conical)
- stability (good root development)
- flavor

Progression of cabbage from head to seed bearer. Starting in late winter, bolting cabbage stalks attempt to penetrate the leaves of the head. To enable the stalks to do this, a carefully made cut may be necessary. Over the next several weeks, the head opens up and the flowering stalks grow forth. With good pollination, each plant develops hundreds of seedpods. Harvest seeds when the first pods have dried and the majority of pods are golden brown, yet still soft. Waiting too long to harvest can result in pods exploding on their own and their seed falling to the ground.

- early ripeness (for storage varieties as well), quick head development
- ability to ripen at your location (site adaptation)
- for storage varieties: dense, tightly packed head
- especially for red cabbage: earliness

CULTIVATION HISTORY Shredding and fermenting is an ancient method of preserving and storing cabbage: sauerkraut was for centuries the primary source of vitamin C in temperate climate diets. The typical white and red cabbage forms were developed in the early Middle Ages in central and western Europe. White cabbage is known practically the world over, but red cabbage cultivation is on the decline, as evidenced by decreased demand in stores and restaurants; it is now grown primarily in central Europe and the Netherlands. Each has its own characteristics. Whereas varieties of white cabbage can be found with any shape of head you can imagine, red cabbage heads do not vary far from spherical in shape. Through breeding, both red and white forms have lent their traits to other cabbages (e.g., the dense, tight heads of some savoy cabbages are derived from white cabbage).

SAVOY CABBAGE

Brassica oleracea convar. *capitata* var. *sabauda*

WHAT YOU'LL NEED

- 10 to 15 healthy plants
- overwintering strategy (may vary by variety)
- insect netting (or absence of cabbage pests)
- trellis or one support pole per flowering plant
- bed sheet or cloth bag

GROWING FOR SEED Savoy cabbage is hardier than other head-forming cole crops, withstanding temperatures as low as 14°F (−10°C). Overwinter plants indoors where it gets colder than this in the winter, especially varieties intended for an autumn harvest. Savoy cabbage is especially sensitive to drying out, which starts with severe wilting of the leaves.

Savoy cabbage is an especially hardy cole crop.

SELECTION CHARACTERISTICS Savoy cabbages are divided into three groups: those with a loose head for spring and summer; a storage variety with a heavy, yellow head; and a light-headed, greenish winter savoy cabbage. Potential selection criteria:

- earliness, quickness in forming head
- flavor
- ability to form a head
- stability (good root development)
- short stalk
- head size
- true-to-type color and head shape (peaked, round, flat-round)
- lack of bacterial or fungal infections
- storage length for storage varieties

CULTIVATION HISTORY Ruffly leaved brassicas were known even in ancient times in the Mediterranean region. Perhaps these Roman crops were the ancestors of the savoy cabbage we know today. Savoy cabbage is widely grown in western Europe, in the western Mediterranean region, and in North America, as a highly prized autumn and winter vegetable. Its leaves are used in soups and in vegetable dishes. Savoy cabbage is rich in minerals, especially phosphorus, potash, and magnesium.

KOHLRABI

Brassica oleracea convar. *caulorapa* var. *gongylodes*

The kohlrabi we know today, with the tender flesh of its swollen stem and its relatively few, small leaves, comes from an older, tankard-shaped fodder form. This fodder kohlrabi has a very large "bulb" (up to 14 in. [35 cm] long and over 6 in. [15 cm] thick) and tall (up to 28 in. [70 cm]), dense foliage. Despite its size and long growing season, the fodder kohlrabi does not become woody and can be stored for many months in the root cellar.

WHAT YOU'LL NEED
- 10 to 15 plants, selected from at least 30 plants
- overwintering strategy
- insect netting (or absence of cabbage pests)
- trellis or one support pole per flowering plant
- bed sheet or cloth bag

GROWING FOR SEED Time the starting of seeds such that plants attain a normal eating ripeness at the time they are to go into storage. When seed is sown too early, plants become overgrown and crack open, which often leads to rotting in storage. Early to mid summer is the right time to sow seeds in most areas.

Kohlrabi is best overwintered in a dirt or gravel-floored root cellar in sand or in

Flowers and seedpods of kohlrabi

Kohlrabi seeds

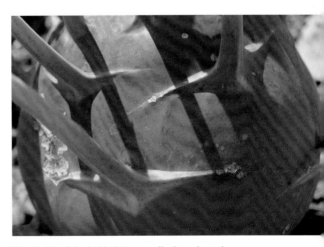

The "bulb" of the kohlrabi is actually the enlarged, swollen stem of the plant.

pots. It is more resistant to rot than cabbage, making it comparatively easy to overwinter. In regions where the temperature stays above 19°F (–7°C) all winter, kohlrabi can be overwintered outdoors. Overwintering is most successful after a dry autumn, which contributes to a low water content of the plant.

SELECTION CHARACTERISTICS Though it is natural for the kohlrabi's swollen stem to become "woody" over time, the direction of selection for the plant has historically been for an ever larger, more tender bulb that gets woody as late as possible. This trait needs to be constantly selected for. Other selection criteria:

- size, shape, and color of bulb
- rapid bulb development or long-lasting tenderness
- flavor
- thin skin and tender flesh
- leaves only at the top of the bulb
- health and disease resistance
- bulb size and storage life for fodder kohlrabi

CULTIVATION HISTORY The earliest documentation of kohlrabi in central Europe is from the 16th century, though several Roman authors described similar plants. It is not certain, however, whether these Roman authors were referring to kohlrabi or rutabaga. Kohlrabi as we know it has existed since the 19th century.

CAULIFLOWER
Brassica oleracea convar. *botrytis* var. *botrytis*

WHAT YOU'LL NEED
- 10 to 15 healthy plants, selected from at least 60 plants
- for biennial forms: overwintering strategy
- insect netting (or absence of cabbage pests)
- trellis or one support pole per seeding plant
- heated growing quarters or mild winter

GROWING FOR SEED Cauliflower is among the most challenging crop plants to grow for seed; in contrast to other cole crops, it develops relatively few flowers and relatively few viable seeds. The part of the plant that we think of as the vegetable portion (the "rose") is actually the fleshy embryonic flower head of the plant. This should not be harvested when growing for seed, as cauliflower does not send up secondary stalks from leaf axils when the primary stalk is removed. Shrub-like flower stalks emerge from the rose. Cauliflower becomes highly vulnerable to rot at this point, leading many seed growers to prune the rose to help stalks emerge; other growers have reported their crops becoming even more susceptible to rot when employing this method. Although cauliflower is one of the few brassicas whose seeds can ripen in one growing season, in some regions it is nearly impossible to get seed to do so. The typical problem in central Europe (zone 6) is that cauliflower blossoms in mid to late summer, and seeds only ripen fully when the weather in autumn is perfect. At Arche Noah, we start seeds in early to mid winter (early varieties in late winter) and plant out in early to mid spring under row cover until the danger of frost has passed. When plants have attained eating ripeness, improvise a roof to prevent water from penetrating the rose. Remove small spots where rot is occurring, or remove entire plants with rot problems.

Cauliflower is one of the most weather-sensitive vegetables. In some years, several small early-blooming florets will appear; in other years, very large flowers develop very late. Some potential counterbalancing measures: using row cover during cold spells; removing row cover in hot weather; consistent irrigation.

An interesting form of cauliflower that seems to have all but disappeared is winter cauliflower, which can overwinter outdoors in mild climates or with sufficient snow cover. It is sown in late summer and produces ripe heads in late spring the following year.

SELECTION CHARACTERISTICS The most important selection happens automatically: selection for ease of propagation. Yet this trait often contradicts other important selection criteria, such as:

- rapid growth and well-developed leaves
- dense, well-developed, sufficiently large rose
- rose that maintains its ripeness for a long time

Cauliflower plants beginning to bloom in late spring

- flavor
- leaves that enclose the rose well (the rose will turn yellow when exposed to direct sunlight)
- shape and color of flowers
- plant health and disease resistance

CULTIVATION HISTORY Cauliflower did not come into being until the modern era (after the Middle Ages). It supposedly originated in Asia Minor. Many varieties come from Italy, where much breeding work has been done. In Germany, the area around the city of Erfurt is the classic cauliflower seed production area, hence the variety 'Erfurter Zwerg' (Erfurt dwarf), introduced in 1902.

BROCCOLI

Brassica oleracea convar. *botrytis* var. *italica*

WHAT YOU'LL NEED
- 10 to 15 healthy plants
- insect netting (or absence of cabbage pests)
- trellis or one support pole per flowering plant
- for biennial varieties: overwintering strategy

GROWING FOR SEED Broccoli is a close relative of cauliflower and what has been said for cauliflower is valid for broccoli, though broccoli is generally easier to grow. The embryonic flowers are green or violet and are not as tightly compressed as those of cauliflower. When growing for seed in zone 6, start seeds and plant out as early as possible in order to harvest seed in late summer/autumn. Broccoli must bloom by midsummer in order for seeds to have enough time to ripen, as seeds often ripen slowly. If this is not possible in your climate, start seeds in late summer, dig up plants before the hard frosts come, and overwinter in a root cellar.

Winter broccoli can be grown only in regions with mild winters. Seed can be sown from midsummer to early autumn. Arche Noah member Monika Sahling, who lives in Tuscany and grows many vegetables for seed, sows broccoli seed in midspring and overwinters plants outdoors. Small broccoli florets are ready for harvest in early spring the following year, and seedpods are harvestable by early summer. Broccoli roses are also harvested before flower stalks begin to form. In Monika's experience, broccoli needs less water than cauliflower.

Broccoli in bloom

SELECTION CHARACTERISTICS

- true-to-type growth pattern, color, and stalk length
- development of a large, dense rose for a single harvest or
- development of many small florets for continual harvest
- rapid growth
- plant health and disease resistance
- late blooming

CULTIVATION HISTORY Broccoli has traditionally been grown in areas with mild climates, such as southern and western Europe. It is presumed to have originated in southern Greece and was then brought to Italy in the 15th century (hence its botanical name). It reached the German-speaking world by the 17th century. Broccoli has become relatively common in home gardens across central Europe only in the last few decades.

BRUSSELS SPROUTS

Brassica oleracea convar. *fruticosa* var. *gemmifera*

For Brussels sprouts, the highly developed axillary buds are used as a vegetable. These buds look like tiny heads of cabbage and are made up of many densely layered leaves.

WHAT YOU'LL NEED

- 10 to 15 healthy plants
- insect netting (or absence of cabbage pests)
- trellis or one support pole per flowering plant

GROWING FOR SEED When growing for seed, sow Brussels sprouts in early summer. Plants grow to be 24–32 in. (60–80 cm) tall the first year. In the second year, the stalk can grow to be up to 60 in. (150 cm) tall. Brussels sprouts are hardier than head cabbage and can take temperatures as low as about 14°F (–10°C). The upper and lower third of the stalk on plants being grown for seed can be harvested for

The "fruit" of Brussels sprouts is the small, compact axillary bud.

Plants of Brussels sprouts can be overwintered outdoors in areas with no killing frosts.

Brussels sprouts; do not harvest sprouts from the middle third when growing for seed. Once the plant has been planted out again in the second year and its roots have re-established themselves, the end of the main stalk can be pruned to encourage earlier flowering.

SELECTION CHARACTERISTICS
- uniform sprout development along the entire stalk
- shape, color, and firmness of sprouts
- sprout flavor (not bitter; cabbage-like)
- winter hardiness
- yield
- final height and width of plant (smaller varieties are often more useful for the home gardener)

CULTIVATION HISTORY Brussels sprouts are the youngest member of the brassica family, first appearing on the Belgian market in 1785. They were first hybridized in 1958, and hybrids have since dominated the market.

KALE
Brassica oleracea convar. *acephala* var. *sabellica*

Kale is a leafy brassica that develops no head but instead wrinkled, curly leaves on tall-growing stalks. It is a much-beloved winter vegetable in northern Germany and other mild climates. Kale's flavor is improved by exposure to light frost, which causes starches contained in the leaves to be broken down into sugars. Curly kale varieties have extremely tightly curled leaves. Northeast Germany is famous for its violet-leaved varieties.

WHAT YOU'LL NEED
- 10 to 15 healthy plants
- insect netting (or absence of cabbage pests)

The leaves of multiple kale varieties take on an ornamental character in autumn and deliver fresh leaf vegetables. Palm kale is pictured in the foreground.

- trellis or one support pole per flowering plant

GROWING FOR SEED Grow for seed as for *Brassica oleracea*. Kale can survive temperatures as low as 19°F (–7°C); some varieties can withstand even colder temperatures. Where winters get colder, overwinter indoors.

SELECTION CHARACTERISTICS There are low, medium, and tall-growing varieties. Potential selection criteria:

- dense foliation; true-to-type leaf shape
- stalk length (varies greatly between and sometimes within varieties)
- flavor
- yield

CULTIVATION HISTORY The non-heading cole crops are the oldest of the species. The ancient Greeks and Romans grew types similar to kale, and paintings from the Renaissance depict similarly shaped plants. In East Frisia (German: *Ostfriesland*), the variety 'Ostfriesische Palme' is famous for its palm tree–like height and is grown for people and livestock alike. Its stalks were once grown for use as rafters in buildings.

COLLARD GREENS

Brassica oleracea convar. *acephala* var. *medullosa*

Collard greens have been selected over the years for thick leaf stalks. The main stalk of the plant can grow to over 3 ft. (1 m) in height and is loosely leaved from top to bottom.

WHAT YOU'LL NEED
- 10 to 15 healthy plants
- insect netting (or absence of cabbage pests)
- trellis or one support pole per flowering plant

GROWING FOR SEED Grow for seed as for cabbage. Like kale, collard greens can survive temperatures to 19°F (–7°C) or even lower, in some varieties. Where winters get colder, overwinter indoors.

SELECTION CHARACTERISTICS
- development of a tall, strong main stalk
- good foliation
- winter hardiness

CULTIVATION HISTORY Collard greens have been cultivated in France since the beginning of the 19th century, spreading thence to England, Denmark, and Germany. The crop was grown in Germany as livestock feed until the 1970s, at which point it was given up in favor of soy imports and increased corn (maize) cultivation.

COURTESY SHUTTERSTOCK/© VERDESKERDE

Collard greens

Brassica rapa

Many vegetables belong to the species *Brassica rapa*. Several of these (turnips chief among them) come from Europe and are woven into the tapestry of its culture; Chinese cabbage and bok choy (or pak choi, as it is exclusively known in UK) are both of Chinese origin.

Overview of *Brassica rapa* crops

COMMON NAME	BOTANICAL VARIETY
turnip	ssp. *rapa*
Chinese cabbage	ssp. *pekinensis*
bok choy (pak choi)	ssp. *chinensis*
broccoli raab, turnip rape	ssp. *oleifera*
mizuna, potherb mustard	ssp. *nipposinica*

Turnips

TURNIP
Brassica rapa ssp. *rapa*

Turnip is the general term for the various forms and varieties of *Brassica rapa* ssp. *rapa*. What all turnips have in common is their rapid growth. Their shapes and sizes differ according to their region of origin. The turnip of the Alps is the *Wasserrübe* (water turnip), which is traditionally shredded and fermented (like cabbage is for sauerkraut) to make the tasty and nutritious *Rübenkraut*; the fermentation not only increases the content and availability of its nutrients, it also preserves the kraut so it can be eaten throughout the winter. Turnips vary greatly, from long and stretched out to plump and spherical in shape; with flesh from white to golden; with skin from red and violet to green or white. Many local varieties that were still being grown in the 19th century have been lost, unfortunately. Early May turnip varieties (*Mairüben*) can be planted in early to mid spring for a late spring harvest of tender, spherical roots. One particularly special turnip is 'Teltower Rübchen', which for centuries was grown exclusively in the sandy soils of Brandenburg, south of Berlin, and is highly prized by gourmets for its unique flavor. Mild-flavored, white, spherical varieties are staples of Japanese vegetable markets. The turnip is not to be confused with the rutabaga (*B. napus*), with which species it does not cross.

WHAT YOU'LL NEED
- 10 to 15 healthy, well-developed turnips
- insect netting (or absence of cabbage pests)

Various shapes of turnips

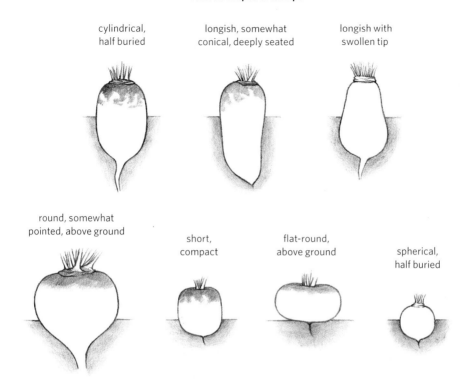

cylindrical,
half buried

longish, somewhat
conical, deeply seated

longish with
swollen tip

round, somewhat
pointed, above ground

short,
compact

flat-round,
above ground

spherical,
half buried

- trellis or one support pole per flowering plant
- overwintering strategy

POLLINATION NOTES Like all brassicas, turnips are insect-pollinated outcrossers. All members of the species *Brassica rapa* can cross with one another, so if, for example, Chinese cabbage, broccoli raab, and turnip all flower in the same garden at the same time, they will without a doubt cross-pollinate each other.

GROWING FOR SEED Growing turnips for seed is not much different from growing cole crops (see *Brassica oleracea*) for seed.

Traditional turnip cultivation involves seeding directly into stubble fields after the grain harvest in mid to late summer, later thinning to 4–8 in. (10–20 cm) spacing. When growing for seed, turnips can be selected directly out of those that are being grown for food. Turnips can overwinter outdoors where temperatures do not drop below 15°F (–9°C) and humidity remains relatively low in the winter. Otherwise overwinter in a root cellar, being certain to place only healthy, undamaged plants into storage. Simply pull selected plants from the ground in late autumn (do not prune roots). Plant roots out in spring deeper than they were when harvested in autumn. Plants flower profusely, with stalks growing to be at least 3 ft. (1 m) tall, thus requiring support.

In some areas, overwintering turnips can be challenging due to their high water content, and suitability for storage varies from variety to variety. In areas with high winter humidity (as at Arche Noah), turnips tend to rot in storage; we now overwinter young plants in pots. To do this, sow seed in pots in late summer, such that they develop turnips about 1 in. (2.5 cm) tall. Place in hoop house, cold frame, or other cold space that will not freeze too deeply. Cover the cold frame or similar

Ripe seedpods being threshed by hand

set-up with straw bales or bubble wrap if extreme cold threatens (remove when this danger has passed). Check planting medium regularly throughout winter to assure that it is not too wet, yet does not dry out.

Those varieties that store less water and have tougher flesh (e.g., 'Blanc dur d'Hiver') can be overwintered outdoors where climate allows.

May turnips, when being grown for seed, should be planted in midsummer like regular turnips. In order to select for quality May turnips, grow them again in the spring from time to time, make your selections, and dig up soon thereafter. Dig up and move plants several times until autumn to stunt growth, prevent cracking, and help plants make it to and through the winter.

Turnip greens, those "turnips without turnips," develop seed in the first year of cultivation.

HARVEST Seed harvest and processing instructions as for *Brassica oleracea*. Ripe seedpods of *B. rapa* crops explode,

Turnips in South Tyrol, Italy

Turnips, usually sown in fields right after the grain harvest, are used for many things in this German-speaking region of the Italian Alps: as livestock feed, as food for people, and as a medicinal. The fresh, blanched shoots of new growth from turnips in storage (*Ruabkeime*) are eaten in salads or steamed. The juice from fermented turnips (*Ruabenkraut* in the local dialect) is drunk to combat fever. And a folk medicinal remedy for swelling and abscesses in livestock is to place rags soaked in fermented turnip juice on them.

releasing their seed to the ground, so harvest before pods attain full ripeness.

SELECTION CHARACTERISTICS For all crops, select for true-to-type characteristics. Additional selection criteria for turnips:

- size, shape, and color of root
- flavor (fresh and fermented); tenderness
- portion of root above/below top of soil
- vigorous growth
- shape, color, and hairiness of leaves
- storage life

Additional selection criteria for turnip greens:

- rapid growth
- leaf yield, leaves harvestable over a long period
- flavor

DISEASES AND PESTS All pests listed for *Brassica oleracea* (which see) can also damage *B. rapa* crops when they are in bloom, especially leaf beetles (*Phyllotreta* spp.).

CULTIVATION HISTORY The turnip was domesticated in the temperate climate of Europe, before the domestication of the rutabaga. It was developed from the wild form of rape. Natural histories and herb books of the ancient Greeks and Romans contain only general and non-specific descriptions of turnips. Fast-growing varieties were mostly grown in Europe as livestock feed in stubble fields after the grain harvest.

CHINESE CABBAGE
Brassica rapa ssp. *pekinensis*

Chinese cabbage has crisp, watery leaves with a mustard-like flavor. Its growth habits are similar to those of romaine lettuce or collard greens, and its leaves are stalk-free, which differentiates Chinese cabbage from bok choy (pak choi), whose leaves always have long stalks. Many varieties come from China and Japan, where European-style legal protections for cultivars are practically nonexistent; this has contributed to the dominance of hybrid seed on the market.

WHAT YOU'LL NEED
- 10 to 15 well-formed heads with roots
- insect netting (or absence of cabbage pests)
- trellis or one support pole per flowering plant
- overwintering strategy

GROWING FOR SEED Growing Chinese cabbage for seed in temperate climates is among the great challenges in gardening—and not one that we would

Chinese cabbage seeds

recommend for beginners. Seed yield is usually relatively small, and large, head-forming types with white hearts are the most difficult to cultivate. Plants cannot handle high temperatures and need sufficient water and fertile soil. Sowing seed in mid to late summer usually brings the best results. Select plants to go to seed from these and overwinter in a root cellar. It can be a feat to bring Chinese cabbage through the winter free of fungal disease and rot. Ideal storage conditions are temperatures as close to freezing as possible (without going below freezing!), medium humidity, and good ventilation. It is easier to overwinter young plants in pots, though this makes it hard to select for head size and shape. Chinese cabbage can also be grown for seed as an annual by seeding very early, though it develops no head, making selection impossible.

HARVEST Ripe seedpods explode, releasing their seed to the ground, so harvest before pods attain full ripeness. Processing instructions as for *Brassica oleracea*.

COURTESY ISTOCKPHOTO/NODEROG

Chinese cabbage, head-forming variety

SELECTION CHARACTERISTICS Head-forming varieties can be oval, tall-oval, or oblong in shape and have a tight, dense heart or not. There are also loose-leaf varieties. Potential selection criteria:

- true-to-type growth form
- good head development and resistance to bolting
- resistance to myriad fungal diseases
- ability to overwinter well
- further details at cabbage

DISEASES AND PESTS Chinese cabbage is susceptible to everything that besets regular cabbage (see *Brassica oleracea* for the full suite), but those same diseases and pests seem to cause even more damage to its tender leaves.

CULTIVATION HISTORY This is an important vegetable in China, with both heading varieties and varieties that form a rosette of leaves. Chinese cabbage is used in salads, sautéed, or fermented like sauerkraut to preserve for the winter. In temperate Europe, it is grown for harvest in late autumn and winter for winter salads, as it withstands colder temperatures and stores well, longer than lettuce.

BOK CHOY, PAK CHOI
Brassica rapa ssp. *chinensis*

Like Swiss chard, bok choy (UK: pak choi) develops wide ribs and long leaf stalks; unlike Swiss chard, it has the mild, spicy flavor characteristic of brassicas. It grows quickly and, whereas most varieties are better adapted to growing in autumn, some varieties tolerate the heat and humidity of summer. If plants bolt before they produce ripe leaves, no worries: flower stalks can be steamed and eaten as well. Young plants can overwinter outdoors in mild-winter areas and leaves can be harvested all winter long.

Propagating bok choy is much easier than propagating Chinese cabbage. Bok choy is grown biennially for seed. Since it grows so quickly, there is plenty of time to select plants to grow for seed from late summer seedings. Where possible, overwinter outdoors with frost protection or overwinter young plants indoors in pots. Bok choy can also be grown as an annual for seed by seeding as early as possible, though selection opportunities are starkly reduced. Bok choy has been grown in China since the 5th century; it is unclear when it first arrived in Europe.

BROCCOLI RAAB, TURNIP RAPE
Brassica rapa ssp. *oleifera*

This subspecies is the oldest crop form of *Brassica rapa*. The wild form comes from northern Africa and the Mediterranean region, though the crop form has been known to naturalize itself. Turnip rape was once one of the most important oil and fodder plants of Europe and the Middle East, the oil being used in lamps and for cooking. It has been grown less and less in the last several decades. Spring varieties are planted in the spring and harvested later that same year; winter varieties are planted in autumn and harvested the following summer. Broccoli raab (also known as broccolette and rapini) is a special variety from Italy that produces no "turnip" but rather swollen flower heads, like broccoli, though these are individual

Brassica rapa ssp. chinensis in the field

Broccoli raab

and ripen one after the other over a long period. Its feathered leaves, which are often sold as entire rosettes, are ideal for winter salads and can be prepared like Chinese cabbage or broccoli. Broccoli raab is fast growing (40 to 90 days to harvest) and produces seed in one growing season. Select those plants that stay in the bud stage for the longest amount of time.

MIZUNA, POTHERB MUSTARD
Brassica rapa ssp. *nipposinica*

Mizuna has been grown in home gardens in the USA for salad greens for about 60 years. Originally from Japan, it is also now being grown in European gardens. The plant grows quickly and its spicy leaves can be used like arugula in salads and sandwiches. It produces seeds the first year; select for plants that flower the latest (bolting resistance).

COURTESY ISTOCKPHOTO/LIGHTHOUSEBAY

Mizuna

RUTABAGA, OILSEED RAPE
Brassica napus

Two crops of large agricultural importance belong to the species *Brassica napus*: rutabaga (ssp. *rapifera*) and oilseed rape (ssp. *napus*). Rutabaga production has decreased in recent decades, but oilseed rape (often as canola) production has increased dramatically in the same time frame. The rutabaga is an old turnip-like (though of a different species) crop that, depending upon the variety, can be used for food by people and/or livestock. Rutabagas for human consumption have blue-green leaves; others do not. Oilseed rape is grown on the field scale, and oil from its seeds is processed into cooking oil, margarine, and biodiesel. Rutabaga is grown as a biennial for seed, whereas rape is grown as an annual. Up until the 1960s, it was common practice in Germany to harvest edible leaves from rape plants before they set flowers. Oilseed rape can also be grown early in the garden for fresh vegetables in mid to late spring, when fresh garden vegetables are otherwise rare; do not use it as a green manure in the garden, as this may invite problems with cabbage diseases and pests.

Rutabagas (also known as Swedish turnips, or Swedes) store well, so they can be enjoyed all winter long. Varieties with yellow flesh (from beta-carotene) such as 'Wilhelmsburger' and 'Gelbe Schmalz' (yellow lard) usually taste better than white-fleshed varieties. Because of its cabbage-like flavor, rutabaga is often made into casseroles with potatoes, onions, and fatty meat. White-fleshed varieties are often grown for livestock, though some ('Mammoth White Russian') are for human consumption.

WHAT YOU'LL NEED
- 10 to 15 healthy plants
- insect netting (or absence of cabbage pests)
- trellis or one support pole per flowering plant

POLLINATION NOTES Rutabaga and oilseed rape are, like all brassicas, insect-pollinated outcrossers. Rutabagas flowering in the home garden will cross with flowering rape being grown nearby. Use an isolation distance of 500 ft. (150 m) in an ideally sited garden, larger distances in less-ideal circumstances (such as if a field of rape is being grown nearby).

GROWING FOR SEED Rutabaga seed is normally direct sown when grown for food, but it can be started indoors when growing for seed. Wait until at least early summer to sow rutabaga seed to avoid overripe roots that can no longer be selected in late autumn. Plant out or thin to 16 in. (40 cm) spacing within and between rows. Smaller rutabagas, with a diameter of 6 in. (15 cm) or less, taste better and overwinter better. Rutabagas will keep for six months in the root cellar.

HARVEST Seeds grow in pods that do not all ripen at once. Harvest either individual ripe stalks over a longer period of time, or the whole plant when most pods are ripe. Processing instructions as for *Brassica oleracea*.

SELECTION CHARACTERISTICS
- true-to-type
- tenderness and flavor (lack of bitterness)
- size, shape, and color of root
- portion of root above/below soil level
- vigorousness and vitality
- shape and color of leaves, healthy foliage
- storage life

DISEASES AND PESTS Pests of *Brassica oleracea* (which see) can also do lots of damage to rutabaga and oilseed rape,

Rutabaga seeds

Heirloom rutabaga 'Wilhelmsburger'

especially during flowering. Leaf beetles can cause complete crop failure.

CULTIVATION HISTORY Rutabaga's origins are unknown, though some botanists have speculated that it comes from a cross between *Brassica rapa* and *B. oleracea*. Rutabaga is grown mostly in northern Europe, Russia, and around the Baltic Sea, though in recent years it has been grown more in the USA, the Middle East, and Siberia. It has been difficult to learn of rutabaga's history because the same word is often used for rutabaga and turnip in historical documents. Unambiguous documentation of the rutabaga goes back only to the 17th century.

During World War I, long-storing rutabagas were sometimes the only source of nourishment for starving people, which could have contributed to its sharp decrease in popularity since then.

Two characteristics make rutabagas easy to distinguish from turnips: the stem-like bulge in the transition area from root to leaves and the blue-green leaves.

MUSTARD
Brassica juncea

This species offers a diverse array of plants: from the extremely hardy 'Green in the Snow', which, as its name suggests, can be harvested throughout the winter, to varieties bred for their high oil content, used to make condiment mustard. Plants of this species have long been grown in India as an oilseed crop. Varieties cultivated in China have been selected for their flavorful leaves. There are four different mustard subspecies, the first of which (mustard greens) is the most widely cultivated mustard crop in Europe:

- *Brassica juncea* ssp. *integrifolia* (mustard greens)
- *Brassica juncea* ssp. *juncea* (grown for its seeds or as livestock feed)
- *Brassica juncea* ssp. *napiformis* (root mustard)
- *Brassica juncea* ssp. *tsatsai* (multishoot mustard, grown for its shoots and leaves)

Mustard seeds

WHAT YOU'LL NEED
- 10 ft.^{2} (1 m^2) of plants
- insect netting (or absence of cabbage pests)
- trellis or one support pole per flowering plant

POLLINATION NOTES Thought it is sometimes described as a self-pollinator in the literature, mustard is an outcrosser, and the various subspecies can all cross with one another. Use isolation cages when growing multiple varieties at the same time.

GROWING FOR SEED Plants produce seed in one growing season. Sow in mid to late spring; expect bloom in late spring/early summer.

HARVEST Harvest seed in early to late summer. Ripe seedpods explode, releasing their seed to the ground, so harvest before pods attain full ripeness. Processing instructions as for *Brassica oleracea*.

SELECTION CHARACTERISTICS Mustard is one of the most diverse of all *Brassica* species, and there are many heirloom varieties. Selection criteria depend on the type of plant. For mustard greens, select for low erucic acid and glucosinolate content. For use as a spice, select for light-colored seeds.

DISEASES AND PESTS The diseases and pests of *Brassica oleracea* (which see) can also affect the flowers and green shoots of mustard.

CULTIVATION HISTORY Mustard is the result of a crossing of *Brassica nigra* and *B. rapa*. In India, Pakistan, and eastern Europe, mustard is cultivated primarily as an oilseed crop, whereas in the UK and

Mustard flowers and pods

Canada, mustard is primarily grown for condiment mustard.

WHITE MUSTARD
Sinapis alba

White mustard is grown for use as a spice (condiment mustard), as a fodder plant, and as a green manure crop. The seeds of white mustard and *Brassica juncea* mustard are the main components of condiment mustard. *Sinapis alba* seeds give hot mustard its spicy flavor. When white mustard, which is not winter hardy, is grown as a "catch crop" (to "catch" nutrients that might otherwise leach away) following a main crop like wheat or beans, the winter-killed remains of the plants can be worked into the ground the following spring.

WHAT YOU'LL NEED
• 10 ft.² (1 m²) of plants

POLLINATION NOTES White mustard blossoms with brilliant yellow flowers that, when pollinated, produce an elongated pod as their fruit, each of which contains three or four spherical seeds. White mustard does not cross with mustard (*Brassica juncea*) or black mustard (*B. nigra*).

GROWING FOR SEED White mustard is an annual, seed of which is sown in midspring. It blossoms in early to mid summer.

HARVEST Harvest seed in mid to late summer. Ripe seedpods explode, releasing their seed to the ground, so harvest before pods attain full ripeness. Processing instructions as for *Brassica oleracea*.

SELECTION CHARACTERISTICS
• yield
• rapid growth
• rapid, uniform ripening of seed
• late flowering (when growing for leaf use)

White mustard is also known as *Gelbsenf* (yellow mustard) in German, for its brilliant yellow flowers.

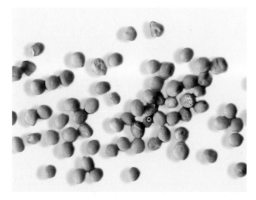

White mustard seeds

DISEASES AND PESTS White mustard is susceptible to many of the same pests and diseases as other brassicas (see *Brassica oleracea*).

CULTIVATION HISTORY The wild form of the plant is spread across the Mediterranean region, the Middle East, and the Caucasus as a weed and ruderal species and has over time been brought to other regions. The crop form of white mustard is mostly grown from Europe through the Middle East to India. In southern and eastern Asia, young plants are used as a leaf vegetable. Prehistoric finds in present-day Iraq are evidence of the long history of white mustard as a crop plant. The plant came to Europe in the Middle Ages and was used as a leaf vegetable and as a medicinal. Intensive breeding of white mustard is a recent development in the UK and Canada.

RADISH
Raphanus sativus

The species *Raphanus sativus* can be divided broadly into two categories: small-rooted summer radishes (var. *sativus*) and longer-rooted winter radishes (var. *niger*). Summer radishes are most commonly white, pink, or red, but there are also varieties with yellow, gray, violet, or black skin. Winter radishes are white, violet, brown, or black. The daikon, a type of winter radish, can grow to be 20 in. (50 cm) long yet remains crunchy; it is almost always white in the USA and Europe, but in China a red-fleshed variety

('Hsin-li-mei', meaning "beautiful deep down inside") is also very popular.

WHAT YOU'LL NEED
- 15 to 20 healthy, flowering plants
- insect netting (or absence of cabbage pests)
- trellis or one support pole per flowering plant
- for winter radishes: overwintering strategy

POLLINATION NOTES Radishes are insect pollinated and, like all brassicas, are

Radish seeds

Most summer radishes have white flowers. Their cylindrical seedpods stand upright and do not explode when ripe.

self-infertile outcrossers: a flower from one plant can only be pollinated by a flower from another plant. Since summer and winter radishes belong to the same species, they can cross with one another; they do not, however, cross with other brassicas like cabbage or turnip. Flowers are normally white or off-white, often with purple veins. Even pure varieties can produce variably colored flowers. Make sure there are plenty of plants flowering at once to reduce the risk of inbreeding. The more plants that flower next to each other, the greater seed yield will be. Isolate multiple varieties of this species by at least 500 ft. (150 m). Isolation distances should be much greater (⅓ mile [500 m] or more) when larger quantities are being grown and when garden configuration is less than ideal (few or no tall plants, one variety downwind from another variety, etc.). Temporal isolation can be achieved by growing, for example, a winter radish variety and a summer radish variety and choosing sowing times that ensure that the two do not flower at the same time. Otherwise, isolate mechanically by growing in cages.

GROWING FOR SEED Summer radishes produce ripe seeds in one growing season. The German heirloom 'Mairettich' is an in-between form that also produces seed the first year. Winter radishes are grown for seed as biennials. Summer radishes are very easy to grow for seed and are an ideal crop for the beginning seed saver. Sowing in early to mid spring makes for ripe seed in late summer to early autumn. Cover radish seed only lightly with soil. When seed is planted too deeply, radishes turn out misshapen. A round radish planted even only ⅔ in. (1.5 cm) deep will develop into a cylinder instead. For this reason, when growing radishes for seed, sow seed in pots or trays on the surface. Observe their development and plant out only the best-shaped plants in the garden to go to seed. Select 15 to 20 plants from 50 to 100 grown in pots.

Pull up radishes again when they are of eating ripeness and select. Replant selected radishes in 12 in. (30 cm) rows at 10 in. (25 cm) spacing within the row to allow plenty of space for flower stalks. Make sure the entire root is underground when planting for the last time to maximize stability. Water well and often after replanting. Stalks grow to be fairly tall, 4–6.5 ft. (120–200 cm); use a trellis or support poles to keep them from falling over. Skipping the step of replanting means missing out on an opportunity for selection.

Sow winter radishes in midsummer when growing for seed. Pull roots in late fall and cut back foliage to about 1 in. (2.5 cm). They can overwinter in a root cellar or in pots in a frost-free unheated greenhouse. Plant out in 16 in. (40 cm) rows, 12 in. (30 cm) spacing within the row. Water well after planting out, especially in dry weather.

HARVEST Flowering and seed ripening takes place over the course of several weeks. Seedpods do not explode when ripe, but we do not recommend waiting too long to harvest as the first seeds (which are often the best seeds) may fall

Below right are summer radishes at eating ripeness, left the seed stalks of another summer radish variety.

victim to various fungal diseases. Harvest when the plant is still green to some degree, but many seedpods have turned brown. The entire plant or just the stalks that are ripe can be harvested at this point and hung up to dry, ideally draped in bird netting, as birds love to snack on the seeds. Seedpods are soft and somewhat elastic even when dry, making for difficult threshing. Seeds are easily damaged by being pounded too hard, so take care. Threshing can be made easier by waiting until winter and setting dried stalks outdoors for a long, hard freezing. Thresh first thing in the morning when stalks and seedpods are still brittle. Seeds are light brown with a hint of red

and round to egg-shaped, sometimes very irregular.

SELECTION CHARACTERISTICS
- true-to-type
- vigor and earliness
- resistance to bolting
- root: size and shape; not fuzzy, woody, or spongy; no cavities; retains eating ripeness for a long time
- flavor: spicy or mild
- length and color of foliage

DISEASES AND PESTS Typical problems in the early stages of cultivation are flea beetles and cabbage root flies; pollen beetles, cabbage seed weevils, and aphids are potential problems during flowering. If any of these pests are problems during flowering, use insect netting to protect plants, as heavy infestations can prevent any seeds at all from forming. In rape- and canola-growing areas, radishes that flower in your garden when rape is done flowering are quickly infested by cabbage seed weevils. The fungal disease white rust (*Albugo candida*) can cause great damage to flower organs and seedpods. Plant at wider planting distances (see earlier) to

Various shapes of summer radish

flat-round　　　spherical　　　elongated, oval　　　elongated, bicolored　　　icicle

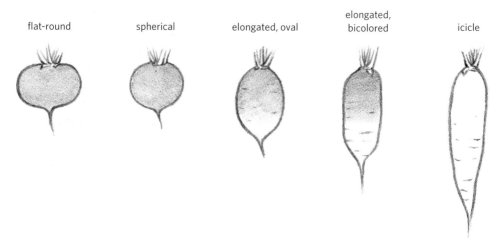

Various shapes of winter radish

round　　round-oval type (e.g., 'Münchner Bier')　　long and pointy, without shoulders　　long, conical, with shoulders　　black, spherical type (e.g., 'Runder Schwarzer Winter')　　daikon

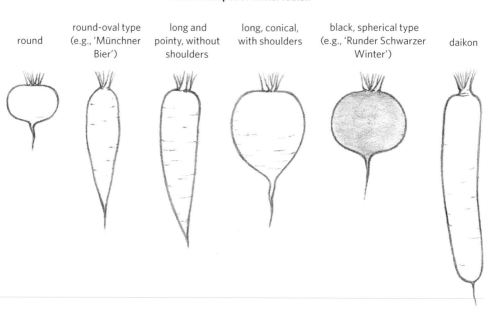

help avoid or reduce white rust. Remove afflicted plants and wait at least three years to grow brassicas in the same bed.

CULTIVATION HISTORY Although they belong to the same species, summer and winter radish were presumably domesticated at different times and places. Overwhelming evidence points to the early use of radish as a leaf vegetable, as its wild ancestor shows no swelling of the root. The plant first started to change when grown in the irrigated agriculture of the Fertile Crescent; from there it made its way to Egypt, where oilseed varieties were bred. The winter radish is one of the oldest crop plants, being grown by the ancient Egyptians, Greeks, and Romans; it was domesticated in either the eastern Mediterranean or southwest Asia. Unique varieties have been developed in China, where the radish has been cultivated since at least 300 BC. The first record of the small-rooted summer radish dates to 16th-century Italy. In India and Indonesia, another variety is grown for its edible unripe seedpods; these rat-tailed radish (var. *mougri*) seedpods are eaten raw in salads or boiled, steamed, or sautéed like other vegetables. Oilseed radishes (convar. *oleiformis*) have long been cultivated in eastern Asia, Egypt and, since the 19th century, in a few European countries; the oil is used in lamps and for cooking.

Rat-tailed radish seedpods

HORSERADISH
Armoracia rusticana

Horseradish is grown for its aromatic, spicy root that is often eaten raw and shredded with beef, sausage, or fish, or made into a condiment. In Austria, raw, shredded horseradish is added to cream or applesauce. Horseradish is one of the oldest cultivated garden plants and is sometimes found naturalized along paths.

WHAT YOU'LL NEED
• several well-developed roots
• a permanent place in the garden or
• overwintering quarters for root scions

POLLINATION NOTES The horseradish plants found in most gardens are self-sterile selections that flower but produce no seed. They can only be propagated vegetatively. Newer varieties are an exception to this.

PROPAGATION In most home gardens, horseradish stays in the same spot for years. Be warned: it is difficult to remove once it is planted (small pieces of root left behind send up new shoots), so site horseradish at the edge of or outside the garden. Horseradish is a perennial, hardy down to zone 3, though a few varieties (e.g., 'Spreewälder Meerrettich') may be significantly less hardy. Horseradish likes fertile, deep soils with plenty of humus and consistently moderate moisture content.

If you have ever wondered how it is that horseradish roots from the market can be so straight, whereas those from your garden are full of twists and turns, follow

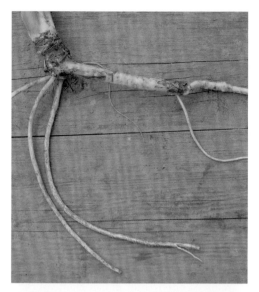

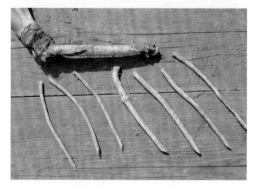

This is how straight horseradish roots begin. Scions growing from the main root are removed with a sharp knife. Cut tops straight and bottoms slanted ("Spreewald method") to make it easier to keep track of which end is which.

this method, which involves harvesting root scions (secondary roots growing off the main root) annually. It was developed by commercial growers in Germany, but it can be used in the home garden as well.

Pull up entire root in autumn and remove scions with a sharp knife. Cut further so you have pieces about 0.5–1 in. (1–2.5 cm) thick and 10–12 in. (25–30 cm) long. The thicker and longer the cutting, the better-looking the crop of horseradish will be. Two to three cuttings can be gotten per plant. Bundle cuttings together and overwinter in a cool cellar in moist sand or in the ground.

In early to mid spring, sprout cuttings and leave them in a heated room underneath a dark tarp (cover cuttings overwintered outdoors with a tarp). After two to three weeks, undesirable shoots can be recognized; rub these off with a towel, leaving those on the upper and lower 1–1.5 in. (3–4 cm) to form roots and shoots. Place cuttings in the ground, one end 2 in. (5 cm) deep, the other 6 in. (15 cm) deep. Old seed-propagation literature suggests aligning all cuttings in the same direction, ideally toward the south. Pack soil well atop the cuttings and water if necessary.

In late spring to early summer, when above-ground shoots are 4–5 in. (10–12 cm) long, free roots from the top (shallow) end (make sure the bottom, deep end remains in the soil). Remove all side roots except the thickest, then cover root again with soil.

SELECTION CHARACTERISTICS There are no varieties per se, but rather selections from areas of traditional horseradish cultivation ('Bayrischer' [Bavarian], 'Österreichischer' [Austrian], 'Steirische Auslese' [Styrian selection], etc.). These selections vary in root size, leaf shape, flavor (spicy or mild), texture of flesh (hard or soft), and resistance to fungal and viral diseases.

DISEASES AND PESTS Diseases are rarely an issue in the home garden. In commercial production, verticillium wilt (*Verticillium albo-atrum*) and white rust (*Albugo candida*) are the main concerns. White rust is a downy mildew fungus. Milky, pustule-shaped spots appear on the tops and bottoms of leaves; they open and spread spores, and these spores can then overwinter in the soil. The fungus can also overwinter as mycelium on roots. In serious cases, leaves die off and root heads rot. Remove and dispose of infected plants.

CULTIVATION HISTORY Horseradish is found in gardens across Europe and in the temperate zones of the USA, sometimes even in mountainous areas of the tropics. It is presumed to have originated in southern Russia and eastern Ukraine, spreading from these native lands to central Europe, with documentation of its cultivation dating back to the 12th century. The top-producing countries are Austria, Poland, and the Commonwealth of Independent States.

ARUGULA, ROCKET
Eruca sativa

Arugula is an old crop plant enjoying a recent resurgence in popularity. It can be used as a pungent, spicy addition to salads or sandwiches, a pizza topping or, combined with olive oil, salt, and Parmesan cheese, a refreshing appetizer. A relative of arugula is perennial wallrocket (*Diplotaxis tenuifolia*), which is slower growing, with narrower leaves and a more intense flavor.

WHAT YOU'LL NEED
• 10 ft.² (1 m²) of late-bolting plants

POLLINATION NOTES Arugula is a strict outcrosser. Its flowers are self-sterile, so at least two plants and pollinator insects are needed for pollination. Flowers are white or cream-colored, sometimes with purple veins. Perennial wallrocket flowers are brilliant yellow. Arugula and perennial wallrocket do not cross with each other.

GROWING FOR SEED Broadcast or sow in rows as early as possible in the spring, so plants do not flower so quickly, allowing more time for selecting for leaf development and to give more time for seed to ripen. Arugula is an annual and can be sown several times until late summer because of its relatively short life (about 40 days). As soon as plants have three pairs of leaves, they can be cut for eating.

HARVEST Arugula seeds have a natural dormancy period of about two months from the time of harvest. Seedpods are up to 1.5 in. (4 cm) long and stand upright on the stalk. Harvest seedpods shortly before fully ripe, as they otherwise fall off. Dry in the shade. Protection from birds may be in order as they like to snack on arugula's

Arugula seeds

Perennial wallrocket (*Diplotaxis tenuifolia*)

oily, spicy seeds. Arugula can also self-sow in the garden.

SELECTION CHARACTERISTICS There are no distinct varieties of arugula per se, only different selections and places of origin, which differentiate themselves in leaf color and size, vigor, and essential oil content, which gives the plant its pungent, spicy flavor.

DISEASES AND PESTS Flea beetles and cabbage seed weevils can cause a lot of damage when plants are flowering. See *Brassica oleracea*.

CULTIVATION HISTORY The wild relative of arugula is found from the Mediterranean to Afghanistan. It was used in ancient Italy as a leaf vegetable, and oil from its seeds was considered to be an aphrodisiac. Arugula was grown in central Europe in the Middle Ages for its pungent leaves but was later all but forgotten. In India, arugula is grown in a polyculture with flax, cereals, or cotton. Seeds are used there as a seasoning, and taramira or jamba oil from arugula seeds is used in pickling and cooking, as a lamp oil, and as a medicinal.

SEA KALE
Crambe maritima

Sea kale is a special vegetable whose blanched, tender leaf stems are eaten like asparagus. Although it has "kale" in its name, it belongs to a completely different genus. Sea kale's large, gray-green leaves look somewhat like kale, but their flavor

is more like cauliflower. Another *Crambe* species, *C. abyssinica* (Abyssinian kale) is an annual from Ethiopia used as a leaf vegetable and oilseed crop.

WHAT YOU'LL NEED
• three to five well-developed plants

POLLINATION NOTES Sea kale is a fully cross-pollinated, self-infertile plant. Its white flowers have a pleasant, honey-like aroma that attracts many insects. Arche Noah has no data on the potential for

Terra cotta cloche for blanching sea kale

COURTESY ISTOCKPHOTO/TRIFFITT

Sea kale in flower

cross-pollination between varieties, but since sea kale is a brassica, it is assumed that out-crossing is the rule and that multiple varieties would easily cross with one another.

PROPAGATION Sea kale is a perennial, hardy to zone 6. It can be propagated by seed (sow seed in early spring in deep, sandy soil or in pots) or by root cuttings, but seeds tend to have very low germination rates (20%), making vegetative propagation the surest method. Dig up plants in autumn when the leaves have died off, and cut roots back to 4–6 in. (10–15 cm). Bundle root cuttings together and overwinter in large flower pots in moist sand, making sure that the "head" of the root points upward. Replant plants. Plant out root cuttings 12 in. (30 cm) apart in spring.

Vegetables from sea kale plants grown from seed can be harvested in the third year, from vegetatively propagated plants

Propagating sea kale by root cuttings

in the second year. Plants can be harvested for eight to 10 years.

HARVEST Each fragile seed is enclosed in its own firm seedpod. To avoid damaging seeds, simply store harvested seeds in their pods and leave inside their individual pods for sowing as well.

SELECTION CHARACTERISTICS Older varieties show the hint of purple seen in the wild plant. Potential selection criteria:

• winter hardiness
• vigor and cold tolerance
• tenderness of shoots

BLANCHING In coastal areas where wild sea kale is found, leaf stems are blanched by drifting sand that accumulates over the winter. Blanched leaf stems can then be collected in the spring. Another technique must be used in the garden: English gardeners use terra cotta cloches for blanching leaf stems. A large flower pot or plastic bucket (20–24 in. [50–60 cm] tall) can do the same job. Simply set them upside down over plants in early spring. The first blanched leaf stems are ready in three to four weeks and a second harvest three to four weeks after the first. After the second harvest, remove the cloche, pot, or bucket you have used to allow the plant to receive light. When grown in this way, sea kale can be used in the same way as asparagus, as a tender early vegetable. Both the wide, blanched leaf stems and the flower stalks with their buds are edible.

DISEASES AND PESTS The biggest danger to sea kale is a late spring frost that freezes tender new growth. Slugs (especially under cloches) and wild rabbits also love to eat young shoots. When plants are planted too close together or in the shade, they may start to rot in hot summer weather. All the pests of *Brassica oleracea* (which see) can also infest and damage sea kale plants.

CULTIVATION HISTORY Sea kale grows in the wild on the coastlines of western Europe and along the Baltic and Black Seas. Up until about 1750, when sea kale cultivation began in England, it was only wild harvested. Sea kale was long somewhat of a culinary status symbol, as its tedious cultivation was attempted only by the professional gardeners of the bourgeoisie. Commercial production is mainly done in England, France, and North America. In the German-speaking world as well as in most of the USA, this brassica is rarely found in markets, and connoisseurs grow it themselves.

GARDEN CRESS
Lepidium sativum

Though it can only be grown for seed in the garden or in large pots, garden cress also makes a fine container plant, growing well in small pots on the windowsill. It is a diuretic, and its sprouts are rich in iron and vitamin C. Larger plants can be used in salads or as a seasoning. Eaten fresh, garden cress cleanses the blood and stimulates the appetite; its bitter taste may be traced to glucosinolates and other compounds.

WHAT YOU'LL NEED
• 10 ft.^{2} (1 m^2) of well-developed plants

POLLINATION NOTES Garden cress is an outcrosser, though there are self-fertile varieties. Its very small, white to pink flowers are seldom visited by bees, yet we have still observed crossing between varieties. Because of this, multiple varieties should be spatially or temporally isolated. Garden cress does not cross with bittercress (*Barbarea vulgaris*) or watercress (*Nasturtium officinale*).

GROWING FOR SEED In addition to water, warmth, and oxygen, garden cress seeds need light to germinate, so simply press seeds very lightly into the growing medium when starting seeds. The plant is an annual and produces seedpods as its fruit. As plants mature to 16–32 in. (40–80 cm) tall, planting distances when growing for seed must be greater than when growing for leaf production by about 8 in. (20 cm). Pods are ripe in midsummer. Plants from seeds sown in summer flower

Garden cress seeds

quickly in the high heat and dry conditions of the season, which makes it impossible to select for good leaf development.

HARVEST Harvest entire plants when they dry and seeds start to turn yellowish brown. Dry completely in the shade.

SELECTION CHARACTERISTICS Different varieties have different growth habits and produce variously shaped leaves and even seeds. They are not always accurately named and described in seed catalogs; the main categories are those with flat leaves, those with curly leaves, those with wide leaves, and golden-yellow English varieties, with the widest leaves. Potential selection criteria:

- leaf curliness
- vigorous growth
- leaf yield
- flavor (spicy or mild)

DISEASES AND PESTS As for many other brassicas, flea beetles can cause great amounts of crop damage.

CULTIVATION HISTORY Descriptions of garden cress are found in antique garden literature, and it was spread across Europe by the Romans. Domestication presumably occurred in the Middle East, where the greatest genetic diversity is found. The wild form of garden cress occurs in Ethiopia as a weed in flax fields.

BITTERCRESS
Barbarea vulgaris

Bittercress is used as a leaf vegetable in France, England, and North America. It grows wild (and in North America is naturalized) in wet meadows and riverbank slopes. Young leaves can be gathered in the spring before the plant flowers for vitamin C–rich spring salads. The cultivated

Garden cress in bloom

Bittercress seeds

form has larger leaves than the wild form and is easily grown for seed where no wild or naturalized plants can be found.

WHAT YOU'LL NEED
- 10 ft.^{2} (1 m^2) of well-developed, well-overwintered plants

POLLINATION NOTES Bittercress is a strict outcrosser and is pollinated by insects.

GROWING FOR SEED Bittercress is relatively easy to grow. Sow this biennial in mid to late summer in fertile, moist soil. Plants can handle some shade. Their dark green leaves develop in a rosette and can be harvested from late fall until flowering in late spring. Plants can be overwintered outdoors down to zone 4. Flowers are a brilliant lemon yellow.

HARVEST Bittercress fruits are seedpods. Harvest as for *Brassica oleracea*.

SELECTION CHARACTERISTICS There are no bittercress varieties per se. Potential selection criteria:

- leaf size
- rapid leaf regrowth

DISEASES AND PESTS We have yet to observe diseases affecting bittercress. For flower pests, see *Brassica oleracea*.

CULTIVATION HISTORY The wild form of bittercress is found in Europe and western Asia. The first European settlers of North America brought bittercress with them and grew it there as a leaf vegetable. Cultivation ceased sometime in the 18th century. Bittercress was once grown as a medicinal (blood cleansing, diuretic, appetite stimulant), and one form of the plant with double flowers as an ornamental.

COURTESY SHUTTERSTOCK/© SLOWFISH

Bittercress in flower

WATERCRESS
Nasturtium officinale

Like other plants named cress, water-cress is a medicinal, stimulating appe-tite, cleansing the blood, and acting as a diuretic. With a biting flavor reminiscent of radish and horseradish, it is often eaten raw in salads but can also be cooked. Its leaves can be harvested from autumn until the following spring, but once the plant flowers, they become fairly bitter. The plant has special ecological require-ments: it needs clean, flowing water and in the wild grows along clear-flowing creeks; it is an endangered species in Austria.

WHAT YOU'LL NEED
- 10 ft.² (1 m²) of well-developed and well-overwintered plants
- a garden bed that can be irrigated and drained

Watercress cultivated in a basin, Wildegg Castle, Switzerland

- a spring or creek with clean, somewhat hard water

POLLINATION NOTES Watercress is an outcrosser.

PROPAGATION Watercress is an herbaceous perennial, hardy to zone 5. It grows to be 12–28 in. (30–70 cm) tall, and its stalks develop runners that creep across the ground near water. It is best propagated vegetatively by cuttings, with seed being useful only when vegetative propagation is not an option. Sow seed in early sum-mer in a very moist mix in containers; seeds germinate between 50°F (10°C) and 59°F (15°C). When the plants have several leaves, the containers can be placed out-doors near running water. When seedlings are 2 in. (5 cm) tall, they can be planted in a watery ditch. The tips of the plants must stick out of the water, and the water surface level can then be slowly raised, in stages.

White flowers appear at the tips of highly branched stalks in late spring, fruits in mid to late summer. Late sum-mer/early autumn is the ideal planting time.

HARVEST Seedpods can be straight or curved like a sickle. Harvest when yel-low ripe (after the milk-ripe stage, slightly before fully ripe), dry further, then thresh.

SELECTION CHARACTERISTICS The many regional selections differentiate them-selves mainly in the intensity of their leaf color, from light to dark green. The brown form is a cross with *Nasturtium* *macrophyllum*; it is sterile and can only be propagated vegetatively.

DISEASES AND PESTS No significant diseases or pests affect watercress. A horticultural center in Switzerland reports problems with a pest not typical in vegetable gardening: wild ducks, which flock to creeks planted with watercress. Colorful plastic bird netting is stretched above the crop to protect it.

CULTIVATION HISTORY Watercress is found the world over, and its exact area of origin is unknown. Its heyday was the 18th and 19th centuries, when it was grown on a relatively large scale in England, France, and Germany as a leaf vegetable; special water beds were established to this end. It is now grown in eastern Africa, southeast Asia, and other countries, mostly on a very small scale, as cultivation is labor-intensive.

SCURVYGRASS, SPOONWORT
Cochlearia officinalis

One common name comes from the plant's apparent ability to cure scurvy (it has a high vitamin C content); it is also said to be effective in problems with the bladder and digestion. Another is a reference to the spoon-like shape of its spicy, cress-like leaves, which can be a pungent addition to salads. Scurvygrass is found wild in salty, moist soils, growing along the coast of the Atlantic Ocean and the Baltic Sea from northern Spain to Scandinavia.

WHAT YOU'LL NEED
• 10 ft.^{2} (1 m^2) of healthy plants

POLLINATION NOTES Scurvygrass is an insect-pollinated outcrosser.

GROWING FOR SEED Scurvygrass has no special needs as far as soil is concerned, thriving even in salty soils. Sow seed in early to mid spring or in late summer to early autumn (summer seedings lead to a strong salty/bitter taste). The plant is extremely hardy (as low as zone 2 in the literature) and flowers in its second year.

HARVEST Ripe seedpods explode, releasing their seed to the ground, so harvest before pods attain full ripeness. Processing instructions as for *Brassica oleracea*.

SELECTION CHARACTERISTICS We know of no varieties per se, only a German

Ripe scurvygrass pods

selection, 'Erfurter Echte Löffelkraut' (true spoonwort from Erfurt). Selection criterium: vigorous growth.

DISEASES AND PESTS Scurvygrass can theoretically be affected by all brassica diseases, but infection seldom occurs. Flea beetles can be an all-too-common unwelcome guest. Timely harvesting and regular soil cultivation can help with flea beetle problems.

CULTIVATION HISTORY Back in the days of long journeys by ship, scurvygrass was brought aboard to prevent scurvy, in the form of dried leaves or distilled. Its cultivation was first documented in Belgium in the 16th century, and soon thereafter it was widely included in the gardens of apothecaries. The plant was grown intensively in the 19th century, and in Jena, Germany, it was a market vegetable until World War II.

Carrot and relatives

APIACEAE

Plants in this family are now categorized as belonging to the family Apiaceae but are still known colloquially as umbellifers, a reference to the umbrella-shaped flower heads formed by family members (the family's former Latin name, Umbelliferae, literally means "umbrella carrier"). Umbellifer blossoms are composed of small symmetrically arranged umbels that together make up the flower umbel. All umbellifers are herbaceous plants and for the most part high in essential oils, the reason they are often used as flavoring and spices; there are, however, many medicinal and also toxic plants in the family. Several crop plants come from this family, the carrot being the most well known, as well as parsley, fennel, and that tasty rediscovered root vegetable, the parsnip. There are also plenty of wild plants from this family: Queen Anne's lace, poison parsnip, caraway, angelica, and cow parsnip.

● ●

GENERAL PROPAGATION CHARACTERISTICS
Practically all umbellifers that are cultivated for their roots or bulbs are biennials, the main exception being skirret, which flowers in the first year. For certain other members of this family, especially those grown for leaves and seeds, it is possible to harvest seed in the first year, for example, turnip-rooted chervil. All umbellifers only rarely self-pollinate and are highly susceptible to cross-pollination, because of which, two varieties of the same species should never be grown close together

Carrot family flowers attract pollinators and other beneficial insects.

Overview of the umbellifer family

COMMON NAME	GENUS	SPECIES	USE	LIFE CYCLE
carrot	*Daucus*	*carota*	root	biennial
parsley	*Petroselinum*	*crispum*	root, leaf	biennial
celery	*Apium*	*graveolens*	leaf, bulb, leaf stalk	biennial
parsnip	*Pastinaca*	*sativa*	root	biennial
fennel	*Foeniculum*	*vulgare*	leaf, bulb, seed	biennial, perennial
skirret	*Sium*	*sisarum*	root	perennial
turnip-rooted chervil	*Chaerophyllum*	*bulbosum*	leaf, fleshy taproot	biennial

in the same garden without some form of reliable isolation (e.g., isolation cage). Umbellifer blossoms are visited by any number of insects, with hoverflies being the most reliable pollinators.

CARROT
Daucus carota

WHAT YOU'LL NEED
- at least 30 (ideally 50 to 100) healthy, well-developed carrots
- mild climate or root cellar
- the absence of wild carrots and/or isolation cage
- support for flowers
- bed linen or cloth bag

Carrot seeds

POLLINATION NOTES Like all umbellifers, carrots are outcrossers and are essentially self-sterile. Because of their high susceptibility to crossing, it is only possible to grow one variety per year for seed without isolation.

The nectar of the large flower umbels attract a large assortment of insects, including beetles, bees, wasps, and hoverflies. In many places wild carrots (Queen Anne's lace) grow in meadows and fallow strips; these are the same species as cultivated carrots and will cross with them if the cultivated carrots are not isolated. The white umbel of wild carrots differentiates itself from all other umbellifers through the purplish black dot that is typically found in the center of its umbel. It is not uncommon to find even commercial carrot seed that is crossed with wild carrot, which can be seen in plants with white, fibrous roots and in plants that flower in the first year. Remove these plants by the root to eliminate possibility of grow-back. Depending upon population size and location of the patch, use a spatial isolation distance of at least 500 ft. (150 m), though if wild carrot is anywhere near, mechanical isolation is a must. When isolation

The beautiful, aromatic umbels of carrots are dried by hanging upside down.

cages or tents are used, hoverflies have shown themselves to be the best pollinators, though flies of the Calliphoridae family (blowflies, carrion flies) will probably also get the job done. Honeybees are not particularly effective pollinators of carrots.

GROWING FOR SEED Carrots should not be sown too early when growing for seed, unless earliness is a trait you would like to select for. Keep in mind that carrots should develop to their full eating ripeness at the time they are dug up in autumn, so early-ripening varieties should be planted relatively late (early summer) and late-ripening varieties should be planted a week or two before the last spring frost. If early carrots are sown too early, there are consquences: they are overly ripe in autumn (and thus will not store well), they are difficult to select, and they do not grow well when replanted in the spring. Ideally, carrots sown for propagation are harvested as late in autumn as possible and are ripe at the same time as eating carrots. This is when the first selection takes place. Store undamaged, clean roots in a frost-proof root cellar and cut the tops (green vegetative growth) back to 1–2 in. (3–5 cm) above the crown of the root. It is of utmost importance not to damage the crowns. Carrots will need protection from drying out and too much warmth throughout the winter, the optimal conditions being 33–38°F (1–3°C) and 90% humidity. A second selection of plants occurs just before planting these carrots out again the following spring: be ready to appraise their longevity in storage and maintenance of taste and lushness.

Roots can be planted out in the spring as soon as the snow has melted and the ground is more or less dry (early to mid spring). A hardening-off period of a few days is recommended to let the carrots slowly adjust to sunlight after a whole winter in the dark. Carrots are vulnerable to drying out at this point, especially if the soil is relatively sandy, so be sure to water adequately and perhaps provide shade from the sun and ground cover to protect from the wind. The ideal conditions for planting out are cloudy, mild temperatures, little to no wind, with rain coming right after planting.

Plant spacing: 16–25 in. (40–65 cm) between rows, 8–12 in. (20–30 cm) within the row, depending upon size of the variety. Plant roots such that only the crown is visible and the roots are well anchored and vertical in the ground. Once they have begun to grow, they will need to be weeded two or three times. With the last weeding, build up soil around the base of the stems to provide more stability. The flowers will need support, but it is not necessary to support each individual plant. Sink a post every 20–40 in. (50–100 cm) in the ground and pull a string taut on each side just below the flowers, such that all stalks between the poles are supported.

A technique for temporally isolating cultivated carrots from wild carrots is to plant second-year roots early (late winter) indoors in pots. Plant five or six roots in a 2.5-gallon (10-liter) pot and keep the pots in a frost-free yet cool place. They can then be hardened off and planted out as just described. Carrots handled thus will blossom several weeks before wild carrots, thus nullifying the risk of cross-pollination.

In warmer climates, where carrots can

Various carrot varieties flowering in their own isolation tents

Since varieties are easily mixed up in the root cellar, be sure to label them for winter storage.

stay in the ground all winter, it is still necessary to dig up carrots in autumn for selection, so that they can then be replanted together in one patch with appropriate spacing for flowering and, if necessary, covered with straw to protect from frost. This method eliminates the possibility of a second selection in the spring, however.

HARVEST As with many umbellifers, the best seeds are typically found on the first umbels that develop on the main stem. To take advantage of this, harvest these umbels first, and harvest seed from later or smaller stems only if you have too little seed. Older seed propagation literature even recommends pruning smaller

and secondary growth, so the seeds from the main umbel are better nourished and become bigger and healthier. Plantings with compact spacing yield a higher percentage of seed from the main umbel because there is too little space for secondary growth.

Carrot seeds ripen over a long period of time, and seeds can be harvested throughout. As soon as the first umbels become brown and dry, they can be harvested, ideally cut with a scissors on a warm, dry day and left to dry further for two to three weeks. In colder zones, the ripening of seeds can be sped up by uprooting the plants in early autumn and spreading them out to dry for a similar amount of time. Thresh dry umbels in a cloth bag

Women in Küttigen, Switzerland, laying out second-year 'Küttiger Rüebli' carrot roots.

or with a coarse sieve. Seed can then be winnowed with finer sieves and with the wind. The seed will be easier to handle if the "lashes" are removed in a cloth bag.

SELECTION CHARACTERISTICS Carrots can be divided into two groups: fodder carrots and eating carrots. Fodder types are late, well-storing varieties with white or golden-red flesh. Eating carrots have a variety of harvest times and uses. Because colors can range from white to yellow, orange, red, and purple (and these can all appear in carrots of different shapes), selection criteria are myriad:

- leaf formation, vigorous growth (potentially an expression of good drought tolerance)
- true-to-type leaf shape and color
- resistance to powdery mildew, carrot leaf blight, and other diseases
- true-to-type shape (conical, pointed, stubby, cylindrical, short, long, etc.)
- root crown: well-formed shoulders, not flat or countersunk, sturdy foliage

Allow cut umbels two to three weeks for drying.

- lack of green collar (top portion of root green or violet in color). This trait can be bred out, if desired, although this can also be a defining varietal trait—as in 'Blanche à Collet Vert', which is a white Belgian carrot with a "green collar."
- smoothness of root surface
- stability
- straight, unbranched roots
- sweetness and aroma (because carrots are outcrossers, individual plants in a patch may have different flavors: sweet, typical carrot, neutral, aromatic or bitter, soapy). There are two options for a taste test: you can either remove the lower third of the root and taste this, or punch out a cylindrical chunk from the bottom half (a core sample) and taste that. Hardcore carrot enthusiasts may want to taste raw as well as steamed. After taste testing, let the wound dry and disinfect it with bone char or wood ash before returning it to storage.
- fine-grained flesh
- inner and outer color of root
- storage life of late varieties
- shorter greens for early varieties

It is not possible to discourage by selection the presence of fine, sinewy side roots, which develop when carrots are left in the ground too long. In this case, the root has reached its full size, and the plant develops finer roots to take up more nutrients for seed production.

DISEASES AND PESTS Carrot leaf blight, caused by the fungus *Alternaria dauci*, can present challenges in carrot seed propagation. The hot water treatment

Various shapes of carrots

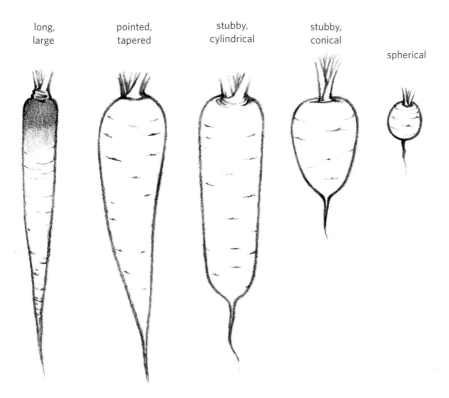

long, large   pointed, tapered   stubby, cylindrical   stubby, conical   spherical

can be used as a preventative measure. In infected plants, leaves turn brown and black, then die off. Even the root can be affected, showing black spots. This disease can be seed-borne as well as soil-borne. Also seed-borne, if rarer, is the fungus *A. radicina*, which usually turns up in storage as black spots and can reach deep into the tissue of the root. Non-seed-borne diseases include powdery mildew and gray mold.

In storage, many fungal diseases can occur. Often the actual infection happens out in the field, and the fungus is brought into storage with otherwise healthy-looking carrots, as with *Thielaviopsis*-caused root rot. Store only fully ripened, carefully harvested, and unwashed carrots that are not too densely layered. If using a storage pit, establish it somewhere other than last year's.

The carrot fly (*Psila rosae*) is a widespread pest in carrot culture. There are typically two generations per growing season, the first appearing after the last spring frost, which in extreme cases can kill young carrot plants. The second generation appears in late summer and can be more dangerous for seed growers because it affects carrots throughout the winter. Carrot flies lay eggs on the surface of the soil, where larvae form,

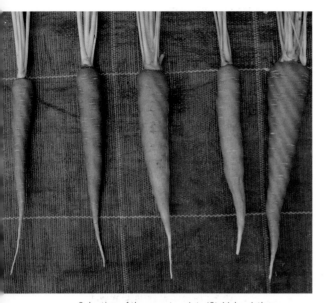

Selection of the carrot variety 'St. Valery': these roots will be planted out the following year for seed production. Not pictured but just as important as the shape: selecting for taste. Often only the best 1–5% of carrots of a given variety grown by professional breeders are used for seed production. Home gardeners need not be quite so strict in their selection process.

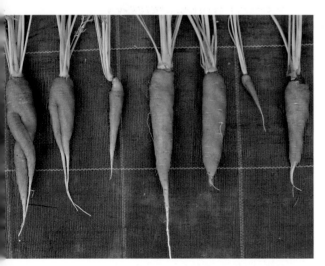

These root types should not be propagated: leggy carrots, green-shouldered carrots, small carrots . . .

which then eat their way into the carrots and fill the channels they've dug with their excrement, causing a rusty brown discoloration. Prevention: use an isolation tent and/or row cover, select a windy plot to grow in, good crop rotation. Hot, dry weather inhibits the growth of young larvae. The classic companion planting of carrots with onions appears to be of no help with carrot fly; we highly recommend undersowing subterranean clover (*Trifolium subterraneum*), which can be extremely effective in preventing infestation, does not go to seed, and winter-kills.

CULTIVATION HISTORY The wild ancestors of the cultivated carrot were originally found spread throughout Europe and Asia Minor. The modern carrot, traceable to two or three subspecies (one of which is native to Europe), can be divided into an Asian type and a Western type. The Asian type was presumably domesticated in central Asia from local wild varieties; individuals were selected for the colors violet-red (attributable to anthocyanins, a flavonoid category) and yellow. The Western type was domesticated in Asia Minor, is biennial, and has unbranched white, yellow, or orange roots. The typical orange (from beta-carotene) carrot sold in supermarkets comes from 17th-century Dutch breeding. Most European carrots are from varieties developed in the Netherlands, England, and France, the latter having developed itself into a virtual carrot-breeding empire in recent decades (seen in varieties like 'Nantaise'). Pale yellow carrots faded from popularity over the course of the 20th century and are now mostly used in soups.

PARSLEY
Petroselinum crispum

There are two main types of parsley: root (Radicosum group) and leaf (Crispum group). Leaf parsley is common worldwide as a seasoning; its leaves are of three sorts: flat and small, flat and large, and curly. Root parsley is thought to have been bred from "transitional" varieties used for both their leaves and roots.

WHAT YOU'LL NEED
• 20 well-formed plants
• overwintering strategy
• support poles and string

POLLINATION NOTES Parsley is insect-pollinated, and insects love parsley blossoms. Leaf and root parsley varieties, being of the same species, will cross

Parsley seeds

with each other. Isolation distances of 300–500 ft. (100–150 m) have worked for us, though the greater the distance, the better; otherwise, use an isolation cage with hoverflies, carrion flies, or common houseflies.

GROWING FOR SEED All forms of parsley are biennial and in the first year are grown for seed in the same way they would be grown for food. Harvest as few leaves as possible for plants slated to be grown for seed, to support good root growth. Plants are theoretically hardy to zone 3, though overwintering success outdoors is less reliable below zone 5, even with ground cover. Plants are most susceptible early in the second year, when they start to send out new growth, only to be damaged by a late frost. To be safe, dig the plants around the time of the first autumn frost and overwinter them in the root cellar. Remove all stems except those arising directly from the center of the root's crown. Plant roots out with 12 in. (30 cm) spacing between rows, 10 in. (25 cm) spacing within the row. Leaf parsley can also be selected for larger roots, which would potentially improve drought tolerance and vigor.

HARVEST Harvest umbels as soon as they become ripe and dry them. Ripe parsley seeds left on the plant too long are easily knocked to the ground by wind and rain. Thresh and winnow as for carrots. Parsley seed is viable for a relatively short period of time, only two to three years.

Curly-leaved parsley

SELECTION CHARACTERISTICS

• fast growth for maximum number of harvests
• powdery mildew resistance in autumn
• root parsley: large, vigorous roots; smooth and unbranched; true-to-type shape (short/plump/stubby, middle-long/conical, long/pointy, etc.); well-defined shoulders
• leaf parsley: lushness and vigor of foliage; true-to-type shape and color (curly-leaved varieties must always be selected for curly leaves); vigor and ability to regrow after cutting; tenderness and full-bodied aroma of the leaf (as a garnish)

DISEASES AND PESTS Parsley is susceptible to septoria leaf spot (*Septoria petroselini*), a seed-borne fungal disease. Affected seed is infested with the fungus's asexual fruiting bodies (pycnidia), which are visible to the naked eye. Some parsley varieties are highly susceptible to powdery mildew in autumn; this can be minimized by

Ancient Chinese secret

Eduard Lucas (1905) described a Chinese seed propagation technique that he found in a memo from the Styrian (Austria) Horticultural Association: "It is well known that the quantity and often also the quality of seed from a given plant is dependent upon the extent of its root development. To encourage the development of root hairs, the Chinese use the following peculiar procedure, which is worthy of emulation. Before they plant out root vegetables in the spring, they make three or four shallow cuts with a sharp knife from crown to tip. Along these cuts, a bulge or ridge develops, out of which innumerable root hairs grow, which contribute significantly to the nourishment and vigorous development of the plants."

quickly removing affected leaves (and, if necessary, plants) and by careful watering.

CULTIVATION HISTORY The original home of wild parsley has not been firmly established but was presumably around the Mediterranean or in western Asia. Root parsley has been used since antiquity; it was the Romans who first brought it north of the Alps, where it especially caught on in what is today Austria, Germany, Poland, and the Netherlands. Parsley is an important component of Suppengrün (soup greens) and other bouquets garnis used to flavor soups and stocks. It reached England in the 18th century (where root parsley is still commonly known as Hamburg parsley, after the first variety to be grown there) and is now naturalized in many parts of Europe.

CELERY
Apium graveolens

There are three main forms of cultivated celery: celery root or celeriac (var. *rapaceum*, grown for its bulbous root), celery (var. *dulce*, grown for its stalks), and leaf celery (var. *secalinum*, used as a spice).

WHAT YOU'LL NEED
- 15 well-formed, healthy plants
- support posts and string
- frost-free overwintering

POLLINATION NOTES Celery blossoms are insect-pollinated, and all three forms, being of the same species, will cross with each other. Because wild celery is found only sporadically on some sea coasts (as far north as the British Isles and Denmark), risk of cross-pollination with it is practically nonexistent. Though it is rare, celery can cross with parsley—an exception to the rule that plants from different species cannot pollinate each other. The resulting seed produces parcel, a plant with parsley-like leaves and a celery-like aroma.

It is early spring, and these celery roots have overwintered well, embedded in sand.

Celery seeds

Isolation distance between celery varieties in an ideally sited garden should be at least 500 ft. (150 m); otherwise, use an isolation cage. As with all umbellifers, hoverflies are the best pollinators, followed by carrion flies and houseflies. Honeybees pollinate minimally at best.

GROWING FOR SEED All forms of celery are cultivated biennially for seed. In the first year it is grown for seed just like it would be grown for produce. It is important to avoid planting too deep when planting out celery seedlings to keep the development of side roots to a minimum. Where late blight is a problem, use 28 in. (70 cm) as plant spacing between and within the row instead of 20 in. (50 cm), which helps prevent the fungus from spreading. Plants for seed production can be selected directly from plots that are otherwise for production. Take care not to injure the plant, because, especially with root celery, small injuries in autumn can lead to significant rotting of the plant in storage. Dig up with a spade and leave the roots alone to encourage better growth in the spring. Remove all stalks down to those coming from the heart and cut those back to about an inch (2 cm). Store them such that the plants do not touch each other, to minimize rot through the winter. They should enter the root cellar dry for better overwintering.

Plants can be overwintered outdoors only in zones free of frost, though hardiness varies from variety to variety. Peter Lassnig, long-time curator for Arche Noah, reports that at his zone 6 farm, small celery plants overwinter better outdoors under row cover (with leaves or straw, as needed) than in the root cellar. In wet weather, pull plant protection away from plants to prevent rot. Straw helps prevent early growth in spring. Remove row cover when the ground has cleared (early to mid spring). Seed yield is typically higher for plants overwintered outdoors, though plants that spent the winter in the root cellar have typically been better observed and more carefully selected.

When planting out in the spring, see to it that roots have good contact with the soil by pressing the soil well around them. Plants should also be deeper in the soil than in autumn, with only the leaves coming out of the heart of the root having direct exposure to the air. Plant at 24 in. (60 cm) between and within the row. Water well, as new root growth is slow. Once the plant has bolted, it may be helpful to tie the stalks up with poles for added stability.

HARVEST Harvest seeds as soon after they become ripe as possible, as wind and rain easily knock ripe seeds to the ground. One can either harvest umbels individually as they become ripe, or the whole plant once the majority of umbels have ripe seeds on them. Hang entire plants upside down with a sheet underneath (to catch falling seeds) to finish ripening and to dry. Unripe seeds harvested from entire plants will have to be sorted out later, as for carrots (which see).

SELECTION CHARACTERISTICS FOR CELERY ROOT Recently we have seen the development of "snow white" celeriac, which is curious as the essential oils, which give the root its flavor and other important nutrients, are found in the yellowish spots in the root. Potential selection criteria:

- leaf: true-to-type growth patterns and size (leaf shape, color, and development; rapid growth; tight onset of growth from crown)
- root bulb: true-to-type shape (round, flat, egg-like, conical); lack of voids (mostly found in very large root bulbs; take a core sample)
- flesh: fine-grained and firm (not spongy)
- roots: no side roots, only at the bottom of the bulb; well-defined connection to the bulb (makes processing easier). A strong root system is, however, important for good plant health and growth, so strike a balance in your selection.
- good celery flavor (not bitter)
- health, lack of disease

SELECTION CHARACTERISTICS FOR STALK CELERY

- stalks: fineness of skin and of stalk; juiciness; aroma
- true-to-type color (green, green-yellow, golden yellow, pink)
- lends itself well to blanching or is self-blanching
- length (up to 15–20 in. [40–50 cm]) and thickness (up to 1.5–2 in. [4–5 cm]) of the stalks
- bolt resistance
- health, lack of disease

SELECTION CHARACTERISTICS FOR LEAF CELERY

- good regrowth

- abundant leaves, vigor
- robust aroma

DISEASES AND PESTS The two most important diseases of celery are seed-borne, so seed savers must take special care to avoid them. Root rot in celery (*Phoma apiicola*) appears first as gray, then reddish brown bark-like crusts on the root bulb that are up to 1/10 in. (2 mm) thick; these then dehisce (rupture). This fungal disease is most likely to appear in damp years but is not particularly common in general. Individual varieties are differentially susceptible to root rot. Late blight of celery, also caused by a fungus (*Septoria apiicola*), appears as light brown to grayish brown spots with black dots on either side of the leaves and dried tissue. Remedy: longer storage of seed before use, which weakens

Celeriac in the field

the fungus; watering plants with warm water; spraying a horsetail compost tea in damp weather. The hot water treatment is also recommended.

CULTIVATION HISTORY Celery is a very old food, medicinal, and spice crop. It has been grown in Egypt since at least 1325 BC, presumably domesticated from wild celery, which requires salty soils and is frequent along sea coasts.

Leaf celery is the oldest domesticated form of celery, verifiably since the 2nd century BC in China. The Romans, who rarely failed to include it in herb gardens around the Mediterranean, brought celery north of the Alps and began selecting for whitened, elongated stalks, although modern cultivated varieties can only be traced back to the late 16th century and came into being through selective breeding. In the 18th century, celeriac cultivation declined in favor of the parsnip. Celeriac has since become one of the most important vegetable crops in Europe, albeit much less known elsewhere. Many stalk celery varieties originally come from England, where celery has been grown and bred since the 19th century.

PARSNIP
Pastinaca sativa

WHAT YOU'LL NEED
- 15 to 20 healthy roots
- overwintering strategy
- support polls and string
- gloves for harvesting seed

POLLINATION NOTES Parsnip is an outcrosser and only rarely self-pollinates. The last few umbels tend to not get pollinated. Blossoms are yellow. Cultivated parsnip will cross with wild parsnip without proper isolation. With an ideally sited garden, an isolation distance of as few as 500 ft. (150 m) from wild parsnip or other parsnip cultivars may suffice; otherwise, use a spatial isolation of at least ¼ mile (400 m) (or an isolation cage).

GROWING FOR SEED Parsnip seeds germinate relatively slowly, sometimes requiring up to three weeks, although later sowings (one to four weeks before last anticipated spring frost) tend to germinate quicker and more evenly than earlier sowings.

Parsnip is an extremely hardy biennial, reliably surviving winters down to zone 3. However, overwintering outdoors risks herbivory from moles and other rodents. It is in any case expedient to harvest in autumn to select ideal plants to grow on for seed. Roots can then either be planted out again immediately (if you

Parsnip seeds

are confident that herbivory will not be a problem) or overwintered in the root cellar. Plant at 15–20 in. (40–50 cm) between and within rows.

Stalks of parsnip plants will grow to be up to 5 ft. (1.5 m) tall and, since they are not as robust as wild parsnip stalks, require support.

HARVEST Once parsnips begin to flower, it can take a month and a half or longer before seeds ripen. The harvest should ideally be carried out in three phases. The first harvest is when the first umbels turn yellowish brown; these will yield the largest, most viable seeds. Harvest two more times as umbels turn color. Parsnip seed does not remain viable for long and should ideally be used the year after harvest.

Parsnip stalks have a rather unpleasant characteristic: they contain an essential oil that in combination with sunlight causes blistering and burning of the skin. Wear gloves and long sleeves when harvesting, and wash hands well afterward. Otherwise, harvest as you would carrots.

SELECTION CHARACTERISTICS In his definitive handbook on the growing and propagation of vegetables, Josef Becker-Dillingen (1938) differentiated between five types of cultivated parsnips:

Two appropriate packing media for overwintering root crops in the root cellar: sand (pictured) and a mixture of peat moss and sawdust.

Parsnip is a delicious storage vegetable. Pictured is the cultivar 'Halblange' (half-long).

Here the wind got a head start on harvesting parsnip seed, so get going, before it finishes the job for you!

- long (up to 15 in. [40 cm]) and white
- long (about 15 in. [40cm]), thicker at crown (2.5–3 in. [6–8 cm]), recessed nodality
- medium long (up to 6 in. [15 cm]) and densely foliated
- medium long (up to 6 in. [15 cm]), short-leaved, and early-ripening
- round (3–4 in. [8–10 cm] long, 4.5–6 in. [12–15 cm] wide) for clayey soils

Since then, round varieties seem to have disappeared, and many more varieties that fit somewhere in between the remaining four categories have been bred and recognized, especially in Great Britain. Potential selection criteria:

- vigor, color, and health of leaves
- true-to-type root shape and size
- true-to-type color (white or cream)
- smooth root bulb
- unbranched root
- pleasant aroma of root
- hardiness (when overwintering in the field)

DISEASES AND PESTS In cool, damp areas, it is recommended parsnip be grown in raised beds, which helps prevent fungal disease by improving drainage. It is not uncommon for white mold to appear in storage during winter; it presents as a dense, cottony growth of mycelia with black spots (sclerotia) that eventually produce a fruiting body. The fungus *Phoma complanata* causes a canker; prevent by storing parsnip between 32°F (0°C) and 50°F (10°C) and removing affected roots. Aphids can be a problem in the first and second year by weakening plants and spreading viruses.

CULTIVATION HISTORY The wild form of parsnip is native to Europe and has tough, branched roots about 0.5 in. (1 cm) in diameter. It was presumably domesticated in Italy. From the time of the Romans up to the 17th century, the same word was often used in the literature for parsnip, carrot, and skirret, which undoubtedly led to confusion and mix-ups; because of this, the history of cultivated parsnip is difficult to reconstruct, but we know for a certainty that it was cultivated in France in the 14th century. The parsnip was the principal root vegetable and fodder crop there and in the Netherlands and England between the 17th and 19th centuries. It first came to North America with the Europeans but was later pushed aside in favor of carrots, celery, and potatoes, except in England, where its popularity never waned. Presently, this tasty, healthy storage crop is enjoying a resurgence of popularity in central Europe. It is hardly known in Asian cuisine.

FENNEL
Foeniculum vulgare

Florence fennel (var. *azoricum*) and sweet fennel (var. *dulce*) are two varieties of the same species and therefore will cross with one another. With Florence fennel, dense leaf sheaths develop, forming the bulb that is used as a vegetable. With sweet fennel, leaves and seeds are used to season dishes or as a tea to aid in digestion.

WHAT YOU'LL NEED
- 15 to 20 well-formed bulbs
- support poles and string
- overwintering strategy

POLLINATION NOTES Fennel is an outcrosser whose tender, yellow umbels are visited by countless insect pollinators, the most effective of these being the hoverfly. Self-pollination can also occur.

GROWING FOR SEED
Florence fennel is grown as an annual for food but is a biennial when growing for seed. It is hardy to zone 5. Fennel is a long-day plant that easily blossoms in the spring. Bolt-resistant varieties allow more time for the bulb to develop; these varieties can go to seed in the first year, if the growing season is long enough. In wine-growing climates, early sowings of fennel can also go to seed in the first year and can be selected for bolting vigor.

Fennel seeds

The thickened bulb elongates as Florence fennel bolts.

Seeds take a long time to ripen, and a cool, damp late summer/autumn can ruin them. To prevent this, cut stalks back to 8 in. (20 cm), pot the plants, and overwinter them in a frost-proof yet dry environment (root cellars are too damp; bulbs rot quickly). Second-year fennel plants bolt quickly, which allows plenty of time for seeds to completely ripen.

Italian heirloom varieties are different: if they are planted too early, they will bolt very quickly, so they should be sown only in mid to late summer, whether for vegetables or for seed. Keep these frost-free through the winter, in pots if necessary. Where winters are mild, overwintering outdoors is a possibility, as fennel can handle light frost. Harvest the bulb for eating in autumn. In the spring, small secondary bulbs develop, which will then bolt, blossom, and go to seed. Florence fennel can be continually harvested for three to four years in mild climates

Sweet fennel is a perennial, hardy to zone 4. It can be sown in the spring, produces no

Bulbs and bolting

Many bolt-resistant varieties have been bred over the last 40 years. The Swiss research institute Wädenswil made a breakthrough in fennel breeding with their 'Zefa Fino', introduced in 1979. This variety was bred from the only two (!) fennel plants not to bolt in a large fennel planting; it is still available from conventional and organic seed companies and traders. But note that bulb development is not just a matter of breeding: weather (drought or heat stress), age, and size of the seedling when planted are also factors.

bulb, flowers, and goes to seed the first year (although the seed harvest the following year will yield higher). Sweet fennel ranges in color from green to reddish bronze.

SELECTION CHARACTERISTICS The most important selection criterion for Florence fennel is bolt resistance: the later it bolts, the more time it has to develop its bulb. Other selection criteria:

- well-formed, round bulb
- consistent, uniform leaf formation
- light-colored bulb
- lack of stringiness of leaf sheaths and stems (easier to select for when growing as a biennial, as the bulb can be harvested in the first year; avoid cutting too deeply into bulb)

Selection criteria for sweet fennel:

- stability (especially for large-scale production)
- synchronous ripening of seed
- resistance to dropping seed
- seed size, yield, and aroma

DISEASES AND PESTS Fennel is loved by caterpillars of the Old World swallowtail butterfly (which, despite its name, is also found in North America). The minimal damage done to fennel crops is fortunately far outweighed by the joy of seeing these beautiful, rare insects.

CULTIVATION HISTORY The native lands of fennel are around the Mediterranean, Asia Minor, central Asia, and Nepal. Fennel was being used as early as 3000 BC in Mesopotamia, whereas the first sure evidence from Egypt is from the first century AD. The ancient Greeks and then Romans also grew it. Seeds and leaves were used culinarily as a seasoning and medicinally to treat cramps and as a relaxant. The Romans brought fennel north of the Alps, where it has only grown in popularity since the Middle Ages.

The only thing known about the development of Florence fennel is that it probably happened in Italy (hence its name). Presumably it was bred directly from wild fennel. Florence fennel has not been grown in central Europe long and has gained popularity with the spread of Italian cuisine.

SKIRRET
Sium sisarum

Though it remains a fairly obscure taste, for the many who seek to rediscover forgotten vegetables, skirret quickly becomes a delicacy. The flesh of the root contains 4–8% sugar (sucrose); it tastes pleasantly sweet and is very agreeable.

Skirret seeds

- plant with strong, well-formed roots
- support poles for seed-producing plants

POLLINATION NOTES Skirret is an outcrosser that is (like all umbellifers) pollinated by insects. Skirret plants of different origins (true varieties do not really exist) can therefore cross-pollinate.

PROPAGATION Most home gardeners find it easiest to propagate skirret vegetatively, with individual root scions. With a bit of deftness, one can "untangle" and separate individual roots; these roots will grow more vigorously. In the spring, small shoots with some roots attached can be cut away with a sharp knife and replanted; in drier areas, we recommend growing these cuttings in pots until the root system is more fully developed (from early spring onward).

Growing skirret from seed in pots and then planting out seedlings is also relatively easy. We at Arche Noah have had the best experience sowing in pots in late autumn in a frost-protected room and then planting out seedlings in the spring. Seeds have a relatively long germination time, needing up to 35 days. For an autumn harvest, sow seed in early to mid spring, though roots develop even more when seed is sown in late summer.

In the first year, skirret develops only a primary root, but from the second year on, it grows 10 to 15 roots that are irregularly formed, about as thick as a finger, and 8–12 in. (20–30 cm) long. Skirret does best in moist, fertile soils and can also be grown where the soil is otherwise too wet for root vegetables. It is hardy to zone 5, although it should in any case be dug up in autumn, and only the plants with the strongest root system should be used for propagating seed. Overwinter these in a frost-free environment.

HARVEST After plants have been selected once, you can harvest seed from these plants from the second year on for many years, although by proceeding in this way, it is not possible to select for root strength every year (which may be the better approach for this underappreciated root crop).

Remove flower stalks from the first year; collect seed only from at least two-year-old plants that have been selected for root quality. Seeds ripen in late summer and early autumn (for tips on harvesting the best seed, see carrots). Often, much of the harvested seed is sterile and germination rates are low.

COURTESY WIKIMEDIA COMMONS/MALTE

Skirret

SELECTION CHARACTERISTICS The most important selection criterion is a well-developed root system. Because cleaning and processing the many gnarled roots of skirret for cooking can be fairly laborious, it seems promising to select for plants that develop one or few relatively thick and straight root(s). Other possibilities: more tender fibers, smooth roots, less side-branching.

DISEASES AND PESTS Disease is a rare occurrence in skirret cultivation. Ascomycete fungi (*Septoria*, *Alternaria*) or various rust diseases can appear. Simply remove affected plants.

CULTIVATION HISTORY The exact origin of skirret is unknown, though it is presumed to have been brought from Russia to central and western Europe. Crop researcher Ursula Körber-Grone surmises that the 16th and 17th centuries were the years of skirret's most widespread cultivation. Before this time, skirret was virtually unknown, and after, cultivation and spread of skirret dropped dramatically, driven to obscurity by the appearance of the sugar beet.

TURNIP-ROOTED CHERVIL
Chaerophyllum bulbosum

Turnip-rooted chervil is challenging to cultivate and is therefore not often found in home gardens, but it is a prized delicacy among gourmets. Its taste does not reach its full potential until a few months after it has lost its leaves. Raw, it is juicy and crispy with a hint of spiciness. Cooked it becomes somewhat mealy, has a smooth consistency, and tastes a bit like roasted chestnuts.

WHAT YOU'LL NEED
- 15 to 20 well-formed plants
- support poles and string

POLLINATION NOTES Turnip-rooted chervil is an outcrosser that is pollinated by insects, especially hoverflies. Where it is naturalized, it is often found in wet habitats. Crossing with wild chervil is possible, though rare. Spatial isolation distance: 500 ft. (150 m).

GROWING FOR SEED Cool conditions (50–65°F [10–18°C]) are required for turnip-rooted chervil to germinate; it can be

Turnip-rooted chervil roots are like small gourmet turnips, albeit of a different botanical family.

sown in autumn in zone 6, in which case seeds will germinate earlier than when sown in the spring. Use the freshest seed you can, because even seed that is only a year old has sharply reduced germination rates. When sowing in the spring, do so six to eight weeks before the last expected spring frost and cover loosely with finely sieved soil and brushwood (turnip-rooted chervil loves partial shade and direct sun exposure should be avoided).

Important conditions for growing turnip-rooted chervil: uniform soil moisture until and throughout the summer and a good, light soil (not particularly clayey). Under these conditions, turnip-rooted chervil will reach a desirable size within about four months. It is not uncommon to come across forms that grow to only about an inch (2 cm) long, but after several years of selection, we at Arche Noah are growing turnip-rooted chervils 4–5 in. (10–12 cm) long. In areas with long winters, the use of row cover is recommended. The roots actually finish growing around midsummer, but they are not ready to eat until mid to late autumn and can be left in the ground or pulled and stored. Select the best (largest, least branched) and most uniform roots for seed, and plant them out 12 in. (30 cm) between rows, 10 in. (25 cm) within the row, right away in zone 6 or above, in the spring in zone 5 or lower. They bolt quickly in the spring and yield prolifically.

HARVEST As for carrots.

CULTIVATION HISTORY Wild turnip-rooted chervil is only rarely found in central and western Europe. In the 16th and 17th centuries, turnip-rooted chervil was described by botanists in Austria, Switzerland, and Germany as a crop plant, but even then it was considered a rare delicacy, reserved for nobility and the rich. The traditional size of turnip-rooted chervil was actually much larger than what is typical today, which points to the need for renewed selective breeding of this species. The closely related Siberian chervil (ssp. *prescottii*) produces a larger root (3–4 in. [8–10 cm]), but it is not as aromatic as the turnip-rooted chervil.

Chinese mallow and relatives

MALVACEAE

The mallow family is made up of more than 200 genera of trees, shrubs, and herbaceous plants with generally alternate leaves. Mallows are monoecious and have perfect flowers. Plants produce fruits in the form of schizocarps (a dry fruit that splits into sections) or bolls (seed capsules). Cotton (*Gossypium herbaceum*), the most widely grown fiber plant in the world, is a member of the family; cotton fibers are made up of monocellular hairs from the boll, which surrounds the seeds. Okra (*Abelmoschus esculentus*) also produces a boll as its fruit; it is an important vegetable in Mediterranean, Arabic, and African cuisines and in the cuisine of the American South. Okra fruits are harvested when still green, unripe, juicy, and soft. Typical mallows grown in Western gardens are marshmallow (*Althea officinalis*), hollyhock (*Alcea rosea*), and plants of the genus *Malva*. The musk or hollyhock mallow (*M. alcea*), tall or high mallow (*M. sylvestris*), or common mallow (*M. neglecta*) are grown in many gardens as medicinals with expectorant properties. The fruits of these plants are schizocarps, whose seeds are joined together in the form of a ring.

● ●

CHINESE MALLOW
Malva verticillata

Not especially well known in the West, Chinese mallow is an old crop plant in China, where several varieties and uses exist. In traditional Chinese medicine, seeds are used to treat swelling and to increase mother's milk production. Curled mallow (var. *crispa*) does have a horticultural tradition in Europe. Its leaves are used like spinach, in soups or salads; flower buds can also be used in salads.

WHAT YOU'LL NEED
• five large plants from a 16 ft.² (1.5 m²) patch

POLLINATION NOTES Chinese mallow is a selfer. Cross-pollination can also occur through insects, but since this plant is fairly rare in the West, it's unlikely that the purity of your variety would be threatened by crossing with plants from a neighbor's garden. If you would like to grow more than one variety for seed, use a mechanical isolation technique. Chinese

Chinese mallow seeds

mallow flowers are white and relatively inconspicuous.

GROWING FOR SEED Plants are easy to grow, and seed can be broadcast or planted in rows in early spring, as soon as the ground is clear. Leaves can be harvested as soon as the plants are 8–10 in. (20–25 cm) tall. When plants are regularly cut back, they can be harvested throughout the entire growing season. Allow at least five plants to go to seed. Flowering plants can grow to be over 6 ft. (2 m) tall. Chinese mallow will self-sow, producing dense, lawn-like growth on the ground below.

HARVEST The seeds are in hard rings that are covered by a husk. Plants produce seeds prolifically, and these ripen relatively uniformly and hold on to the plant well. Seed stalks can all be cut at the same time. Dry stalks, thresh and winnow seed.

The aibika (*Abelmoschus manihot*) is another edible mallow family plant. Here is one flowering in front of the pavilion at the Arche Noah display gardens.

Mallow flowers

Seeds tend to stick to one another; a seed-cleaning machine can be helpful to separate seeds from leaves and one another.

SELECTION CHARACTERISTICS There are many distinct varieties grown in China; not so in the West. Potential selection criteria:

- size and tenderness of leaves
- rapid growth of young plants
- vigorous leaf growth
- curliness of leaves

DISEASES AND PESTS We have yet to observe a disease problem; not even hollyhock rust (*Puccinia malvacearum*) affects Chinese mallow. What we have found is a beetle that we have yet to identify. It is about ⅛ in. (3 mm) long with an orange head, causes extensive leaf damage, and also infests hollyhocks. Treatment: neem oil pesticide.

CULTIVATION HISTORY The wild form of curled mallow is unknown, though the plant is presumed to have originated in central Asia and the southern Himalayas. Once a prized vegetable in China, mallow is now seldom grown; it was grown in the former USSR as a fodder and fiber plant and was once grown more frequently in European home gardens as a vegetable and medicinal plant. It came into Arche Noah's collection through Austrian member Bertram Sonderegger, who inherited the variety from his grandmother; he remembered her giving him mallow flower buds when he was young, so he would grow up to be big and strong.

The leaves of curled mallow at eating ripeness

Corn and relatives

POACEAE

Grass family plants are found all over the world, and they are the basis of agriculture in the Old and New Worlds. What all cultivated grasses have in common are starch-rich seeds that are highly suitable for storage. In agricultural communities, the decision to sow, harvest, and process grain has far-reaching consequences for the rhythm of life. The seeds of grasses, which have slowly been enlarged over thousands of years of selection, are the fruits of their labor. Intensive and extensive root penetration of the soil and rapid growth from seeds or runners are characteristic of grasses. Crops of the grass family include Old World cereal grains like wheat, rye, oats, and barley as well as New World plants like corn (maize) and certain millet species. Though all cultivated grasses can also be called cereal grains, "cereal grains" is generally used in this book to refer to the various wheats, rye, oats, and barley; these are combined in the first entry, with individual entries on millet, sorghum, and corn following.

● ●

GENERAL PROPAGATION CHARACTERISTICS
All grasses are monoecious; cereals and millet have perfect flowers clustered together to form an ear. Grasses have no colorful, conspicuous flowers because individual species are either selfers or wind-pollinated outcrossers. With few exceptions, cereals are annuals. Grow at least 300 plants to maintain genetic diversity. Corn (maize) is different from the cereals: it has separate male and female flowers and 100 to 150 plants should be grown to maintain genetic diversity. In general, though, for genetic diversity, the more plants grown, the better.

Khorasan wheat (*Triticum turanicum*) produces beautiful bearded ears; Kamut brand wheat belongs to this species.

The starch-rich seeds of the grass family

Overview of the grass family

COMMON NAME	GENUS	SPECIES	POLLINATION BEHAVIOR
wheat	*Triticum*	*aestivum*	selfer
durum wheat	*Triticum*	*durum*	selfer
spelt	*Triticum*	*spelta*	selfer
emmer	*Triticum*	*dicoccum*	selfer
einkorn	*Triticum*	*monococcum*	selfer
khorasan wheat	*Triticum*	*turanicum*	selfer
rye	*Secale*	*cereale*	outcrosser, wind
oats	*Avena*	*sativa*	selfer
barley	*Hordeum*	*vulgare*	selfer
corn (maize)	*Zea*	*mays*	outcrosser, wind
sorghum	*Sorghum*	spp.	outcrosser, wind
foxtail millet	*Setaria*	*italica*	selfer and outcrosser, wind
millet	*Panicum*	*miliaceum*	outcrosser, wind

CEREAL GRAINS

Triticum spp., *Secale cereale, Avena sativa, Hordeum vulgare*

When someone says "wheat," one usually thinks of common wheat used for bread. Common wheat has many cousins in the genus *Triticum*, however. Some, like spelt and durum wheat, are still grown more or less frequently, whereas others, such as einkorn (literally, "single grain"), are now hardly cultivated. Rye tolerates more extreme climatic conditions than wheat and is grown at elevations of up to 6200 ft. (1900 m), higher than any other grain in Europe. Nevertheless, many Alpine farms have switched from growing grains to grazing livestock, which has contributed to the recent disappearance of many Alpine heirloom grains. The Alps had been seen as a secondary center of diversity for cereals, making this loss of genetic diversity all the more keenly felt. Many varieties could be preserved in home gardens; they produce ears with stunning symmetry, bizarre contortions, or impressive coloration and, if nothing else, make for uniquely beautiful ornamentals.

WHAT YOU'LL NEED

- 10 ft.^{2} (1 m^2) of plants or a field planted to grain
- for rye: isolation

POLLINATION NOTES All cereal grains, with the exception of rye, self-pollinate. It is still necessary to grow different varieties of the same species far enough away from each other that the ears cannot touch, so that cross-pollination does not accidentally occur.

Rye is a strict outcrosser, and different varieties must be either spatially or mechanically isolated from one another by 1000 ft. (300 m) when growing garden-sized parcels, 1.5 miles (2.5 km) for field-scale parcels. Peer Schilperoord, grower of many heirloom grain varieties in Switzerland, recommends separating rye varieties with a 10 ft. (3 m) wall. It is likely easier

Black emmer

to isolate temporally by growing only one variety per year. At the former Institute of Plant Breeding and Seed Testing in Rinn, Austria, heavy plastic tarps (3 by 4 ft. [100 by 120 cm]) with a 1.5 by 1.5 ft. (50 by 50 cm) hole cut out of them, were stretched horizontally between poles at the four corners of beds of rye about 1.5 ft. (50 cm) above the ground. This technique by no means hermetically seals the bed, but rather causes a chimney effect, wherein the air in the bed tends to move upward, and the rye plants of each individual bed pollinate each other and not those of other beds.

GROWING FOR SEED All true grains have either spring varieties (planted in the spring for harvest in late summer/early autumn) or winter varieties (planted in autumn for harvest the following summer). Grains develop roots quickly and send them very deep in the ground so they do not freeze in the winter.

Support long-stalked varieties grown in small quantities with a trellis or by tying the ears together to prevent lodging (plants flattened to the ground because of bent stalks).

HARVEST Grains are harvested at the dead-ripe stage (when plants are completely dead, brown and dry) when harvested by machine, but when harvesting by hand, grains should be harvested just after the milk-ripe stage (when seeds are soft and "milky" when squeezed). At this yellow-ripe stage, the base of the plant will have already turned brown and dry, but the rest of the plant is still somewhat green and

seeds are relatively hard. For larger quantities, use an Austrian-style scythe with a small bow-style attachment on the snath to make a grain cradle; avoid American-style scythes, which were designed for sugar cane harvesting and are relatively ineffective when harvesting cereal grains. For small quantities, use a hand scythe, sickle, or even a very sharp scissors; cut stalks at the base, tie into sheaves (bundles of stalks with ears all facing the same direction), and stand several sheaves up by leaning the ears together, forming what are called shocks in the USA, stooks in the UK. Leave the cut grain in shocks for another two weeks to finish ripening and drying. Cover shocks with cloth or bird netting, especially for smaller quantities, to protect grains from hungry birds. Thresh when ears have fully dried. Emmer, einkorn, spelt, and most oat and barley varieties are hulled grains, meaning

The delicate ear of einkorn wheat

that they have inedible hulls that must be removed before eating (see ltras.ucdavis.edu/files/Grain%20huller.pdf for instructions on how to build a hand-cranked spelt huller). Hulls should, however, remain attached for grain being used as seed. The hulls of emmer and spelt contain multiple seeds.

SELECTION CHARACTERISTICS Many heirloom varieties are conglomerates or mixtures of multiple ecotypes (strains within the variety adapted to specific environmental conditions). They visibly vary from each other, in the presence and absence of beards, the color of the hulls, and so forth. Be sure that seeds are collected from all forms to maintain genetic diversity. Selection criteria that apply to all varieties:

• true-to-type appearance
• stability (resistance to lodging)
• yield
• good tillering (production of side shoots or multiple stems)
• resistance to various fungal diseases (rust, mildew, bunt, etc.)
• adaptation to local conditions (moisture, temperature, etc.)

DISEASES AND PESTS A long list of diseases affects the cereal grains but, fortunately, they rarely pose a problem when the grains are being grown on a small scale. Several are seed-borne: loose smut of barley (*Ustilago nuda*) and wheat (*U. tritici*) (symptoms: the ear transforming into a black/brown spore deposit), bunt (*Tilletia caries*, symptoms: stunted growth, grain

replaced with spore-containing balls, "dust" of spores when threshing), various fusarium blights (symptoms: spiral distortions of seedling growth, reddish web of mycelia under snow cover), diseases of the ear (ears containing nonviable seed), barley stripe disease (*Pyrenophora graminea*, symptoms: stunted growth, shrunken grains, nonviable seed), and barley net blotch (*P. teres*, symptom: yellowing of tissue).

Treatment: Tillecur (85% yellow mustard powder), warm or hot water treatment of seeds. The hot water treatment can be tricky, as it is crucial to maintain exact temperatures for an exact amount of time to avoid damaging seeds. Warm water treatment: leave seeds in 113°F (45°C) water for two hours. Hot water treatment: leave seeds in exactly 125.6°F (52°C) water for exactly 10 minutes. These water treatment methods are being intensively studied, as they are extremely useful in organic agriculture. Synthetic chemicals are used in conventional agriculture, often in the form of a coating on the seed.

CULTIVATION HISTORY Many of the various grains have been cared for by people for thousands of years. The oldest finds of cultivated wheat are 9,500 years old. Wheat domestication began in the Middle East, where wild wheat species are native. Wheat and barley were the most important crop plants of early Old World agriculture. Rye and oats were domesticated in a roundabout way: originally weeds in grain fields, they were slowly transported by people to other climates, where they sometimes thrived better than the crop they were intending to grow. Almost all the world's rye is now grown in Russia, Germany, and eastern Europe.

MILLET, SORGHUM
Panicum miliaceum, Setaria italica, Sorghum spp.

Millet is an umbrella term for various grass species that produce similar edible seeds. It is the most important grain crop in Africa but is hardly grown in the USA and Europe. Proso or common millet (*Panicum miliaceum*), depending on the variety, can be 1 ft. (30 cm) to up to 6 ft. (180 cm) tall. It does not contain gluten and thus cannot be made into traditional breads; it is usually consumed as a porridge or flatbread and is also used as a fodder crop. A panicle (a kind of flower head) up to 8 in. (20 cm) long produces legions of small round seeds. The Latin name is a variation on the word *mille*, suggesting that each plant produces a thousand seeds. In German agriculture, millet was once grown as a row crop and was considered a "poor man's food" until the 19th century.

Foxtail millet (*Setaria italica*) is the most widely grown millet of the genus *Setaria*. The plant itself is strong and sturdy, its stalks standing up straight. Ears of the plant can be so heavy that they hang down, giving the appearance of the tail of a fox. Ears can be fed whole to caged birds. Foxtail millet is grown on a large scale in Africa, India, northern China, and Russia. It is relatively easy to cultivate and is often grown as livestock feed where corn does not do well. The seeds of

Proso millet (*Panicum miliaceum*)

Foxtail millet (*Setaria italica*)

Sorghum (*Sorghum bicolor*)

Ripe proso millet

the various foxtail millet varieties come in many different colors but are otherwise very similar to proso millet seeds.

Another genus of plants with millet-like seeds is *Sorghum*. The cultivated species, *S. bicolor*, produces edible grains that are simply called sorghum. Sorghum's growth habit is very similar to that of corn (maize); plants grow to be very tall, sometimes over 13 ft. (4 m), and the panicle, which sits atop the plant like the tassel on corn, can be used as a broom. Some varieties are specifically for popping like popcorn. Sorghum needs lots of heat, which is why it is so often grown in tropical climates.

WHAT YOU'LL NEED

- 20–30 ft.^{2} (2–3 m^2) patch or a field planted to grain

POLLINATION NOTES Millet and sorghum are generally wind-pollinated outcrossers, though foxtail millet primarily self-pollinates, depending on the weather. Separate multiple varieties of the same species by 1000 ft. (300 m) or more. Millet can be mechanically isolated with row cover, as with amaranth.

GROWING FOR SEED Sow millet in spring, after all danger of frost is past (it is very sensitive to frost); plant in 10 in. (25 cm) rows, 10 in. (25 cm) apart within the row. Sowing time and planting distances for sorghum are the same as for corn (maize).

HARVEST Sorghum requires a long season to ripen seed. Millet seeds are ripe 60 to 90 days after sowing, so seed sown in late spring means harvesting in mid to late summer. Seeds of proso millet generally do not fall from the plant, so they can be allowed to fully ripen on the plant before harvesting, and there is no need to further dry stalks after harvesting; for proso and foxtail millet, it is likely that birds will come to snack on seeds before the harvest. Cover well with bird netting. There is no such danger with sorghum, as seeds are attached firmly to the plant.

SELECTION CHARACTERISTICS Compared to the cereal grains, millet is practically an afterthought in Europe, and this has been the case for many centuries. There is not a lot of knowledge, therefore, about growing and selecting seed in temperate climates. Potential selection criteria:

- earliness and tendency to produce ripe seed (tropical selections do not tend to ripen well in temperate climates)
- stability
- proso millet: tillering, synchronous ripening of seed, size and flavor of seed, many highly productive panicles
- sorghum: ideal traits for intended use (popcorn, porridge, broom-making, etc.), seed size
- foxtail millet: compact ears

DISEASES AND PESTS The only problem we at Arche Noah have had in growing garden-sized patches of millet and sorghum are the aforementioned birds, which can be thwarted with the help of bird netting.

CULTIVATION HISTORY Eastern Asia is the center of genetic diversity for proso millet, but the area of origin is unknown. It is speculated that it was domesticated in northern China, where the oldest finds in the world reside (4th millennium BC). Seeds have been found in Switzerland dating back to the Stone Age, and millet was an important grain crop of the Neolithic period in eastern and central Europe. Since millet is highly drought tolerant, it was an important crop in poor, dry soils in the Middle Ages. Millet cultivation in Europe all but ended with the introduction of the potato, and it is now little more than a relict crop. Foxtail millet is also not among the early grain crops of the Middle East, instead being domesticated (probably) in China (5500–5000 BC) and later in Europe (2nd millennium BC, finds in central Europe and France). Durra-type sorghum is widely grown from Nigeria to Ethiopia, where it is eaten cooked like rice. Broomcorn varieties of sorghum were once frequently grown in far southern German-speaking areas like southern

Ripe foxtail millet

Styria, Austria, and South Tyrol, Italy. *Sorghum bicolor* is mostly grown as livestock feed; it was gathered as early as 6000 BC in southern Egypt and was domesticated in the Sudan and Chad.

CORN, MAIZE

Zea mays

Corn (UK: maize) is far and away the most important crop plant to come from the New World. After wheat and rice, it is the third-most-cultivated grain worldwide, the largest producers being the USA, China, Brazil, and Mexico. Corn is also one of the most important crops in the world of plant breeding, and many genetically modified varieties are now grown in several different countries; all corn varieties grown industrially, mostly to feed livestock, are hybrids. Worldwide there are at least 3,000 different varieties of this highly adaptable plant, and innumerable open-pollinated varieties are still being bred locally to this day.

WHAT YOU'LL NEED
• 100 to 150 plants or a field of corn
• paper bags for isolating flowers
• time for hand pollination
• sufficient space

POLLINATION NOTES Corn is a wind-pollinated outcrosser. All varieties can cross-pollinate one another. Growing a flint corn and a sweet corn for seed in the same year means pollinating by hand or growing the varieties far enough apart that they cannot cross. Isolate by ¼–⅓ mile

Categories of corn varieties

TYPE	DESCRIPTION OF KERNELS	USE
flint corn (convar. *indurata*)	hard, glassy, non-mealy	eating, livestock feed, silage; robust, can be grown in northerly regions
dent corn (convar. *indentata*)	resemble molars, indentation at the tip, tissue otherwise keratinous	eating, livestock feed; cornmeal
popcorn (convar. *microsperma*)	small, glassy, yellow, soft inside, pops when heated	eating, ornamental
sweet corn (convar. *saccharata*)	shrink when ripe because sugar is not transformed into starch	vegetable corn, rich in fat and protein; canned corn; ideal for cooler regions due to harvest at milk-ripe stage; stalks have a high sugar content (similar to sugar cane)
wax corn (convar. *ceratina*)	hard and smooth outside (waxy coating of amylopectin), waxy inside	eating; for making pudding, powder, and glue
flour corn (convar. *amylacea*)	rich in starch	eating; cornmeal, beer (*chicha*) production; grown in Peru, Bolivia, Colombia, seldom in Europe

(400–500 m) when growing relatively small quantities in a diverse garden landscape. Isolation distances of several miles are used in professional breeding. Do not forget to consider commercial cornfields, pollen from which can travel for several miles, when calculating isolation distances in

Flint corn

Popcorn

Dent corn

Flour corn

Sweet corn

your area. The simplest method would be to grow only one variety per year of corn for seed in an area at least several miles away from large cornfields. Harvest ears from the middle of the patch for seed.

Cross-pollination between varieties is often visible in first-generation seed (it

This dynamic heirloom corn from Oaxaca, Mexico, brings a reliable yield and can be used for many dishes. It is far from uniform yet has many uses.

can be tasted in sweet corn). This is normally not the case for crop plants, where crossing is evident only by growing outcrossed seed.

HAND POLLINATION Hand pollinating corn is time-consuming but not difficult. You will need a sharp pocketknife, tape (e.g., masking tape), a stapler, and rip-resistant paper bags. Bags made of opaque parchment paper work very well. They shed water, and you can see inside without removing the bag. Use 8 by 16 in. (20 by 40 cm) bags for the tassel, 6 by 12 in. (15 by 30 cm) bags for the ear. Timing is crucial in hand pollination. Tassels (male flowers) must be bagged before they release pollen, ears (female flowers) must be bagged before the silks (which receive the pollen) become receptive. Normally hand pollination of a variety takes place over the course of two to three days, unless the variety ripens non-synchronously.

Divide the patch of corn in half. One half will be used as father plants, the other as mother plants (ideally at least 50 of each). Remove tassels from mother plants with a sharp knife. Implementation is as follows:

Day 1. Bag and cut ears from mother plants (B–E). Correct timing: as many ears from mother plants as possible should be just about to send out their silks. These should, however, not yet be visible as these have likely already been pollinated by natural processes. Carefully remove the leaf that contains the ear so a bag can fit around the ear. Then cut off the tip of the husk leaves with a sharp knife. When the cut is too far down the ear, not all silks will be cut. Practice on a few ears, if you have enough plants, to get a feel for where the cut should be. Immediately after cutting, place a bag over the ear and close with binder clips between ear and stalk. Make sure there is space between the bag and the tip of the ear to avoid the ear splitting the bag.

Day 2. Bag the tassels of father plants (A). Wait until they just start to shed pollen (they start to look kind of dusty and scraggly). When tassels are bagged too early, they often cease development and produce no pollen. Shake tassels just before bagging to remove pollen from other plants that may have landed on the tassel. Put the bag over the tassel with the tassel in the side folds of the bag. Fold the opening of the bag over twice to ensure that pollen cannot fall out and staple shut.

Day 3. This is when actual pollination takes place (F–H). The ideal time for pollination is late morning, when much pollen has collected in the bags. There should be no strong winds. Shake the tassel well while it is still in the bag to maximize pollen collection and minimize pollen that blows away from the tassel once the bag is off. Then remove the bag very carefully, pulling toward the side and down. Pollen is bright yellow and fine as flour. Filter all the pollen of a variety through a metal or porcelain colander and into a bowl. Remove the bag around the ear of each mother plant individually as you get to each plant. Silks should have grown to be about 1–1.5 in. (3–4 cm) long by now.

Hand pollination of corn. Preparation:

A. bagging tassels

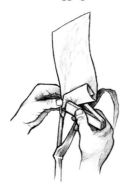

B. removing leaf covering the ear (which is not yet showing silks)

C. cutting off husk leaves at the tip of the ear

D. cutting tip of ear to expose silks

E. bagging ear following cut

Hand pollination of corn. Pollination:

F. corn pollen (emptied from tassel bags into a bowl)

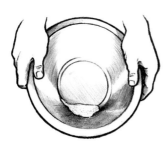

G. exposing silks (now grown out) and brushing pollen onto them with your finger

H. rebagging ears and taping shut

Brush pollen onto the silks with your finger (pollen is accepted by the silks along their entire length, not just at the tip). You will need about a teaspoon of pollen per ear. Replace the bag over the ear immediately after pollinating and close well with tape (not so tight that growth is restricted, not so loose that wind can blow in pollen or blow the bag away). Leave the bags on the ears until they are ripe. This not only serves as a label for which ears were hand pollinated, it also protects the ear from herbivory by birds.

Note: Pollen that has been rained upon and sticks together is no longer useful. Re-bag tassels (tassels produce pollen for 10 to 14 days, the same length as the female flowering period) and try again.

GROWING FOR SEED Corn is grown for seed more or less like it is grown for eating. Sow seed when it is typically sown in gardens in your area (local farmers may use early-planting varieties that can be planted earlier than most open-pollinated varieties). Even if the growing season is long enough in your area to produce ripe seed from seeds sown outdoors after the last frost, it may still be worth it to start seed indoors to prevent planted seeds from being picked from the soil by birds. Seeds can usually be started in mid to late spring and planted out after the danger of frost has passed. Plant at wider planting distances than is seen in field corn. Plant at even wider distances if hand pollination is planned so you will have enough space to move between plants in the patch. Most old varieties tiller (produce

side shoots); remove these. Plant in 2 ft. (60 cm) rows, 12–14 in. (30–35 cm) spacing within the row. Hill up soil around base of plants once or twice in early summer. When hand pollination is not being used, plants should be in a block (not in one long row); orient the patch parallel to the main direction of the wind to help maximize pollination.

HARVEST Corn is ready to harvest when the husk leaves are completely dry and seeds are hard. Harvest ears with their husks and stems. Then remove husk, cut back stem, and hang upside down indoors, somewhere with good air circulation and below 86°F (30°C), to dry. They can also be dried outdoors, under an eave, for example, but be sure that birds cannot access the seeds. Harvest all hand-pollinated ears, even if you do not need that much seed, to maximize the passing on of genetic diversity. In general one can say that fewer kernels from many ears is better than many kernels from fewer ears. Inbreeding depression shows up quickly in corn, which is avoided by having a diverse seed stock. Harvest ears from the middle of the patch if you have used the wind to pollinate your corn. Seed from the middle of the ears is normally better developed than seed from either end. If you do not have access to a traditional corn sheller, rub two ears together to separate kernels from cobs.

SELECTION CHARACTERISTICS It is not absolutely necessary to be strict about varietal purity. If it interests you, you can experiment with crossing varieties intentionally or just let yourself be surprised by each year's new crossings by foregoing the techniques just described, which are mainly important for maintaining varieties of open-pollinated corn. Without hand pollination (and, to a small degree, even with hand pollination), there is always the danger that genetics from hybrid or genetically modified varieties from nearby fields could make their way into open-pollinated varieties.

Exact selection criteria are highly dependent on the variety. Adaptation to local conditions (drought tolerance, production of ripe seeds in your climate) is important to all varieties. Additional general selection criteria:

- handsome, well-developed ears (well covered by husks)

- true-to-type kernels organized in a true-to-type way (e.g., double rows, single rows, offset)
- good-looking plant (many older varieties, from which seed was saved from too few plants, show inbreeding depression in the form of stunted growth or poor tassel and/or ear development; remove these plants before they flower)

Potential selection criteria for sweet corn:

- many (two or three) sweet, soft ears per plant
- good, sweet, typical corn flavor (taste one or two ears per plant, leave one ear to ripen, note which plants were tastiest)

DISEASES AND PESTS The most common fungal disease of corn is corn smut (*Ustilago maydis*), affecting sweet corn in

Bagged corn after hand pollination

particular. It causes drastic deformations of the ears (fist- to softball-sized galls) but can also afflict stalks and leaves. Blue-black spores develop inside the gall, which then spread and can survive for several years. Remove infected plants, rotate crops, and grow future crops with wider spacing in an area with better air circulation. Modern varieties from central Europe and the USA are mostly resistant to corn smut, whereas in Central and South America, galls are considered a delicacy and eaten. Ripe spores are also used medicinally like ergot. Smutted corn is also used by some farmers as silage. Aphids like to attack smaller stands of corn; use standard organic aphid treatments. Finally, European corn borer caterpillars (*Ostrinia nubilalis*) can damage corn crops. Symptoms: caterpillars eat superficially of the leaves and male flower parts; later they dig into ears and stalks and overwinter in the lower parts of the stalk. Early varieties are especially vulnerable, as is sweet corn. Treatment: remove tassels after flowering, apply *Bacillus thuringiensis* (Bt) insecticides. Prevention: remove entire plants from the garden and compost well. Harvested ears may be infested with Mediterranean flour moth (*Ephestia kuehniella*). Treatment: place fully dried ears in the freezer, store seed in sealed containers.

CULTIVATION HISTORY We are still in the dark about exactly how and where corn came to be domesticated and developed into the plant we know. Many authors name Central America's teosinte (*Zea mexicana*) as corn's wild ancestor; their growth habits differ significantly, but a loose flower head turning into corn's compact ear could be a spontaneous mutation. In Central America, corn has been the most important grain crop for several millennia. The oldest finds are from southern Mexico circa 5000 BC, and it seems to have reached South America at around the same time, with a second center of corn diversity establishing itself in Peru. Corn was a holy plant to the ancient tribes of Central America, a gift of the gods and source of life (the indigenous name for the plant, *mays*, means "that which sustains our lives"). Scouts from Columbus's expedition brought corn to Spain in 1493 and within 30 years it was being grown on a field scale in Andalusia. Documentation of corn cultivation dates back to 1542 in the southern Alps (Carinthia, Austria). It spread throughout central Europe via the Middle East, however. In some areas of Austria corn is still known as *Türkisch Korn* (Turkish grain), as corn's origins were otherwise unknown when it was introduced there. Corn appeared as *Türkisch Korn* in Hieronymus Bock's and Leonhard Fuchs's botanical works of the early 16th century. Corn was not widely grown on a field scale in Europe until the 18th century.

Corn salad and relatives
VALERIANACEAE

The valerian family is composed of eight genera and about 400 species, most of which are found in the temperate climes of the northern hemisphere. Plants have mostly opposite (pinnate) leaves and tapering stamens. Seeds develop a characteristic aroma as they dry. The best-known genera for gardeners are *Valeriana*, of which garden valerian is a member, and *Valerianella*, which includes corn salad. The roots of garden valerian are dried for their essential oils and administered in the form of valerian drops as a calmative. *Valerianella* literally means "small valerian," and many plants of this genus are known by the common name corn salad, though most often corn salad is associated specifically with *V. locusta*.

● ●

CORN SALAD
Valerianella locusta

Corn salad (also known as lamb's lettuce or mâche) got its name from its appearance as a weed in grain fields. Rosettes can be harvested in winter and early spring down to zone 5. The plant contains vitamins A and C, and folklore holds that it can hold spring fever at bay.

WHAT YOU'LL NEED
• 50 plants (approx. 10–12 ft.^{2} [1 m^2])

POLLINATION NOTES Corn salad is self-fertile but cross-pollinates readily through insects. Its flowers are perfect.

Spatial isolation: distances of 100–175 ft. (30–50 m) are typically sufficient between two varieties in a diversely planted garden plot, especially if there are taller plants

Corn salad seeds

in between. Temporal isolation: in zones 5 and above, one variety can be planted in the autumn and one in spring, which results in the two varieties flowering at different times, thus eliminating the possibility of cross-pollination.

GROWING FOR SEED Sow in early autumn or as early as possible in spring. Do not harvest leaves of autumn-planted corn salad for the table in the winter if you intend them for seed production.

HARVEST Corn salad seeds are ripe between late spring and early summer, depending on planting date. The seeds do not ripen all at the same time but rather over a long period, so pay attention to when the majority of seeds become ripe (when the bolls burst open), at which point harvesting should commence. Because ripe seeds will fall out by merely brushing

the plant, lay the entire plant directly on a sheet or tarp, or in a pillowcase, and hang it all up to dry. Dried plants aren't so much threshed as they are simply patted and rubbed with the hands. Seeds that are harvested by hand are best. Those that are harvested mechanically are smaller, less ripe, and germinate poorly. Winnow with a sieve. Freshly harvested seeds are often pale in color but become darker in storage. Corn salad seed does not begin to germinate well until a month or two after harvesting; a year later the germination rate is even better. Because of this, always use the previous year's seed.

SELECTION CHARACTERISTICS
- resistance to fungal diseases
- size, shape, and color of leaves
- stalk sturdiness
- hardiness
- strong and large rosettes

DISEASES AND PESTS There are two important seed-borne diseases of corn salad: a foliar disease caused by *Phoma valerianellae* and downy mildew caused by *Peronospora valerianellae*. *Phoma*-infected seed can sometimes, but not always, be identified by a dark discoloration. Symptoms: some seedlings will die shortly after germination; red stripes develop on roots, shoots, and leaves, followed by the appearance of brown or black spots on the leaves. The lower leaves on older plants shrivel and die. Prevention: hot water treatment. Downy mildew appears most frequently during damp weather in autumn. Symptoms: yellowish discoloration; plants that stay small and attain only a pale green

Corn salad

Corn salad in full bloom

color; pale green mycelia visible on the undersides of leaves. Prevention: water in the morning. Seek out varieties that are resistant to downy mildew.

CULTIVATION HISTORY Native to Eurasia, corn salad can be found in vineyards and similar habitats and was originally foraged. It is one of the few crop plants that was domesticated in Europe: it presumably arrived in central Europe in the late Neolithic period via grain seed, was sown with the grain, then thrived after the grain harvest, like an intentionally undersown crop. All through the Greek and Roman empires and Middle Ages, there is no evidence of its intentional cultivation. It was not until around 1700 that selective breeding of cultivated varieties began in gardens. Around the turn of the 20th century, corn salad began to be grown as a cash crop. Today, it can still be harvested "wild" from fields, though only from those where no mineral fertilizer is found: fallow grounds, vineyards, and organic gardens and farms.

Flax and relatives

LINACEAE

The flax family is made up of several genera and a total of about 90 species; these are found around the world, with the greatest species diversity in the southwest of North America and in the Mediterranean region. Everything from herbs to trees can be found in this family. Plants are generally easy to grow, thriving even on nutrient-poor soils; leaves are simple and alternate, and flowers are radial with a double whorl (perianth). Some family members are wild plants native to Europe: fairy flax (*Linum catharticum*) is found in calcareous grasslands and low-moor bogs. The endangered yellow flax (*L. flavum*) is found in dry grasslands and forest edges. One of the most important oil and fiber crops in human history, flax itself, is of course also a member. Several species are grown as ornamentals, such as the annual red, scarlet, or crimson flax (*L. grandifolium*) or the perennial blue flax (*L. perenne*), with its large, pure blue, funnel-shaped flowers. It is worth noting that toadflax (*Linaria* spp.), an ornamental, belongs not to this but to the plantain family (Plantaginaceae).

● ●

FLAX, LINSEED
Linum usitatissimum

Flax seeds, linseed oil, linen: all come from the same plant. Fiber flax (convar. *elongatum*) produces little-branched stalks up to 3 ft. (1 m) long, from which fibers are obtained and spun to make the prized textile linen. Oilseed flax (convar. *mediterraneum*), a low-growing, bushy plant with many seed capsules, is grown for its large, oil-rich seeds. Flax or linseed oil is a nutritional edible, high in linoleic and linolenic acids; it can also be used for technical purposes, as it dries quickly (boiled linseed oil). Seeds of both forms can be used, but fiber flax seeds are smaller.

WHAT YOU'LL NEED

• 50 to 100 plants

POLLINATION NOTES Flax self-pollinates, though insects can (rarely) cause cross-pollination. There are both spring and winter flax varieties (these last are favored in the Alps), and multiple varieties can be grown a few yards (a few meters) apart and still be kept pure. The tender plants produce white, pink, or blue flowers and add an ornamental note to the vegetable garden.

GROWING FOR SEED Fiber flax thrives best in a temperate, moist climate, oilseed flax in a hot, dry climate. Spring flax should be sown as early as possible (early to mid spring), as it is a long-day plant that may not flower if sown too late. Flax seeds germinate at temperatures as low as 36–37°F (2–3°C) and tolerate late frosts as low as 23°F (−5°C). When flax is sown in 8 in. (20 cm) rows, it is easier to weed. Weeding is especially important early, until plants are 4–5 in. (10–12 cm), at which point they begin to be able to suppress weeds on their own.

HARVEST Seeds ripen in mid to late summer. Capsules of convar. *usitatissimum* remain closed; those of convar. *crepitans* open upon ripening and therefore must be harvested before fully ripe (crepitans flax is rarely grown today). Cut entire plants when they turn brown and seeds rattle inside the capsules. Plants must then completely dry, indoors if necessary. For

Flax seeds

Green-ripe and dead-ripe flax seed capsules

The blue flowers of flax are nearly as heavenly as the sky.

larger quantities, draw plants across a bed of nails to remove capsules from stalks. Thresh in a cloth bag, winnow with the wind and sieves.

SELECTION CHARACTERISTICS In general, the faster the development of young plants, the more likely the plant will produce seeds.

- oilseed flax: high number of seeds (plants richly branched, many capsules)
- fiber flax: height, length, and lack of branchiness of primary stalk

DISEASES AND PESTS Wait five to seven years to grow flax at the same location again. Several fungi (*Sclerotinia, Fusarium, Pythium, Rhizoctonia*) can attack roots and shoots and cause stunted growth. Many fungal diseases can also be seed-borne. Prevention: do not harvest seed from sick plants, long crop rotation, not following legumes or sunflowers in crop rotation.

CULTIVATION HISTORY Flax was the first crop plant used for weaving clothing. The oldest archaeological finds of gathered wild flax (9200–8500 BC) and domesticated flax (6250–5950 BC) are from Syria. Ancient Egyptians wore clothing made of flax fibers. In Neolithic settlements around Lake Constance and lakes in Switzerland, charred linens and knotted fishing nets have been found; there are finds from the later Neolithic in present-day Poland and southern England. Flax cultivation began in Ireland and Scotland after the Bronze Age (1800 BC). Flax is found in many paintings and descriptions of crop plants from the Middle Ages. By the 19th century, flax was the most important fiber plant in Germany and Austria, but since the turn of the 20th century, it has taken a back seat to cotton.

Legumes

FABACEAE

Legumes are the third-largest plant family in the world, after the composites (Asteraceae) and the orchids (Orchidaceae). The family is found the world over and consists of over 17,000 species. There are three subfamilies: the Mimosoideae and Caesalpinioideae contain many perennial and woody species; most vegetable legumes are found in the Faboideae. In practically all agricultural societies, legumes are an important plant source for protein. Legumes have a symbiotic relationship to certain bacteria (*Rhizobium* spp.) in which nitrogen gas from the air is "fixed" in root nodules, thus making nitrogen available to the plant in a usable form (ammonium or nitrate); and the plant, in turn, leaves nitrogen behind in the soil when it dies.

● ●

BOTANICAL CHARACTERISTICS The pods that develop on legumes are fruits. Legume flowers attract many insects and are mostly outcrossers. For certain species, like common beans and soybeans, self-pollination is the rule. Many species are climbing vines. People have also selected for non-climbing varieties, e.g., bush beans (*Phaseolus vulgaris* var. *nanus*).

Not all legume pods are "green beans."

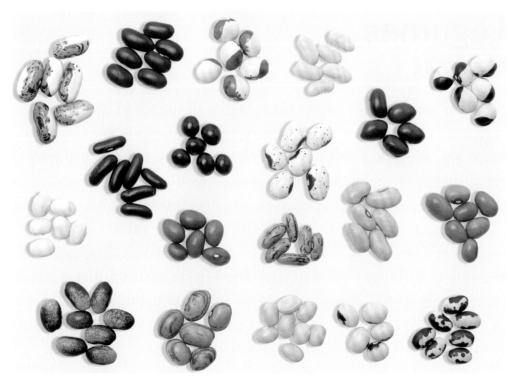

Beans (*Phaseolus vulgaris*)

Overview of the legume family

COMMON NAME	GENUS	SPECIES
bean	*Phaseolus*	*vulgaris*
runner bean	*Phaseolus*	*coccineus*
hyacinth bean	*Lablab*	*purpureus*
lima bean, butter bean	*Phaseolus*	*lunatus*
fava bean	*Vicia*	*faba*
pea	*Pisum*	*sativum*
cowpea, black-eyed pea	*Vigna*	*unguiculata*
mung bean	*Vigna*	*radiata*
soybean (soya bean)	*Glycine*	*max*
chickpea, garbanzo	*Cicer*	*arietinum*
asparagus pea, winged bean	*Tetragonolobus*	*purpureus*
lentil	*Lens*	*culinaris*
peanut	*Arachis*	*hypogaea*

BEAN
Phaseolus vulgaris

Both pole beans (var. *vulgaris*) and bush beans (var. *nanus*) belong to the species *Phaseolus vulgaris*, and both can simply be called beans or common beans. Although pole beans are climbing vines, botanically speaking they do not develop tendrils to climb; rather, the plant itself winds around whatever it encounters. Bush beans have limited growth and as such are relatively undemanding in their cultivation. In-between forms develop short, weak tendrils and grow 3–4 ft. (1–1.2 m) high, making them ideal for a companion planting with corn (maize): corn acts as a trellis for the bean, and the bean fixes nitrogen from the air for the corn, a harmonious symbiosis between plants not unlike the *milpa* growing techniques of Mesoamerica. The practice of growing corn and beans together is also found in southern Austria, Croatia, and many other countries of southeastern Europe. Two varieties of this in-between growth habit hail from Switzerland: 'Schwefleren' (a yellow shell bean) and 'Schnutzla'.

WHAT YOU'LL NEED
- at least 10 healthy, high-yielding plants
- a climate allowing for full ripening of beans
- for pole beans: poles or trellises

POLLINATION NOTES The common bean almost exclusively self-pollinates, with pollination usually taking place before flowers even open (cleistogamy). Specialist literature indicates cross-pollination rates of no more than 1%. In areas where flowers are few and far between (and especially when bees are active), cross-pollination is much more likely (up to 20%!). Bumblebees in particular can bite flower buds open and cause cross-pollination. Carpenter bees (*Xylocopa* spp.) and other large insects are able to force their way so far into the flower bud that they reach the style and pollinate it. Isolation distances of 15–30 ft. (5–10 m) between varieties are in any case recommended. Cross-pollination is evident on pods and beans the first year; remove those that are not true-to-type.

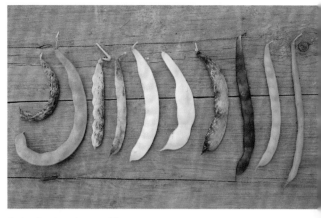

Pods of various bean cultivars

Bean flowers can be white, cream, violet, or pink, depending on the variety. Plants bloom for 20 to 26 days. Flowers open from about 6 to 10 o'clock in the morning, and once they are open, they stay open.

GROWING FOR SEED Because common beans originated in subtropical and tropical regions, they are highly frost sensitive, so do not sow seed until after the last spring frost. Beans require temperatures of at least 46°F (8°C) to germinate. Presoaking beans before sowing is usually not recommended, as seed may rot in cool, wet weather or seedlings may desiccate in dry weather. When tall enough, soil can be hilled up around the base, especially around bush beans, to improve stability.

Beans germinate faster with higher temperatures. The faster they germinate, the less likely they are to be affected by damping off or other fungal diseases. Quick-germinating seeds are also less likely to be nibbled on by the larvae of bean seed flies (*Delia florilega* and *D. platura*). They are

Pods in various stages of ripeness (the pod on the left is completely ripe)

should sow seeds farther apart than when growing for food so the plants do not grow together. For pole beans, it's one plant per pole or grow along a trellis, so you can tell the plants apart; site them 16 in. (40 cm) apart within the row, 3 ft. (1 m) between rows. Bush beans: 6 in. (15 cm) within the row, 16 in. (40 cm) between. Increasing the number of pole beans around a pole typically has no effect on yield, as sunlight and nutrient availability are both factors affecting yield. Ideally, pole beans should be pruned at 6 ft. (2 m) to encourage more beans at a harvestable height.

HARVEST Mark plants selected for seed harvesting conspicuously, as it is nearly impossible to tell them apart at harvest time. Beans are ripe when the pods have significantly changed color and are brittle and dry. In areas with a shorter growing season, some later-ripening varieties may not ripen at all as the pods turn glassy with the first frost. The following trick often helps: before the first autumn frost, pull entire plants—roots and all—and hang them upside down indoors. This accelerates ripening and may save your crop.

Harvest dried pods in dry weather and allow them to dry for another two to three weeks in a warm, breezy spot (though not in the sun or in extreme heat). This is not only a drying process but an extension of the ripening process, which will help ensure a high germination rate for the seed. When pods are completely dry, they break open and beans are easily freed. Beans are dry enough for storage when it is no longer possible to make a mark on

typically the cause of missing cotyledons and eaten-away-at stems. Algal limestone can be lightly applied or algal extract can be used in watering as a preventative measure. Beans should be planted flat and shallow, so that the plant rises quickly from the ground. It is generally a good idea to maintain long crop rotations and to plant beans in an open and windy location.

Bush beans are ripe before pole beans planted at the same time, but pole beans ripen over a longer period of time. Harvest the first robust pods for seed and use the rest for culinary purposes (this is especially important in areas with a short growing season, as later pods will not necessarily ripen before the first frost). Those who would like to observe individual plants for desirable traits (vigor, yield, etc.)

them with your fingernail. If they are not this dry when removed from the pod, dry the beans longer.

SELECTION CHARACTERISTICS The common bean is an example of crop diversity that is almost unfathomable. Seeds can be colored in any tone imaginable, whether single-colored or multi-colored. They can be large or small, flat or spherical. Even the pods come in a wide array of colors: green, yellow, blue, mottled. Different varieties are adapted to different climates, and people have selected for every conceivable trait: time of ripeness, stringless, use as green bean, use as dry bean, to name but a few. Other selection criteria:

- plant: adaptation to given local growing conditions (day length, temperature, etc.); time of ripeness (earliness); healthy, robust foliage that does not wilt; height; resistance to diseases and pests; root quality (good nodulation)
- pod: quantity, flavor, lack of string, thickness of flesh, tenderness, length and width, number of beans per pod, size of beans
- seed: true-to-type shape and color
- bush beans: lack of "tendrils," ease in harvesting, synchronous ripening
- pole beans: development of new pods after picking for increased yield
- usage: for example, in polyculture with corn, not especially vigorous growth that ripens with the corn

DISEASES AND PESTS Of the diseases that can come up in bean cultivation, several are seed-borne, the most important being anthracnose, brown spot, and viruses. The bean weevil can also be spread through sowing infested seed. Bean rust (fungus: *Uromyces appendiculatus*) is not seed-borne. Symptoms: in spring white, in summer red pustules on leaves, stalks, and pods. Prevention and treatment: keep afflicted plants out of the compost pile, disinfect bean stalks.

Anthracnose (fungus: *Colletotrichum lindemuthianum*) mainly affects bush beans. Symptoms: leaves, stalks, pods, and seeds can be affected. Look for brown spots, with dark or red edges, that are somewhat sunken into the tissue. Wet weather encourages spreading and heightens the intensity of this disease. Prevention and treatment: do not use affected seed. Do not grow beans in the same plot for at least three years, burn affected foliage, or compost well. Brown spot (bacteria: *Pseudomonas syringae*) is a bacterial

The tender, violet flowers of a pole bean

disease. Symptoms: "water-soaked" spots on leaves, stalks, and pods that spread. Pole beans are affected less often. The bacteria can be spread from affected to healthy seed during seed cleaning. Remedies: do not use affected seed, thinner plots in the field, do not plant in wet areas. Remove afflicted plants; do not grow beans in the same plot for at least three years. The black bean aphid (*Aphis fabae*) can also affect the common bean.

The most important of the viral diseases affecting the common bean is the bean common mosaic virus (BCMV). Aphids are the most common vector of this disease, though it can also be seed-borne. Symptoms: leaves becoming lighter in color, eventually exhibiting a light and dark green mosaic. Dark green leaf parts bulge like blisters. Infections at the time of pod development do not affect yields but can infect seeds. Remedies: remove plants suspected of being infected, carefully fight aphids.

The bean grower's most feared pest is the bean weevil (*Acanthoscelides obtectus*). This storage pest was brought to Europe from America via aid shipments after World War II. The insect is brownish black and is ⅛–¼ in. (3–5 mm) long. An infestation can be recognized by small circular holes in the seed the weevil has eaten out. It cannot handle low temperatures but is happy to eat holes in beans in the pantry all winter long. Serious cases are usually caused by female weevils laying their eggs directly on seeds in a pod that has burst, which can happen when still on the plant or during drying, after harvest but before threshing. Larvae then

The more you eat, the more you toot?

Beans are said to be difficult to digest. Perhaps this is why beans are consistently absent from lists ranking the most popular vegetables. This is unfortunate because protein-rich beans need only to be properly prepared to make them digestible. Cultures that eat a lot of legumes have learned how to handle them. One of the most important rules is to never cook legumes with salt or acid (e.g., vinegar, tomatoes) because this often results in undercooked and thus indigestible beans. Beans should always be soaked overnight to neutralize their phytic acid content (pour off the water and use fresh water, with seasonings if you like, to cook). Add salt and acid-containing vegetables only after the beans have completely cooked. This stops the cooking process, which helps keep beans intact for any preparation that follows. And when beans are eaten often, bodies tend to adjust to them in time. Adding summer and winter savory (*Satureja hortensis* and *S. montana*), with their essential oils, makes beans even more agreeable.

eat their way into the seeds. Remedies: do not use infested seed, harvest ripe pods immediately, dry under row cover, close storage containers tightly, store seed dry, cool (under 54°F [12°C]), and clean. Place infested seed in a deep freezer (−4°F [−20°C]) for two weeks to kill weevils. Beans must, however, be very dry to avoid being killed by water contained in the seed expanding into ice.

CULTIVATION HISTORY The wild ancestors of common beans are found in Central and South America, from Mexico to Costa Rica, Colombia to central Argentina. Common beans were brought to Spain in the 16th century, and German illustrations from the year 1534 are taken as evidence of its cultivation in Germany at

that time. Like many New World crops, it was initially a curiosity and did not become widely distributed until the 17th century. In the few centuries of bean cultivation in Europe, a vast number of diverse regional varieties were developed. Because changes in colors and patterns on beans are very conspicuous and because these changes are the result of only slight genetic mutations, gardeners could easily select for these changes and establish new varieties. Bush beans were bred from pole beans. One trait that has been intensively selected for since the 1940s is the absence of a string in the pod. Though these strings can be an annoyance in the kitchen, they are important to the plant, serving as a supporting framework for the pod.

Long-time Arche Noah member Lukas Heilingsetzer harvests 'Irmtraud' bush beans and hangs them under an eave to dry.

RUNNER BEAN

Phaseolus coccineus

Runner beans are not as diverse as common beans, and colloquially, they are often simply lumped in with pole beans. While this is morphologically correct, it is botanically false, as runner beans are their own separate species of bean. In addition to appearance, runner beans differentiate themselves from common beans in that their cotyledons remain underground after germination (hypogeal germination) instead of rising above ground (epigeal germination). Runner beans are vigorous, robust, not particular about the weather, and, thanks to the often blazing colors of their edible blossoms, also interesting as ornamentals. Their other common name, scarlet runner beans, is an allusion to the brilliant red flowers of many varieties; other varieties have white, reddish white, or pink blossoms. As greenery in the summer they can be planted by gazebos, shaded benches, or along fences. The long and always green pods of runner beans are rough and somewhat gnarled; their seeds are typically eaten as dry beans, though young pods make for tasty green beans.

WHAT YOU'LL NEED
- at least 10 healthy, high-yielding plants
- a climate allowing for full ripening of beans

POLLINATION NOTES Runner beans are outcrossers that are pollinated by insects—mainly honeybees and bumblebees. Multiple varieties grown without isolation are very likely to cross with one another. Small-scale home growers should use an isolation distance of at least 500 ft. (150 m), although if there are no barriers like hedges, tall plants, or houses, 1600 ft. (500 m) is recommended. Some white-flowered varieties are able to self-pollinate. Although it happens seldom, it is not unheard of for runner beans to pollinate common beans. In our increasingly common hot summers, yields of runner beans are greatly reduced, because, though runner beans flower in such heat, they produce no pods.

Runner beans

Runner beans have either red, white, or pink blossoms.

GROWING FOR SEED Seeds can be sown once the ground has reached 46–50°F (8–10°C). Runner beans are less fussy about temperature than their relative, the common bean. They love cool, wet weather, and they thrive at high altitudes, much better than common beans. Runner beans do not handle hot weather well, however. They are very vigorous growers that require very tall trellises, though a few bush varieties do exist. Runner beans are perennials in their native climate but not winter hardy, so they can be dug up, taproot and all, and overwintered in the cellar like dahlias. Plant out the following year after the last spring frost. These plants will produce ripe fruits before first-year plants.

HARVEST Because runner beans take longer to ripen than common beans, it is best in most climates to reserve the first pods for the seed harvest and eat later pods fresh. It is however still recommended to designate specific plants for seed production, because each plant stops blossoming as soon as their first seeds ripen. Seeds can be harvested when they rattle noticeably in the dried pod, as they do with the common bean. Seeds are in various shades of violet to reddish brown, with dark marbling and spots, plus pure white, light green, and black.

SELECTION CHARACTERISTICS As for common beans.

DISEASES AND PESTS Runner beans are generally more rugged than common beans (which see), but they are still susceptible to bean weevils and bean rust.

CULTIVATION HISTORY The three wild subspecies of runner beans grow in cool, moist mountain regions from northern Mexico to Panama at 3200–9600 ft. (1000–3000 m) elevation; here, both wild and cultivated varieties are perennial. The runner bean came to Europe in about 1654, later than the common bean, and quickly found its way into Parisian flower bouquets and garlands. It is grown mainly in central and northern Europe as a crop and as an ornamental, appreciated for its high resistance to disease, robustness, and

Runner beans develop gnarly pods that are only usable as a green bean when young.

A southern Swiss special

Runner beans have been grown (and grown well) since their introduction to Switzerland, and from the municipality of Poschiavo comes a special variety of runner bean, 'Fasöi dalla minestra da Dumega', whose ripe *fasöi* (beans)—a mixture of white and violet-black—were eaten as a side dish to barley soup. The former derive from red blossoms, the latter white.

adaptability; with its lower heat requirement (when compared to common beans), it can be grown to ripeness in southern Norway and at 4000 ft. (1200 m) in the Alps of South Tyrol, Italy. It is rarely grown in southern Europe and northern Africa.

LESSER-KNOWN BEANS for adventurous gardeners

A multitude of cultivated beans, not just the common bean and the runner bean, stand ready to enliven any home garden. Because of their need for heat, many of these have yet to gain popularity in the milder climes of Europe, though in warmer lands they are important staple crops. Those who give these lesser-known beans their attention are rewarded with plants that serve well as ornamentals, ground cover, extravagant meals, or sprouts. The blossoms and pods of hyacinth beans make for wonderful ornaments, lima beans and mung beans are delectable, cowpea blossoms exude a glorious fragrance and develop long, spaghetti-like pods, and the young pods of the asparagus pea taste just like their namesake.

WHAT YOU'LL NEED

- 10 healthy plants
- trellis for climbing varieties
- for mild climates: greenhouse or an unusually warm summer

POLLINATION NOTES The five species considered here, being of various genera, do not cross with each other, but different varieties of the same species often do cross with each other when not grown in isolation. Plan for a spatial isolation of at least 500 ft. (150 m) or for mechanically isolating individual flowers or whole plants with row cover.

- hyacinth bean: self-fertile outcrosser; blossoms attract lots of insects; varietal purity can be all but guaranteed through spatial isolation or isolating individual flowers with tea filters
- lima bean: self-fertile outcrosser that (though it is of the same genus) does not cross as often as runner beans; very attractive to bees
- cowpea: selfer, though honeybees may cause some small amount of crossing; flowers emit an exquisite fragrance
- asparagus pea: predominantly self-pollinates, though honeybees and other insects can cause some crossing
- mung bean: selfer, with crossing (through insects) happening only rarely

Hyacinth bean (*Lablab purpureus*)

Lima bean, butter bean (*Phaseolus lunatus*)

Cowpea, black-eyed pea (*Vigna unguiculata*)

Asparagus pea, winged bean (*Tetragonolobus purpureus*)

GROWING FOR SEED For all these legumes, start seed indoors two to four weeks before the last anticipated spring frost and plant out after the last frost, unless you live in a Mediterranean climate or warmer. Hyacinth and lima bean seeds typically ripen in mid to late summer. Cowpeas and especially mung beans need a particularly long summer in order to ripen. Only the mung bean needs to be grown indoors in central Europe (zones 5 to 7) to reliably produce ripe seed. Asparagus peas are the least picky of this group

Mung bean (*Vigna radiata*)

as far as climate is concerned. For most of these beans, there are bush as well as climbing varieties. If seeds of the variety you are growing do not ripen because the season was not long enough, try a variety that is more suited to your locale.

HARVEST Harvest pods when they are dry and brittle (for most varieties, they will also be brown at this stage). Cowpea and

The racemose flowers of the hyacinth bean can be purple, white, yellow, or pink.

Cowpea blossom

Hyacinth bean cuisine

In our gardens, hyacinth beans are most appealing as ornamentals, but in countries that grow them the most, they are important food and medicinal plants and sometimes fodder crops. In India they are widely eaten as green beans, and ripe seeds are split to make dahl (note: ripe seeds contain cyanide and should be soaked and cooked well to neutralize it). In Indonesia, blossoms are eaten like vegetables. Often seeds are soaked, sprouted, and then dried and stored for later use as a vegetable or ground into flour. Hulled, they can be ground into a paste, heavily seasoned and fried; Egyptian falafel (*ta'amia*) is sometimes made from hyacinth bean flour. Roasted seeds are also eaten, in addition to the root stock.

mung bean pods burst open easily, so harvest these carefully, just before they are fully ripe, and give them extra time to fully dry. Hyacinth bean pods, however, can be difficult to thresh and are best threshed by hand. For more detailed harvesting and drying instructions, see common beans.

SELECTION CHARACTERISTICS In Europe, distinct varieties of these peas and beans are often not available, but where they are widely and commonly grown, crop diversity is large. For all these legumes, use the same selection criteria as for common beans, as well as the following:

• adaptability to local growing conditions
• earliness
• cold tolerance
• pod tenderness

DISEASES AND PESTS We have found hyacinth and lima beans and the asparagus pea to be relatively robust: we have yet to observe any disease or pest on any of them. All five species (with the exception of the asparagus pea) can be affected by the bean weevil; in their countries of origin, however, numerous diseases and pests affect these plants. Hyacinth beans, cowpeas, and mung beans, typically grown in greenhouses in temperate zones, are susceptible there to spider mites. Prevention: well-ventilated greenhouse, keeping plants well watered. Treatment: targeted use of beneficial insects (predatory mites).

CULTIVATION HISTORY There are divergent opinions as to the native land of the

Lima bean pods usually contain only one to three seeds.

Asparagus pea pods are characterized by four symmetrically arranged, lengthwise ridges (hence the alternative common name, winged bean).

hyacinth bean. On the one hand, it is presumed to come from east Africa because the wild subspecies is found there. On the other hand, the oldest (prehistoric) finds are from the Indian subcontinent, where a great diversity is found and the beans are widely grown.

Lima beans come from Central America (Mexico, Guatemala) and South America (Peru, Ecuador) and were domesticated in two separate events. Wild lima beans were an important food source for regional native peoples, who also used lima bean roots medicinally. Spaniards and Portuguese brought the lima bean to Europe, where it later spread to Asia and Africa.

The cowpea (or black-eyed pea, to the New World) is one of the traditional legumes of the Old World, originating in sub-Saharan Africa. The ancient Greeks and Romans grew it, calling it "phase(o) lus." Around 1250, Dominican monk and naturalist Albertus Magnus wrote a detailed description of it. But when the common bean (*Phaseolus vulgaris*) was introduced from the New World, the name *Phaseolus* was assigned to it instead—a source of much confusion. Long-podded cowpeas were most likely bred in southeast Asia.

The asparagus pea grows wild from the Mediterranean region to the South Caucasus. It has been grown in Germany since the 17th century. It is grown for food in home gardens in India, Bangladesh, Indonesia, Burma, and New Guinea.

Wild mung beans (var. *sylvestris*) grow in the northern regions of the Indian state of Maharashtra. Archeological finds show their use since 3500–3000 BC.

FAVA BEAN
Vicia faba

The fava bean is a very old protein-rich plant that has been grown in the Near East since the late Neolithic period. It forms one primary stem and grows mainly vertically, rather than forming a short, compact bush, though sometimes more than one primary stem can form. The variability of the fava bean is enormous, with varieties existing for myriad growing conditions and intended uses. Varieties for field-scale growing distinguish themselves largely on the basis of their thousand-seed weight:

- small-seeded, var. *minor* (field bean): used mostly as a protein feed for livestock
- midsize-seeded, var. *equina* (horse bean)
- large-seeded, var. *faba* (broad bean): used as green bean or dry bean

WHAT YOU'LL NEED
- 10 healthy plants with good fruit set

Fava beans

POLLINATION NOTES Though most varieties of fava beans are selfers, both self- and cross-pollination (via the insects they attract) can occur. Thus, isolate by at least 500 ft. (150 m) or use isolation cages. Fava beans have white, or less frequently purplish red flowers with a small black spot at the base of the petals.

GROWING FOR SEED Fava beans can handle lower temperatures (as low as 17°F [−8°C], depending on the variety) than common beans or peas and can be sown in most places in late winter or early spring. Earlier sowings tend to yield higher and have fewer disease issues. Planting distances: 6–8 in. (15–20 cm) in the row, 20–24 in. (50–60 cm) between rows. Lower pods are typically larger and contain more viable seed. Fava beans cease to set fruit when it becomes too hot and need lots of water when flowering.

HARVEST Harvest pods when they have turned black. The pods of a few varieties explode easily when dry, but most can be allowed to dry right on the plant. If the weather is wet when pods are drying, harvest them when half ripe and allow them to ripen and dry in a dry place. Open pods by hand or otherwise use great care in threshing. Seeds come in myriad colors; in Europe, browns and greens are most common, but there are also reddish brown, black, and lavender-colored varieties.

SELECTION CHARACTERISTICS
- whole plant: earliness, height, and uniformity of the stand; good root development (stability); disease resistance;

absence of viruses; synchronous ripening of pods
- pods: number of pods per plant; number of beans per pod; bean size and color; flavor; upright or hanging pods; non-exploding pods

DISEASES AND PESTS Several seedling diseases and forms of foot rot affect fava beans. Soaked seeds and seedlings started indoors that are planted out when the soil is still too cold are particularly susceptible. In general: do not soak seeds, do not

'Grossbohne vom Lötschental' (large bean from Lötschental), a Swiss fava bean variety with black-speckled white blossoms

grow where a legume was grown the previous year, and sow as early as possible.

The most common pest infestation is that of the black bean aphid (*Aphis fabae*). Remove affected shoots as early

Broad bean with tell-tale exit hole of the broad bean weevil

as possible. Earlier sowings help prevent infestations. Spray rhubarb compost tea for mild infestations, a pyrethrum-based or other natural insecticide for more serious infestations. Aphids are often vectors for viral infections, which cause visibly stunted growth. Their excretions encourage colonization by *Botrytis fabae* fungi and the resulting chocolate spot disease. Do not further propagate affected plants. Chocolate spot disease appears as chocolate-colored spots, about 0.25 in. (5 mm) in diameter, whose centers are often more lightly colored. *Botrytis fabae* typically infests plants only when there is high humidity, so low-lying, dense stands in wind-protected areas are at higher risk. The fungus overwinters on infected plant tissue in the soil. This relatively widespread fungal disease can be seed-borne, so remove and dispose of affected plants

An heirloom recipe

The foundation of *Ritschert*, a hearty stew, is broad beans, millet, and pearl barley (barley that has been hulled and polished to remove the bran), to which is added cured pork or roast goose and bones (marrow bones, knuckles, feet, etc.), to provide gelatin for the broth—not that this dish is intended to be like a soup; rather, it is reduced in the oven to a soft, grainy mush. Greens, salt, pepper, garlic, onions, vinegar, and herbs provide the seasoning.

Archaeological finds in abandoned underground shelters in the salt mines of Hallstatt, Austria, show that broad beans, millet, and barley were the primary foodstuffs of ancient salt miners. This Styrian stew matches their diet so perfectly, it is hard to resist the conclusion that this is a 3,000-year-old culinary tradition (Arche Noah 2001).

(compost only if you are confident your compost pile gets hot enough to kill pathogens). Prevention: sow early and not too densely.

The seed-borne broad bean true mosaic virus is spread by aphids. Leaves show a mosaic-like brightening, and the plants are noticeably vertical and misshapen. Remove affected plants; the virus can also affect other legumes.

Downy mildew (fungus: *Peronospora viciae*) also overwinters on infected plant material in the soil. It is most likely to spread at temperatures of 60–68°F (15–20°C). The stands most at risk are those where the fungus starts spreading early in the growing season. Symptoms: reddish brown, irregularly formed spots, first on the undersides of leaves, later all over; bright layer of spores on undersides of leaves. Leaf and stem rust of beans (*Uromyces* spp.) is not seed-borne. Symptoms: small brown sporocarps (fungal fruiting bodies) on leaves and pods.

Check harvested seeds for broad bean weevil (*Bruchus rufimanus*) infestation and remove affected seeds. For more details on killing bean weevils, see the earlier entry on the common bean.

CULTIVATION HISTORY Though the wild ancestor of the fava bean is unknown, it is presumed to have been domesticated in the Near East or eastern Mediterranean region. The oldest fava bean find is from the 7th century BC in Israel. Its introduction into central Europe did not occur until the late Bronze Age. There are many fava bean finds from the first millennium AD from Austria, southwest Germany, Switzerland, and east Germany. Until the 16th and 17th centuries, when the common bean arrived and "demoted" them, fava beans were among the most important crop plants. In certain areas in Greece, southern Italy, Portugal, Great Britain, France, northern Germany, and also in a few valleys in the Alps of South Tyrol, Italy (Ulental, for example), broad beans are still grown and eaten in traditional dishes. Over the course of the 20th century, fava beans were rediscovered in central European cuisine, and they continue popular.

PEA
Pisum sativum

Peas can be categorized in many different ways. We will divide them here into three categories. The first, shell peas (convar. *medullare*) have seeds that (when they are dry) are wrinkled. The pods of shell peas have a parchment layer; they are harvested green and shelled, and they are *the* pea for freezing and canning. Dry peas (convar. *sativum*) have smooth, yellow or green seeds that are high in starch; their pods too have a parchment layer. They are dried for later cooking. The third kind are snap peas (convar. *axiphium*); these are eaten like green beans, with the pod, which develops no parchment layer. Unripe pods are very tender when they are young and can be eaten raw or steamed; snow peas and sugar snap peas fall under this category. Shell and snap pea seeds, once dried, do not soften when cooked.

WHAT YOU'LL NEED
- 50 plants
- trellis
- ideally a growing environment free of pea weevils (rare)

POLLINATION NOTES Peas are fairly strict self-pollinators, though insects (honeybees and bumblebees) can cause cross-pollination. Grow different varieties at least 50 ft. (15 m) apart. Flowers are greenish white, pink, or purplish red to violet.

GROWING FOR SEED When growing for seed, space plants 8 in. (20 cm) apart, more than when growing for food, so that individual plants can be better assessed. Provide something for the peas to climb. Dry peas can handle light frosts and can be sown in early spring when the ground has reached 35–41°F (2–5°C). Shell and snap peas are more sensitive to cold; wait until midspring when soil temperatures are 41–46°F (5–8°C) to sow these. As for many other species, the warmer the soil, the faster peas will germinate. Still, sow all

pea varieties as soon as practicable so that the plants can grow for as long as possible in short-day conditions. Peas are long-day plants: flowering is encouraged when days are long, discouraged when days are short. When peas are sown later, temperatures are often too high when the plants are in bloom. When temperatures climb above 86°F (30°C), pods cease to develop. Do not grow peas immediately after other peas or legumes. We have had the best experience with selecting individual plants to harvest seed from and harvesting only seed from these plants (flag young, still-green plants). Harvest pods for eating only from plants that have not been flagged. In Switzerland there are also many winter pea varieties, which are sown in late autumn/ early winter and overwinter in the field as small plants, much like winter grain. Cover with row cover or straw when extreme temperatures threaten. Winter peas at Pro Specie Rara had no problem with a winter when temperatures never rose above 32°F (0°C) and dropped as low as 5°F (−15°C) for a period of six weeks.

Shell peas (convar. *medullare*)

Snap peas (convar. *axiphium*)

HARVEST Harvest pods when completely ripe; be sure that they are completely dry (brittle). Since they ripen so early in the summer, they can stay on the plant until completely dry. Winter peas are ready for harvest about one month earlier than spring-planted peas. Remove peas from pods by hand or thresh on a soft underlay. Caution: since peas are relatively large, they can be damaged relatively easily by threshing. It is important to check for pea weevils after threshing (and do not let them get away!). Infested seeds are recognized by a small dark spot or a small circular hole, which should be sorted out.

SELECTION CHARACTERISTICS First, check seed for general trueness-to-type (color, etc.). Other selection criteria:

- entire plant: early ripening, plant height, resistance to fungal and viral disease, strong root system, stability, synchronous ripening of pods, long harvest period
- pod: good flavor, number of pods, length and width of pods, number of peas per pod, size of peas
- shell peas: suitability for freezing or canning (e.g., maintaining green color after preserving)

DISEASES AND PESTS To help prevent all the diseases treated here, it is important to practice good crop rotation. We recommend not growing peas in the same plot for five years.

In prolonged cold and wet periods, peas can experience reduced vigor in growth and become more susceptible to fungal and bacterial diseases. Stagnant water and poor soil aeration as a result of hardpan can also contribute to crop damage. Any measures that encourage rapid vertical growth of the pea plant plus a good crop rotation discourage disease proliferation: open, sunny beds; weeding; no nitrogen fertilizer.

Downy mildew (*Peronospora pisi*) and powdery mildew (*Erysiphe pisi*) are probably not seed-borne. Even viruses (pea early browning virus, pea seed-borne mosaic virus) are usually not transmitted by seed but rather by aphids. Downy mildew affects yield only when it infects young plants; it appears especially in cold, wet weather. Symptoms: yellow spots on the tops of leaves, a carpet of spores on leaf

The white flower of 'Gommer', a Swiss heirloom dry pea

bottoms. Treatment: five-year crop rotation. Powdery mildew thrives in warm, dry weather and usually makes its first appearance in late summer, meaning that it rarely affects yield. Symptoms: white, powdery layer on leaves. Pea rust (*Uromyces pisi*) can also appear in late summer. This, too, is not seed-borne.

The most important pest is the pea weevil (*Bruchus pisorum*), which causes direct damage to the seed. It cannot reproduce in storage. Infestation is recognized by a small circular hole, caused by larvae eating their way into the pea, closed with a thin membrane. Discard affected peas.

The pea moth (*Laspeyresia nigricana*) is another potential pest. It is an olive-brown moth that lays eggs on the undersides of leaves. Larvae then eat their way into pods and discolor them with their brownish, crumbly excrement. Infested pods often burst. Dry peas are especially susceptible. Prevention: sow early, grow in a windy area, weed often, rotate crops, cover peas with insect netting.

Warm, dry weather is ideal for the pea leaf weevil (*Sitona lineatus*), who nibbles on pea leaves. It is active in late spring and early summer, eating bow-shaped holes in leaves up to 4 in. (10 cm) off the ground. Treatment: encourage vigorous vertical growth. The pea aphid (*Acyrthosiphon pisum*), thrips (*Thrips* spp.), and the pea midge (*Contarinia pisi*) are other pests that can damage pea crops. Do not save seeds from infested plants, as the seeds' growth and development have been impaired.

Remembrance of peas past

In South Tyrol, Italy, dry peas and barley have long been cultivated in a polyculture. The specific varieties have grown up together, so to speak, and they ripen together, whereas modern peas ripen later and would not work here. One farmer from Anterivo had this to say about her "special kind" of yellow-seeded heirloom: "We sowed this pea with the barley, harvested them both together, and ate them together in a barley pea soup" (Heistinger 2001).

Dry peas have been grown in the Swiss Alps since time immemorial. 'Gommer' and 'Lötschentaler', well known in the mountain valleys of the Valais, are old varieties that thrive even at high altitudes. They were grown for use in soup and grew to be over 5 ft. (1.5 m) tall in warm areas and around 4 ft. (1.2 m) tall up in the mountains, heights that are almost unheard of today.

CULTIVATION HISTORY Peas, along with lentils, were staple foods of the first tillers of the soil in central Europe, the pair being the only legumes grown in Europe during the Neolithic period. Together with emmer, einkorn, and, depending on the region, barley or millet, peas formed the basis of European plant-sourced food. The various pea forms have been developed over thousands of years in different areas. Snap peas and peas with tender shoots were bred in Asia, where varieties with edible leaves and tendrils have been grown for a long time. Snap peas have only been popular in Europe since the 19th century and especially since the introduction of the sugar snap pea in 1906.

SOYBEAN, SOYA BEAN
Glycine max

Soybeans (UK: soya bean) are day-length sensitive, with varieties suited to areas with long or short day lengths. The soybean is the most cultivated oil and protein plant in the world. Its seeds contain 13–25% oil and 30–50% protein, a combination that lends itself to the soybean's seemingly limitless uses: miso, tempeh, soy milk, tofu, sauces, and sprouts. Soy can even be found indirectly in meat as it has become one of the most important components of livestock feed in confined hog, chicken, and beef cattle operations. The largest producers of soy as a cash crop are the USA, Brazil, China, and Argentina, countries in which the most genetically engineered varieties are grown. In east Asia and in the USA, unripe soybeans are also prepared as a vegetable, much like peas and beans. Ripe soybean seeds are toxic when raw and must be soaked and cooked for a long time. Soy oil is a cooking oil that is mainly extracted from yellow-seeded varieties; darker-seeded varieties are typically higher in protein.

WHAT YOU'LL NEED
• 10 healthy plants

POLLINATION NOTES The soybean predominantly self-pollinates. The stigma is capable of receiving pollen 24 hours before the flower opens, so fertilization often happens in the unopened flower bud. Cross-pollination through insects occurs at a rate of about 0.5%. Soybean flowers are small and not particularly interesting to insects. Flowers are found in pairs or larger clusters in the leaf axils and open early in the morning. In cool conditions, the flowers of some varieties develop no petals and the flower buds never open. Flowers in a cluster will blossom over six

Soybeans

to eight days, while all clusters on a given plant will blossom over the course of two to six weeks.

GROWING FOR SEED Soybeans are sown in central Europe (zone 6) in mid to late spring, with later sowings leading to late ripening and lower yields. Early varieties ripen—depending upon location—in late summer, early autumn, late varieties in midautumn. The soybean sends down a taproot as much as 6.5 ft. (2 m) deep that develops multitudinous lateral roots. Planting distances: 2–3 in. (5–8 cm) within the row, 10–14 in. (25–35 cm) between rows. Row spacing for some very bushy varieties may need to be larger. Home gardeners with a shorter growing season may find starting seeds indoors helpful, with cultivation methods (tillage, fertilization, watering) being the same as for the common bean. Weeding regularly during the first few weeks is important, as it takes plants this long to grow together and cover the ground.

HARVEST Harvest entire soybean plants, rather than individual pods, which are sharp, pointy, and difficult to open by hand. Thresh smaller amounts in a bag, larger amounts with a belt thresher (a machine with lower and upper conveyor belts that move at different speeds, rubbing the pods until they open). Seeds can be bright yellow, golden yellow, brown, green, black, brindled, spotted, or marbled.

SELECTION CHARACTERISTICS The soybean is a diverse crop, with an estimated 15,000 varieties distinguished by growth habit (bush or climbing), height, flower color, seed size and shape, harvest time, and nutritional content. Only a relative few (early varieties with a short growing

Soy—hidden in plain sight

Many different uses for the soybean have been developed throughout the world. The entire plant can be used as fodder or green manure. Flour from soybean seeds turns up in everything from cereal flakes to powdered spices, milk, and even as an industrial impregnating agent or paper glue. Soy oil is found in candles, candies, cosmetics, and in mayonnaise. Unripe soybeans are dried, pickled, or canned.

Ripe soybeans are eaten as a vegetable, made into tofu, and slipped into ice cream or pasta. Even this long list of uses is far from complete. In recent years, large amounts of GM soy has been used in industrial food processing; Roundup-Ready soy, which was bred to tolerate that general herbicide, is one of the most widely grown varieties in the USA and Brazil.

season) are appropriate for cultivation in central Europe's zone 6 climate. Potential selection criteria:

- early ripening
- higher number of pods per plant, number of seeds per pod, pod resistance to explosion
- large seeds
- cold tolerance
- stability (lodging resistance)

DISEASES AND PESTS There are no significant diseases or pests of soybeans in Europe, as they are grown only in limited areas; Arche Noah has yet to observe any problems.

Early-ripening varieties of soybeans can be harvested in late summer.

CULTIVATION HISTORY The soybean comes from the wild *Glycine soja*, which is found along the Amur and Ussuri rivers in Russia as well as in Korea, Japan, Taiwan, and China. The soybean itself is known only in its cultivated form. The oldest documentation of the soybean comes from northeast China and dates back to the 11th century BC. Soybeans are a traditional source of protein in south and southeast Asia. Around 1740, they were introduced into European botanical gardens; and a century later, the first attempts at growing soybeans agriculturally were made in France, Austria-Hungary, upper Italy (especially in Istria and South Tyrol), the Ukraine, and Germany. The introduction of cold-tolerant varieties has made growing soybeans possible in the temperate climes of Europe and North America, with large-scale soy cultivation in North America dating back to 1924. Currently soy is being grown only on a relatively small scale in central Europe; it is mostly imported from the USA and Brazil.

CHICKPEA, GARBANZO
Cicer arietinum

There are but few chickpea varieties that fully ripen in central Europe's zone 6 climate, as the chickpea needs lots of heat. In many warm-temperate and subtropical countries, the chickpea is among the most important legumes. Monika Sahling, who lives in Tuscany and has for years grown heirloom chickpeas, also grows (and, through Arche Noah's yearbook, offers) a local Tuscan variety. She tells us that chickpeas were commonly grown throughout her province until very recently, when they acquired the reputation of being "poor people's food."

Seeds are eaten either cooked or pureed to make a spread (the most well-known being that traditional Arabian spread,

hummus). Young pods and leaves are also edible. Chickpeas can also be used as sprouts.

WHAT YOU'LL NEED
- 10 to 15 healthy plants
- dry weather in summer

POLLINATION NOTES Chickpeas are selfers, albeit with a marginal potential for crossing, as their flowers are often visited by insects. Association Kokopelli, a French seed-saving organization, reports crossing rates of up to 1%. Chickpea flowers can be white, pink, or blue and are found individually or in pairs in leaf axils.

GROWING FOR SEED Chickpeas do well in garden-quality soil, but they require a hot, dry summer and are easily damaged

Chickpeas

Chickpeas grow in upright bushes and have pinnate leaves.

by watering and stagnant moisture. Some varieties can be planted just before the last spring frost; other varieties must be planted thereafter. In warm areas, seeds ripen in early to mid summer, though in cooler areas they may not ripen until the first autumn frosts. Grow chickpeas as you would bush beans. Starting seeds indoors in temperate climates increases your chances of harvesting ripe seed.

HARVEST The method of seed harvest depends on the variety. For varieties that flower over a long period of time, harvest individual pods as they ripen. For varieties whose flowers blossom more or less at once, pull entire plants, hang to dry, and thresh. In both cases, harvest just before full ripeness to avoid losses via exploding pods. When autumn frosts threaten, harvest full plants and dry in a frost-free environment. Depending upon the variety, seeds can be yellowish, brownish, dark brown, or black.

SELECTION CHARACTERISTICS Chickpeas are not particularly well adjusted to the harsher climates found in central Europe. An important selection criterion is therefore adaptation to the local climate. Other selection criteria:

- cold tolerance
- high yield
- resistance to fungal diseases
- straight, vertical growth

DISEASES AND PESTS Growing chickpeas in the same plot within four or five years of the previous culture increases the risk of fungal root diseases. Fungal infections can kill plants in a matter of days.

CULTIVATION HISTORY The chickpea is one of the Neolithic crops from the Middle East, with archaeological finds in Israel and Syria dating back to the 7th millennium BC. These finds presumably contain the cultivated form of the chickpea as the

COURTESY ISTOCKPHOTO/FABIO BIANCHINI

Chickpea harvest in Pitigliano, Italy

original wild form is unknown. By the 3rd or 4th millennium BC, the chickpea had spread to Greece and by the 2nd millennium BC to India. In the Mediterranean region, Asia Minor, and western Asia, it is still grown as a traditional crop, though it is waning in importance. India is the world's largest producer of chickpeas, with Pakistan, Ethiopia, Turkey, and Spain also growing them on a large scale.

LENTIL

Lens culinaris

Lentils are among the original cultivated plants of the Old World. This protein-rich plant with a short growing season is ideal for the sandy, relatively infertile soils of arid environments. Lentils love lime-rich soils yet do less well on soils with added lime. They yield well in dry summers and hardly produce at all in wet summers. There are two subgroups of lentils: the large-seeded (Macrosperma) and the small-seeded (Microsperma), though there is no exact dividing line between the two.

Lentils

WHAT YOU'LL NEED
- 10 to 15 healthy plants
- relatively infertile soil
- dry weather in summer

POLLINATION NOTES Lentils are selfers with a potential for out-crossing. They are often treated purely as selfers in the literature, but cross-pollination has been observed many times at Arche Noah. Bernd Horneburg, who led a three-year comprehensive study of lentils, reported cross-pollination rates of 0.5–5%. Honeybees and bumblebees often visit lentil flowers.

GROWING FOR SEED Lentils are sown in mid to late spring. Plant in 6–8 in. (15–20 cm) rows, or broadcast. Lentils can be grown successfully only in sandy soils with good drainage. In fertile garden soil, they are highly susceptible to fungal diseases. Dry weather is required when the seeds are ripening.

For large-scale cultivation, we highly recommend a polyculture with cereal grains, especially barley and oats. The lentils then use the stalks of grain to climb and are less likely to lodge, which helps them ripen better and set fewer, though larger, seeds. Yet another advantage: in drier years the lentils yield higher, whereas in wetter years the grain yields higher. Select grains that will ripen at the same time as the lentils. Bernd Horneburg (2003) has published a book (in German) about growing lentils in polycultures and the history of lentil cultivation.

HARVEST Pull entire dry plants from the ground and lay on a bed sheet to finish drying. Thresh and clean seed with a sieve.

SELECTION CHARACTERISTICS Remove seeds that are not true-to-type. Other selection criteria:

- taste, palatability, appearance of the seeds
- good, vigorous growth
- rapid ripening
- setting lots of pods
- stability
- high yield

DISEASES AND PESTS Lentils have a poorly developed root system that is highly susceptible to fungal diseases in cool, wet weather. Rotate crops such that lentils, or for that matter any legume, are not grown more than once in five to six years in the same plot.

CULTIVATION HISTORY The lentil was among the first domesticated plants in the Old World, one that contributed to people choosing a settled versus a nomadic life. It was domesticated in the Middle East, where its wild ancestor, *Lens culinaris* ssp. *orientalis*, can still be found. Lentils

Lentils are not without their ornamental qualities.

have been grown in Europe since the Neolithic period, traditionally in drier areas, as evidenced by variety names like 'Steinfelder Tellerlinse' (stony-field eating lentil) from Austria or Germany's 'Kyffhäuser Linse' and 'Mährische Linse', both named after specific regions. In India, where large amounts of lentils are produced, ripe seeds are used whole or split for flour, soups, and other dishes; young pods are eaten as vegetables; and whole seeds are salted and deep-fried.

PEANUT
Arachis hypogaea

We call peanuts "nuts," but this is a misnomer. It is an edible seed that grows in pods like all other legume seeds. The pods grow on stalks, first above ground; but then the stalks elongate and push pods below ground to finish ripening. Four groups of cultivars are typically grown: runner (peanut butter), Spanish (peanut butter, salted nuts), Valencia (large), and Virginia (shell peanuts).

WHAT YOU'LL NEED
• 10 healthy plants

POLLINATION NOTES Peanuts are selfers, but their flowers attract bees and other insects, which can lead to cross-pollination rates of 30% or more between varieties.

GROWING FOR SEED Isolate multiple varieties by 500 ft. (150 m) in gardens with

plenty of distractions for insects, up to a mile (1600 m) or more in less ideal conditions. Or isolate mechanically by growing in cages. Peanuts are usually direct seeded, but if starting indoors, do not start too early, as plants grow quickly. Whether direct sowing or planting out seedlings, wait until the soil is fully warm. Peanuts need lots of heat, and pods do not ripen until at least 120 days (up to 150 days) after planting.

HARVEST Harvest entire plants when they have dried and turned yellow. Dry for an

COURTESY WIKIMEDIA COMMONS/H. ZELL

The pod at the end of this peanut stalk is now ripening below ground.

additional two to three weeks indoors in a place with good air circulation, then strip pods from vines. Peanuts should be fully dry before going into storage.

SELECTION CHARACTERISTICS
- resistance to disease
- true-to-type shape of peanuts, pods, and pattern on pods
- size of peanuts
- yield
- number of peanuts per pod

DISEASES AND PESTS Late leaf spot (*Cercosporidium personatum*) appears later in the growing season as dark spots on leaves. It can lead to defoliation and reduced yields. Peanut rust (*Puccinia arachidis*) is a fungal disease causing reddish brown spots (masses of spores). It does not overwinter in the USA but is instead imported by subtropical storms like hurricanes. Use wide planting distances to encourage drying out and discourage spreading of these fungal diseases. *Aspergillus flavus*, a mold fungus, can occur in peanuts in storage. Be sure that stored peanuts are fully dry.

CULTIVATION HISTORY Peanuts are a very old cultivated crop, with the oldest finds being from Peru over 7,000 years ago. Spanish conquistadors brought the plant from Mexico to Europe, and it later spread worldwide. George Washington Carver famously developed over a hundred recipes for the peanut through a USDA program to encourage peanut production and consumption. Around 0.5% of people are allergic to peanuts; these people must strictly exclude peanuts and peanut products from their diets, as an allergic reaction results in anaphylaxis in severe cases, which may be fatal.

Malabar spinach and relatives
BASELLACEAE

The Basellaceae is a family of herbaceous climbing plants from tropical America and Asia, whose members for the most part have large, fleshy leaves. Three basella family plants are used as vegetables. Both leaves and tubers of the Madeira vine (*Anredera cordifolia*) are harvested in South and Central America (in non-tropical climates it's known as a winter-blooming houseplant). The starchy tubers of the ulluco (*Ullucus tuberosus*) are relished by many natives of the Andean highlands, from Ecuador to northern Argentina. The third is our subject here.

● ●

MALABAR SPINACH, CLIMBING SPINACH
Basella alba

Malabar spinach is native to India, where it is the best-known member of the basella family. It is a beautiful perennial climbing vine (hence its alternative common name), but it is not winter hardy, preferring a hot, humid climate. Several varieties have a blazing red stalk, which makes them interesting as ornamentals, and its fleshy, juicy leaves can be used just like common spinach (albeit they develop a somewhat

Malabar spinach seeds

slimy consistency when cooked). An advantage Malabar spinach has over common spinach is that it can be harvested continuously; its leaves taste like baby corn and are not bitter. It is increasingly grown in the West, but in many areas, it is best cultivated indoors if it is to achieve its full, fascinating potential.

WHAT YOU'LL NEED
- five to 15 healthy plants
- trellis
- gloves for seed cleaning
- greenhouse or Mediterranean climate

POLLINATION NOTES Malabar spinach plants have perfect flowers which typically self-pollinate, though they do occasionally out-cross. Different varieties do not cross with each other. Blossoms are white or pink and appear as small "ears" in the leaf axils. A short-day plant, it will blossom only when there is less than 13 hours of daylight.

GROWING FOR SEED Malabar spinach should be started indoors about a month before the last spring frost, at which point it can be planted outdoors or in the greenhouse. Seedlings require lots of warmth. Provide plants with climbing opportunities. Seeds don't become ripe until very late in the year. Malabar spinach is a perennial and can be pruned back and overwintered indoors. It can also be propagated vegetatively with cuttings.

HARVEST Each seed is encased within its own individual fruit. These fruits start out green but are black by the time they are ripe. Harvest black fruits from as many plants as possible. In a food processor with plenty of water, reduce the harvest to small pieces; or press the fruits through a sieve with a pestle or your hands (with gloves on) and leave them in cold water for 24 hours (for details, see "Wet Processing Without Fermentation"). Then wash seeds well, put them in coffee filters (a teaspoon of seed per filter), and allow to dry. In India, where Malabar spinach comes from, seed is often distributed by birds.

SELECTION CHARACTERISTICS In Europe, there are no named Malabar spinach cultivars, though plants from different source areas have variously colored stalks and leaves with different shapes and hues. Potential selection criteria:

- large, fleshy leaves
- cold tolerance

Malabar spinach's succulent leaves

Malabar spinach is a climbing vine that is both a vegetable and a beautiful ornamental (seen here in early autumn).

DISEASES AND PESTS Arche Noah has yet to observe any disease or pest problems with Malabar spinach.

CULTIVATION HISTORY Malabar spinach is found wild in India. Cultivated varieties thrive in tropical and subtropical environments, where they are eaten with other vegetables and in salad. In India, it is not just used as a leafy vegetable: the black fruits it produces are pressed for their juice, which is then used as food coloring or as a coloring agent in cosmetics. It has been grown in France since the 19th century but has never threatened to replace common spinach.

Mints

LAMIACEAE

The mint family is known for its herbs and medicinal plants: basil, sage, savory, lemon balm, marjoram, rosemary, peppermint, hyssop—the list goes on and on. All in all more than 3,500 species belong to the mint family, many of them native to Europe. Insects love mints and crawl deep into the flowers to reach their aromatic nectar. Some apiculturalists use mint family plants to make tasty sage or lavender honey. Mints are among the vegetables that are predominantly or exclusively propagated vegetatively (in this family's case, mainly by runners).

• •

BOTANICAL CHARACTERISTICS Herbaceous and woody mint family plants can be recognized by their four-sided stems, strong aroma, and flowers with petals in the shape of a lower and upper lip (hence the former family name, Labiatae). They contain essential oils and often bitter compounds and tannins. Plants are monoecious and flowers are perfect, each having two longer and two shorter stamens and a pistil with a two-sectioned stigma.

CHINESE ARTICHOKE
Stachys affinis

The Chinese artichoke is easy to grow in the home garden. Its runners form a dense ground cover of elliptical leaves that, raw, are reminiscent of lemon balm or peppermint; and the white tubers that develop on its roots, like a string of pearls, can be made into many tasty dishes over the winter.

WHAT YOU'LL NEED
• 10 to 15 healthy plants

POLLINATION NOTES Plants flower only rarely and do not produce viable seed.

PROPAGATION Chinese artichoke is usually propagated vegetatively, by division of runners or tubers. Start in pots in early spring, as plants will grow faster this way. Plant out in 10–12 in. (25–30 cm) rows, 4–6 in. (10–15 cm) spacing within the row. Plants are perennial and can be left in the same spot for up to three years before the soil tires out. Harvest annually to keep plants from competing with one another. A rhizome barrier can be helpful in the home garden to prevent the plant from spreading.

HARVEST Since tubers do not develop until short-day season, the harvest has to wait until at least midautumn, when harvest can proceed continuously as long as the ground is clear. It is all but impossible to harvest all tubers; simply take what you need at any given time, as tubers quickly turn brown and do not store well. At Arche Noah we put tubers in a pot covered with lightly moistened peat or cocopeat with wood shavings; in this way, they can be stored all winter in a cool cellar. Do not allow to dry out.

SELECTION CHARACTERISTICS Select only healthy (virus-free) tubers and good-looking plants for propagation. Potential selection criteria:

- yield (number and size of tubers)
- flavor and ease in processing (not too tangled = easier to clean, cut)
- early tuber development

Mint family flowers appear to form an upper and lower lip with their petals. Pictured here are the large, fragrant flowers of clary sage.

Root tubers

DISEASES AND PESTS Chinese artichoke often succumbs to that classic problem of vegetatively propagated crops: viral disease. Viral diseases were the reason that Chinese artichoke cultivation nearly ground to a halt in the 1970s, until virus-free plant material from Swiss tissue cultures became available. Symptoms: stunted growth, reduced yield, discoloration and wilting of leaves. Treatment: select only healthy plants for propagation, remove infected plants. Viruses are spread by aphids, usually in warm, dry years. Prevention: insect netting. The red spider mite (*Tetranychus urticae*) can be a problem in dry years, but in cooler, wetter years it poses no threat. Treatment: remove infested plants as soon as possible, cover plants with row cover to increase humidity.

CULTIVATION HISTORY Wild Chinese artichoke is native to the northern provinces of China and has been eaten by the Chinese and Japanese for millenia. Albeit never hugely popular outside of its native lands, it has since the mid 1800s been of some importance to gardeners in central Europe. It arrived in France in 1887 via Japan and has been cultivated in small circles there ever since as *crosne du Japon*. French and Japanese plant breeders are on the front lines of selecting and improving Chinese artichoke.

Chinese artichoke is atypical of the mint family in that it rarely blossoms and develops root tubers.

New Zealand spinach and relatives

AIZOACEAE

The botanical name of the family comes from the Greek *aizoon* ("eternal life"), because many of its members thrive under extreme conditions. Most species are succulent plants from the dry areas of southern Africa and Australia; many are sold as "living stones" in flower shops. Common ice plant (*Mesembryanthemum crystallinum*) has naturalized in coastal California; it gets its name from the salt crystals that develop on its edible leaves and stems through evaporation. It is not well known in central Europe but can be found at markets in Australia, New Zealand, France, and Spain. Ice plant requires warmer conditions than New Zealand spinach, one of the few other vegetables in the family.

● ●

NEW ZEALAND SPINACH
Tetragonia tetragonioides

New Zealand spinach is a drought-resistant plant that produces even in high summer, when common spinach is bolting. Two to three plants can cover the needs of a whole family. These plants are perennials in their native climate but are grown as annuals in temperate regions. They branch out readily and grow into small, low bushes with shoots up to 3 ft.

New Zealand spinach seeds

(1 m) long. The triangular, fleshy leaves grow alternately along the stem and can be harvested continuously.

WHAT YOU'LL NEED
• 10 healthy plants

POLLINATION NOTES New Zealand spinach has perfect flowers and self-pollinates, though insects can in rare instances cause cross-pollination. One small individual flower is found in each leaf axil.

GROWING FOR SEED Seed is slow to germinate, needing up to six weeks. Soaking seeds for 24 hours can be helpful; the warmer the growing medium, the faster they germinate. Seed can be started in late winter and planted out after the last spring frost. Plants start to grow vigorously at soil temperatures of 77°F (25°C) and can eventually cover up to 10 ft.[2] (1 m²) of garden bed space. It is important to keep this area weed-free until the plant reaches its full size.

Although New Zealand spinach is very drought-resistant, it grows more vigorously and yields better when well watered.

HARVEST Seeds are found individually in capsules in the leaf axils. Since ripe capsules fall easily from the plant, harvest them when brown and dry them; they will then turn black. The large, hard seeds have four points or "horns," hence the generic name *Tetragonia*. Plants can also be cut at the base and laid out on an underlay to dry. Further cleaning of the seed is not necessary. It is not uncommon to see volunteer plants the following year, whose leaves will ripen later than plants started early indoors.

SELECTION CHARACTERISTICS In Europe there are no known individual varieties, as little breeding work has been done on New Zealand spinach. Selection possibilities include:

• vigorous growth
• cold tolerance
• tender leaves

DISEASES AND PESTS Arche Noah has yet to encounter a disease affecting

New Zealand spinach leaves and blossoms

New Zealand spinach in a negative way. Aphids, which occasionally visit plants individually, could potentially spread cucumber mosaic virus.

CULTIVATION HISTORY Although this plant obviously has its common name from New Zealand, it can also be found growing wild along the coasts of Australia, Japan, and China. The naturalist Sir Joseph Banks took New Zealand spinach with him to England in 1770, since when it has been grown as a vegetable of nominal importance in Europe.

New Zealand spinach and tomato polyculture

At Arche Noah, we have developed a unique companion planting technique: New Zealand spinach covers the ground beneath tomatoes, acting as a living mulch and helping prevent late blight. A light feeder, New Zealand spinach does not compete with tomatoes for nutrients. Its leaves prohibit fungus-infested splash-back of raindrops from spraying on tomato plants. And since tomatoes are typically well watered, New Zealand spinach benefits from its close proximity to them.

Onions

AMARYLLIDACEAE

Alliaceae was once considered to be a taxonomic family in and of itself; now it is ranked as a subfamily of the Amaryllidaceae. Crop plants of this Allioideae subfamily are still known colloquially as onion family plants or alliums (after the genus *Allium*). Onions, leeks, and garlic are mainstays of most home gardens. Their pungent, spicy flavor lends an unmistakable flair to many vegetable and meat dishes. The strong aroma of onions and garlic comes from allyl sulfide compounds in the leaves and bulb.

Botanically speaking, onions are made up of a tightly clinched basal rosette, which supports leaves, called scales, which act as thick storage organs. The bulb is an underground storage organ in onions, garlic bulbs, and shallots, an above-ground reproductive organ in other alliums like topsetting onions and the scapes of garlic.

• •

GENERAL PROPAGATION CHARACTERISTICS
Allium flowers are perfect but self-infertile. Individuals are located in an umbel-like, spherical cluster and open over the course of about 30 days, with most opening during the second week. Anthers of individual flowers emit pollen for three days before the female flower organs are able to receive pollen, which prevents self-pollination.

Many alliums are grown as ornamentals, for their beautiful buds and flowers. These flowers catch the eye of not only gardeners but also a wide variety of

This is no ornamental onion: the flowers of the cultivated leek are also a thing of beauty.

insects. Bees, wasps, and hoverflies are the most important pollinators of alliums; the wind, on the other hand, hardly plays a role. In commercial seed production, isolation distances of at least 1 mile (1.5 km) are used. In diverse home gardens, 500–650 ft. (150–200 m) should suffice, meaning that growing more than one variety of the same species in one garden per year is likely not possible, unless mechanical isolation or hand pollination is used.

Many alliums produce no seeds and are propagated vegetatively. Garlic and topsetting onions, for example, produce bulbils instead of flowers; they do produce flowers when under stress, but these are usually sterile. Alliums that normally produce seed (leeks, for instance) can produce bulbils when they are under stress.

A thorough process of selection is important for all alliums. Remove plants with atypical leaves or those that flower early as soon as possible. Propagate only true-to-type bulbs, bulbils, or topsets.

Overview of the onion family

COMMON NAME	BOTANICAL NAME
onion	*Allium cepa* var. *cepa*
shallot	*Allium cepa* var. *aggregatum*
topsetting onion, tree onion	*Allium* ×*proliferum*
Japanese bunching onion, Welsh onion	*Allium fistulosum*
leek	*Allium ampeloprasum* var. *porrum*
pearl onion	*Allium ampeloprasum* var. *sectivum*
chives	*Allium schoenoprasum*
garlic	*Allium sativum*
garlic chives	*Allium tuberosum*

Insects like to visit onion flowers. Seen here is *Eumenes pomiformis* (potter wasp).

ONION

Allium cepa var. *cepa*

Vegetable or seasoning? Depending on the variety, the common onion is either the former, the latter, or both. The complex flavor of the onion is a combination of sweet, pungent, and spicy, caused primarily by essential oils, especially allyl sulfide compounds and alpha hydroxy acids. Available in markets year round, onions are a crop that many gardeners grow every year. They are natural antibiotics thanks to the organosulfur compound allicin, which also has anti-fungal properties and is purported to strengthen the immune system. Onions are diverse in shape and also color: they can be red-violet, white, brown, or yellow. Red onion varieties mostly have a mild, sweet flavor and do not store as well as yellow varieties.

WHAT YOU'LL NEED
- 15 to 20 good-looking onions
- overwintering strategy or mild climate
- support poles or trellis
- isolation covers (if multiple varieties are being grown for seed)

Onion seeds

POLLINATION NOTES The onion is a strict outcrosser. Its large flower heads are attractive to a diverse array of insects, making it crucial to isolate multiple varieties to avoid crossing. Crossing with the Japanese bunching onion is also not out of the question, but onions do not cross with chives or leeks.

Isolate multiple varieties spatially by at least 500–650 ft. (150–200 m), much more when barriers like bushes and buildings are not part of the garden or if there are few other flowers to distract pollinating insects in the garden. Use mechanical isolation when spatial isolation is not possible. Make sure flowers cannot touch the netting of the isolation cage, lest insects pollinate flowers from outside the cage. The European hoverfly (also known as the drone fly, *Eristalis tenax*) is the best pollinator for isolation cages. Otherwise use mason bees (*Osmia rufa*) or blowflies (Calliphoridae spp.), though these may only pollinate at rates around 35%. Greater success may be had by hand pollination, for which onion flowers must be dry. Simply brush flowers with a 1.25–2 in. (3–5 cm) brush daily for 14 days (use a separate brush for each variety).

GROWING FOR SEED Onions grow best in full sun in sandy-loam soils with good drainage and not too much nitrogen. In temperate climates, sowing seed in spring, harvesting bulbs in autumn, and setting bulbs out again the following spring for a summer harvest is the most reliable method for producing seed. Do not save seed from onions that produce seed in the first year. Sow onion seed as early in spring as possible, whether growing for food or for seed (outdoors in midspring, or start seeds indoors). Onion sets (dried, immature onions from densely seeded plots) can be planted as soon as the danger of hard frosts has passed. If the growing season is too short in your area or if seed was sown too late, grow your own onion sets, plant them out the following spring, overwinter mature bulbs indoors, then harvest seed in the third growing season.

Initiation of bulb formation is dependent on day length and temperature. Short-day varieties form bulbs with 12-hour days; long-day varieties need 14-hour days to form bulbs. Select the 15 to 20 best, most true-to-type bulbs for seed production. Dry these 10 to 12 days in a warm place with good air circulation until the outer scales are well dried. Remove the vegetation that sits atop the bulbs, or leave on and braid several together. To prevent early sprouting of bulbs, store either at high temperatures (77–95°F [25–35°C]) or low temperatures (32–45°F [0–7°C]). Root cellars are less suited to onion storage than are attics or garages. Wherever they are stored, the room should be frost-free (stored onions exposed to freezing conditions quickly rot). Check bulbs regularly; remove rotting onions.

Onions go through a dormancy period and will not sprout even under ideal conditions when they are still dormant. The

Various shapes of onions

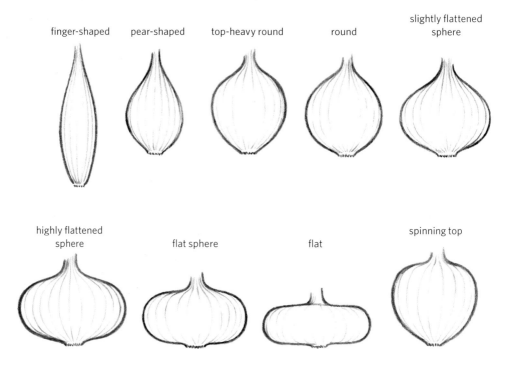

finger-shaped pear-shaped top-heavy round round slightly flattened sphere

highly flattened sphere flat sphere flat spinning top

length of the dormancy period varies from variety to variety. After dormancy, onions sprout as soon as humidity and temperatures (54–59°F [12–15°C]) fall into the onion's comfort zone.

Plant out onions in the spring deeper than they were the previous autumn, all the way up to the tip (make sure bulbs are vertical in the ground). Plant in 10 in. (25 cm) rows, 6 in. (15 cm) between bulbs within the row.

Flower stalks can grow to be over 3 ft. (1 m) tall and need support (poles or trellis). As day length increases, each onion sends up one to three flower stalks; plants bloom in mid to late summer. Plants slowly dry as seeds ripen.

Onions can also be propagated vegetatively: harvest bulbils from mother plants after flowering is completed. When these are planted in the spring, they normally go to seed the same year.

HARVEST Onions produce small pods as fruits, with seeds encased therein. Seeds typically become ripe in late summer and are colored black. Pods break easily; wind or rain can cause seed to fall to the ground. Harvest seed stalks as soon as pods become dry and brown. Place seedheads in a paper bag when harvesting, then break off stalks

Dry seedheads in a loosely packed cloth bag for several days in a warm place with good air circulation. Seeds will now easily fall out; thresh the rest. Freeze seedheads for several hours when seeds do not thresh easily, then try again. Winnowing: use sieves to separate seeds from dried pods by swinging, shaking, and blowing. It is not uncommon for onions to produce many infertile seeds. To separate these out, place all seeds in a bucket of cold water. Fertile (viable) seeds sink to the bottom, infertile seeds float at the top and can be (carefully!) poured off with the water. Dry seeds immediately, using, for example, coffee or tea filters.

SELECTION CHARACTERISTICS
- healthy, vigorous growth in first year
- true-to-type bulb shape
- uniform bulb development; no double or multi-bulbs
- high-quality, sturdy scales with no tears
- true-to-type scale color
- drought tolerance
- flavor
- slim neck of onion (= stores better)
- long storage length
- synchronous, complete ripening
- minimal susceptibility to downy mildew

DISEASES AND PESTS Crop rotation is very important in onion cultivation: wait at least five years before growing onions again in the same bed. Never fertilize with fresh manure or unripe compost as this delays ripening and encourages onion flies (*Delia antiqua*). These look like small houseflies and lay their eggs on young onions. The larvae then eat these young onions, turning leaves yellow and killing them. Later generations can then infest larger plants later in the year. Onion fly attacks inflict the most damage in hot weather when the soil is dry. The second generation eats its way into bulbs from the soil in mid to late summer; sometimes a third generation appears later. Prevention:

insect netting at the time of egg laying (around the time of the last spring frost), not fertilizing with fresh manure, not growing onions after spinach. Polyculture with carrot and undersowing subterranean clover (*Trifolium subterraneum*) are said to help keep infestations under control. Treatment: remove and burn infested leaves (to kill maggots, thus interfering with their reproductive cycle). Infestation of the seed stalks in the second year can cause major problems for seed growers. Onion fly maggots can attack seed stalks from within until they die and fall off. Observe plants closely.

Downy mildew (*Peronospora destructor*) occurs especially in wet years and in plots with little wind. Symptoms: onion foliage with elongated, greenish brown spots, sometimes with a violet-gray carpet of spores. In serious cases, onion leaves can entirely die off, bulb growth is stunted and harvested bulbs do not store long. A primary source of infection is infected plant debris in the soil. Prevention: grow in windy areas, maintain loose soils, apply horsetail slurry, five-year crop rotation, thorough removal of plant debris from garden beds. Treatment: remove infected plants and compost thoroughly or burn.

Dried allium seedheads

Onion neck rot (*Botrytis aclada*) is a disease that pops up in storage. The fungus can enter the plant through dead leaves in the fall or through injuries sustained during the harvest. After a few weeks in storage, the upper part of the onion appears glassy and looks like it has been cooked until soft. A layer of gray fungus with black spots also forms on the onion. Onions ultimately shrivel and rot into a smelly porridge. The fungus is seed- and soil-borne (spread by the wind when soil-borne). Prevention: do not excessively fertilize with nitrogen, sow seed early, protect crop from rain as it ripens (tarp), wait until leaves are completely dead before harvesting, harvest only in dry weather. Treatment: check stored onions regularly and quickly remove infected ones.

Bacterial soft rot (pathogen: *Erwinia carotovora*) is a bacterial disease that can affect onions in storage. Onions can be infected in the garden, especially in wet years or when the soil is generally wet, but symptoms do not appear until they are put into storage. The disease can be recognized by the especially sulfurous odor it causes. Remove infected plants immediately. The leek moth (*Acrolepiopsis assectella*) sometimes attacks onions. Thrips and stem nematodes are also known to infest onions. Prevention: insect netting.

CULTIVATION HISTORY The common onion is known only in its cultivated form, making it one of the few crops where domestication led immediately to the establishment of a new species. The oldest evidence of the cultivation of onions are illustrations from around 2665 BC in Egypt. The oldest evidence from the Mediterranean comes from Crete (2000–1400 BC), which had trade relationships with Mesopotamia and Egypt. Romans spread the onion to the north. Onions are found in central European texts starting in the early Middle Ages. Doctor and botanist Leonhard Fuchs described red, yellow, and white varieties in 1543. A lot of breeding work has been done on the onion in the last 50 years; commercial varieties are predominantly hybrids.

SHALLOT
Allium cepa var. *aggregatum*

Shallots are more difficult to find on the market than onions; for one thing, they are much harder to peel, leading many people to decide not to bother with them. Top chefs, however, swear by their aromatic qualities. They also have their advantages in the garden, as they ripen before onions. Young leaves can be used as green onions. Shallots are smaller than onions, but they are spicier and sweeter, yet at the same time milder. And if you reflect on how often halved onions have gone bad in your refrigerator, their smaller size starts to seem all the more sensible.

Shallots are the best-known multiplier onions. There are others (sometimes known as potato onions, which have larger bulbs and no peel that holds the whole bunch together), but these are rarely propagated by seed.

WHAT YOU'LL NEED
- 20 handsome shallots
- overwintering strategy

POLLINATION NOTES Shallots rarely flower and produce seed even less often. They have a very low tendency to bolt, making them ideal for growing in the tropics.

PROPAGATION Shallots are propagated vegetatively. They are hardy to zone 3 and can be planted from early to late autumn or in late winter to early spring about 2 in. (5 cm) deep in 10–12 in. (25–30 cm) rows at 4–8 in. (10–20 cm) spacing. Stalks will grow to be about 8 in. (20 cm) tall and are hollow. By summer, five to seven new shallots will have grown. Long days and high temperatures encourage bulb development. Plants do not handle competition well; keep the soil loose and free of weeds.

HARVEST Harvest shallots as soon as leaves have wilted, usually in midsummer. Store as for onions.

SELECTION CHARACTERISTICS
- good "family" development, healthy and vigorous growth in first year
- uniform, true-to-type shape (finger-shaped, pear-shaped, top-heavy round, round)
- high-quality, sturdy scales with no tears
- true-to-type scale color (white/yellow to white/reddish violet)
- drought tolerance
- flavor

Individual shallots multiply to form a new shallot "family."

- synchronous and complete ripening
- minimal susceptibility to downy mildew
- long storage life

DISEASES AND PESTS Shallots are more robust than common onions but can be affected by the same diseases. Do not grow shallots where other alliums were recently grown.

CULTIVATION HISTORY Wild shallots are found in the Middle and Far East. Cultivated shallots are used like common onions in Europe. In Charlemagne's *Capitulare de Villis*, "cepas" (common onions) were differentiated from "ascalonias" (shallots).

TOPSETTING ONION, TREE ONION
Allium ×proliferum

The topsetting onion is a true curiosity of the onion family. A nest of bulbils forms not in the soil but above ground, at the ends of its stalks; these then sprout and form another level of plant growth, which eventually produces its own set of bulbils, producing a third story, as it were. The bulbils are eaten raw, sautéed, or as a seasoning. Young leaves can be used as green onions in soups and salads; young bulbils can be pickled. Topsetting onions are not grown commercially but make for an interesting addition to home gardens.

WHAT YOU'LL NEED
- five handsome, healthy plants

POLLINATION NOTES Plants rarely produce flowers. When they do, they can cross with neighboring common onions.

PROPAGATION Topsetting onions are perennial, and various sources list them as being hardy to zone 3 or 4. They can only be propagated vegetatively, which is a relatively easy task: simply collect the newly formed bulbils and plant (ideally in late summer). Rejuvenate older "stories" every three or four years. Plants sometimes do this themselves, by falling over when they get too tall; bulbils then send out new roots.

The little bulbils of topsetting onion grow in the air, above ground.

SELECTION CHARACTERISTICS

- vigorous growth
- plant health
- size and color of bulbils (red, white, yellow)

DISEASES AND PESTS Plants are susceptible to the same diseases as onions, though topsetters are usually more robust than onions. The onion fly is the most likely pest to cause major problems as infested shoots fall over.

CULTIVATION HISTORY Topsetting onions are known only in cultivation. They are seen as hybrids of common onions and Japanese bunching onions; though how exactly the cross occurred is unknown, plants first appeared in England in the 18th century.

JAPANESE BUNCHING ONION, WELSH ONION
Allium fistulosum

This onion family plant is an herbaceous perennial that produces relatively weak bulbs. It also grows strong, vigorously growing, hollow, tube-like leaves that look like a combination of leeks and chives. There are two main approaches to cultivating the plant. In Europe, it is grown as a perennial clump-forming plant. It needs less heat and sprouts earlier than chives. In the kitchen, it is used as an addition to salads and steamed vegetables. In China and Japan, plants are grown as annuals and the entire plant is used: leaves, then later the small bulbs and the long, white, often blanched scapes. The different growing techniques and different uses of the plant have led to the development of different types, with the European type more closely resembling chives and the Asian type more closely resembling leeks (the two common names do not necessarily reflect these different types). Intensive breeding work is currently being conducted on bunching onions in Japan; this form is increasingly popular in Europe as a source of green onions.

Japanese bunching onion seeds

Japanese bunching onions can be propagated by seed or vegetatively by dividing plants.

WHAT YOU'LL NEED
• four or five healthy plants or one dense cluster

POLLINATION NOTES Like all alliums, Japanese bunching onion is an outcrosser, whose white flowers are visited by many insects. It can cross-pollinate with common onions when they flower at the same time, though not with leeks, chives, or garlic.

PROPAGATION To maintain multiple varieties, remove flowers and propagate by dividing plant clusters. Rejuvenate plants every two to three years by digging up, dividing, and replanting at a new location in the garden. Plants send up flower stalks in the second year, soon after sending out leaves. Growing from seed is relatively easy, as they grow to ripeness most anywhere.

Hardiness varies by variety, with Asian selections often being hardy only to zone 6 and other varieties being hardy to as low as zone 3. Hoop houses or other season-extension techniques may be necessary to help less-hardy varieties survive the winter in your area.

HARVEST Seeds fall easily from the plant. Harvest and cleaning as for onions.

SELECTION CHARACTERISTICS
• vigorous growth
• fineness of hollow leaves
• production of long scapes (for blanching)
• true-to-type leaf color (white, green, red, violet)

DISEASES AND PESTS Japanese bunching onions are very robust and rarely succumb to disease. Onion flies can, however, cause damage (for more on this pest, see onions).

CULTIVATION HISTORY The Japanese bunching onion is known only in cultivation. The earliest evidence of its cultivation comes from China in the first millennium BC. It arrived in Europe during the Middle Ages, presumably via Russia. Scapes are an important market crop in China and Japan, where they are often dried for winter storage.

LEEK
Allium ampeloprasum var. *porrum*

The leek is a cherished winter vegetable. It is protected against the frosts of winter by sulfur-containing essential oils. The mild, white, more-or-less swollen base of the leaves is the part that is typically eaten, though the green leaves are also

Leek seeds

delicious. Whereas overwintering leeks, which are harvested in the spring following the year they are planted, are grown more commonly in Europe, summer leaks, grown and harvested in the same growing season, are grown more commonly in England. The latter have lighter colored, less densely packed leaves and are not winter hardy. The related kurrat or Egyptian leek (var. *kurrat*) is cultivated in the Arab world; kurrat produces no stalks, and the leaves are used in salads or as seasoning. Another crop plant is elephant garlic (var. *ampeloprasum*), which grows and looks like garlic but is botanically a leek. Its cloves are up to five times as large as typical garlic cloves; its stalks can grow to be 5 ft. (150 cm) tall. Elephant garlic is used in the kitchen as a milder-flavored garlic, and its leaves are also edible.

These leeks were overwintered in sand and have been laid out in preparation for planting.

WHAT YOU'LL NEED
- 10 to 15 healthy plants
- overwintering strategy
- isolation strategy, if multiple varieties are being grown for seed

POLLINATION NOTES Like onions, leeks are outcrossers. See onions for information on isolation and pollinating insects. Cultivated leeks do not cross with chives, onions, or bunching onions; they do, however, cross with many wild varieties of *Allium ampeloprasum* and with pearl onions. Summer varieties often do not flower; when they do, flowers are sterile.

PROPAGATION Leeks are grown for seed as biennials. Grow the first year as you would for eating. Plants may flower in the first year; do not save seed from these plants. Contrary to what suits the onion, cool, wet weather makes for ideal growing conditions for the leek. Depending on the variety, leeks are hardy to zone 3 or 4 and can be overwintered outdoors down to these zones, even when a few leaves suffer some frostbite. Overwintering indoors may be safer, however, depending on your local conditions.

Summer leek varieties are usually propagated vegetatively. They are hardy only to zone 5 at best and should be overwintered indoors below zone 5 in a relatively dry cellar or in a heated greenhouse. In general, the darker and tougher the leaves, the more winter hardy the variety is. Blue or violet hues in ripe leaves also indicate winter hardiness. Plant out leeks in the spring as soon as the ground can be worked. Plants send up a tall flower stalk in the spring. A long-tipped husk develops at the end of the stalk by midsummer, which then falls off, exposing the typical allium flower head. Leeks bloom later than onions and have stronger stalks, though they still need support.

HARVEST Seeds ripen relatively late. Remove seedheads of slower-ripening plants and hang to dry in a cloth bag indoors with good air circulation. If no plants ripen seeds by the end of the growing season, cut entire stalks, bind into sheaves, and dry indoors with a tarp underneath the sheaves.

Leek seeds sit in their husks more firmly than onion seeds in theirs; nonetheless, the process for threshing is the same as for onions.

SELECTION CHARACTERISTICS Cultivated leek varieties differ primarily in leaf color, winter hardiness, length and thickness of leaf sheaths, and the number of bulbils in their root zones. Plant selection takes place in autumn and again in spring. Potential selection criteria:

- length and thickness of leaf base
- leaf color
- leaf structure and configuration
- flavor
- resistance to bolting (use as summer or overwintering leek)
- resistance to drought, frost, and diseases
- development of underground bulbils (= "false pearl onions") in second year
- overwintering leek: winter hardiness
- summer leek: rapid growth

DISEASES AND PESTS As with the common onion, downy mildew can be a problem in leek cultivation. Purple blotch (pathogen: *Alternaria porri*) is a seed-borne fungus that can also be spread by infected plant debris. Elongated, oval spots appear mainly on the upper halves of leaves. Infected leaves rip open, contort, and ultimately die. The fungus prefers warm, moist weather. Prevention: mulch, mulch, mulch. Leek rust is caused by the fungus *Puccinia allii* and is spread by plant debris in the soil or from plant to plant when plants overwinter outdoors. Symptoms: many small, elongated yellowish brown to orange spots and rips on the top surfaces of leaves. Round yellow spores in summer quickly contaminate all surfaces. Bad cases lead to stunted growth. The fungus spreads most in late summer and early autumn in the form of winter spores. Plants deal with infection better

Ripe seeds in leek flower head

The underground bulbils of the leek

when weather in autumn is cold and wintry. Prevention: sufficiently wide planting distances, not overfertilizing. Treatment: remove infected leaves and plants. Onion flies (*Delia antiqua*) and leek moths (*Acrolepiopsis assectella*) are pests that are easily controlled the first year with insect netting. The white, shiny eggs of the leek moth can be washed away by heavy rain or by watering. The gray-green blackheaded caterpillars of the leek moth can eat their way into the hearts of leeks and kill leaves. Plants can be protected the second year with taller isolation cages, though pollinating insects will need to be introduced. Plants can be affected by all diseases and pests in the second year as well and are especially susceptible when flowering.

CULTIVATION HISTORY The highly variable wild form of leek occurs in Portugal, northern Africa, and from Turkey to Iran, growing in undisturbed soils, coastal cliffs, and sandy beaches. The cultivated leek is an ancient garden vegetable that has been grown in the eastern Mediterranean region for 4,000 years. Leeks are mainly grown in North America and western Europe; many old and interesting varieties are to be found in the UK and France.

Digging deeper

One special feature of *Allium ampeloprasum* var. *porrum* is unknown to many, as it is hidden underground. When plants overwinter outdoors, they form underground bulbils, or pips. These can be used to vegetatively propagate leeks.

Bulbil growth can be encouraged by pruning flowers before they open, which stimulates a division in the growth zone at the base of the plant. In this way, two to five independent bulbils form, which can then be separated from the mother plant. Because they have no protective outer leaves, they must either be replanted or stored in sand. Bulbils are genetically identical to mother plants and can be used to maintain varietal purity. Switzerland's Pro Specie Rara uses this trait to its advantage when two or more varieties are near each other in the display garden but only one should flower.

Bulbils are harvested in summer. If they are not needed or wanted for propagation, they should be eaten, as they are a delicacy—much milder than onions, almost reminiscent of radish in flavor. Simply slice up and eat on buttered wholegrain sourdough bread for a quick and delectable evening meal from the garden.

PEARL ONION
Allium ampeloprasum var. *sectivum*

Pearl onions are a winter-hardy variant of leeks. They develop numerous small bulbils in the root zone with white to silvery scales. They have no brown outer peel like onions and look like pearls. Pearl onions are mainly grown in a narrow band from Italy through Austria and Germany to the Netherlands, and even in this swath they are mostly a crop for home gardeners. Commercial production is mainly for pickled pearl onions (and it is worth noting that most "pearl onions" from supermarkets are actually small, white common onions that are grown in dense patches and harvested early). Pearl onions are excellent stewed, for refining sauces, or, thanks to their mild yet spicy flavor, raw in salads. Leaves can be harvested for green onions.

WHAT YOU'LL NEED
• five healthy plants

POLLINATION NOTES Pearl onions cross with leeks. Plants can produce seed but not reliably every year.

PROPAGATION Vegetative propagation is the norm for pearl onions and easily accomplished. Plant bulbs in late summer 4 in. (10 cm) apart, 1–1.5 in. (3–4 cm) deep. They love humus-rich, sandy soils. Plants do not need much space, and most varieties grow to be 12 in. (30 cm) tall, though some can grow up to 24 in. (60 cm) tall. Bulbils develop as days grow longer and can be harvested as soon as leaves die back. When bulbils are left longer in the ground, they separate from one another, which makes harvesting more difficult. Unearth with a digging fork and select by hand: larger pearl onions for the kitchen, smaller ones for further propagation. The bulbils do not store well and must either be eaten, replanted, or pickled right away. When plants are left in the ground for another year, the yield is greater.

SELECTION CHARACTERISTICS
- vigorous growth
- yield
- plant health

DISEASES AND PESTS Diseases and pests are the same as for the leek, but these are rare for pearl onions, as the vegetative period is relatively short.

Pearl onions

CULTIVATION HISTORY As with the leek, the wild form of the pearl onion is found around the Mediterranean and the Middle East. As for domestication, it is hard to tell if older descriptions are referencing leeks or pearl onions (because leeks also form bulbils when the flower stalk is pruned), but it is safe to say that cultivation of pearl onions has always been rather limited; despite a nod from Becker-Dillingen (1938), who recommended them to the canned food industry, commercial production too has remained small.

GARLIC
Allium sativum

Garlic is grown on every continent, and the individual cloves of the garlic bulb are an absolutely essential ingredient in cuisines from Thailand to Mexico, with signature stops throughout the Mediterranean region. A kitchen utensil has even been invented specifically for garlic: the garlic press, which is found in many households, though professional chefs swear by garlic that is finely chopped by hand. Raw garlic minimizes water loss through the skin when eaten, making the body require slightly less water. Fresh, sometimes blanched leaves of the garlic plant are used in the Asian kitchen. Rocambole is a class of garlic varieties that produce scapes (spiral, elongated stems).

The many heirloom varieties all came into being by spontaneous mutations and simple selection. Since garlic is propagated vegetatively, individuals within varieties are genetically identical clones.

WHAT YOU'LL NEED
• 10 good-looking plants

POLLINATION NOTES Nearly all garlic varieties send up a stalk that produces bulbils; rarely (usually as a reaction to stress), flowers also form, but these are usually sterile. Heirloom varieties can only be propagated vegetatively, thus no isolation is necessary.

PROPAGATION Garlic is propagated vegetatively via individual cloves or via bulbils. An entire garlic bulb grows from each planted clove. Plant cloves in early to mid autumn, and harvest bulbs the following summer. Cloves can also be planted in early to mid spring (at the latest), though bulbs will be smaller and will ripen about four weeks later. Bulbils harvested from the stalks of plants are edible and can also be used to grow bulbs. Growing from bulbils may help work against the accumulation of viruses in garlic. Growing from cloves yields garlic bulbs the following year; growing from bulbils, not until the third year. Bulbils sometimes sprout while still on the stalk, like topsetting onions.

Garlic thrives in full sun in warm, loose soils (and not in wet, heavy soils). Plant in a spot in the garden that is not otherwise irrigated. Once leaves have yellowed, plants should be protected from rain to let leaves dry; otherwise, they are much more likely to contract fungal diseases.

HARVEST Harvest bulbs when stems have withered. Harvest immediately after ripening (midsummer), as bulbs are susceptible to fungal diseases when left in the ground too long and individual cloves may sprout. Pull out of the ground and dry in a dry, shady place with good air circulation in bundles or in crates. Braid the stalks of dried garlic or store in paper bags; do not remove the outer peel. Bulbs store for six to eight months in cool, dry conditions. They sprout quickly in early spring when stored at temperatures that are

Flower buds developing alongside bulbils

The scape of a rocambole garlic variety

When bulbils (left) are used as seed garlic and planted in autumn, each yields a small single-cloved garlic bulb the following year (these may be even smaller than pictured here). Plant these small bulbs again in autumn to harvest fully developed bulbs (right). When individual cloves are used as seed garlic, fully developed bulbs can be harvested the following summer.

too high. Separate bulbs into individual cloves for selection before planting.

SELECTION CHARACTERISTICS Varieties differ in length of dormancy before they begin to sprout, in sensitivity to day length, and in the color, thickness, and number of layers of the outer peel. Potential selection criteria:

- size of clove and bulb
- size of bulbil ($\frac{1}{8}$–$\frac{3}{8}$ in. [3–10 mm])
- length and thickness of neck
- storage life (good, stable peel)
- uniform size
- vigorous growth
- plant health
- flavor (mild or strong)
- color of peel (white, pink, violet)
- drought tolerance

DISEASES AND PESTS When grown where it likes to be grown, garlic is for the most part free of diseases and pests. But since plants can only be propagated vegetatively, they are vulnerable to the accumulation of viruses, which are spread by aphids and other biting/sucking insects. Seed garlic tested to be virus-free is available commercially. If you are maintaining an old heirloom variety, you can help it stay healthy by using insect netting or isolation cages to keep disease-spreading insects out. One way to help reduce concentration of viruses is propagating from bulbils. Embellisia skin blotch of garlic is caused by the fungus *Helminthosporium allii*. Infection is not visible until shortly before harvest, when a black layer can be seen on the base of the cloves. Infections are usually limited to the outer skin. More serious infections make their way into the tissue and turn cloves gray. Cloves then no longer store well. Prevention: use only healthy seed garlic, avoid excessive moisture during cultivation, harvest the moment cloves become ripe. Treatment: clean affected bulbs well and put only healthy bulbs/cloves into storage. Bacterial rot (pathogen: *Erwinia carotovora*) can affect garlic in wet summers. Symptoms: glassy spots, sulfury odor. Prevention: drier growing location, raised beds. Treatment: remove infected plants. The garlic fly (*Suillia univittata*) can infest garlic patches. Larvae eat the innermost, newest leaves throughout the spring, warping and contorting them. Spring-planted garlic is not attacked as severely as fall-planted garlic. Garlic growers in Austria's "wine quarter" report that heirloom varieties are attacked by garlic flies less frequently and survive attacks better than commercial varieties.

CULTIVATION HISTORY Garlic is a very old crop plant. It even has a name in Sanskrit, which can be interpreted as evidence of its cultivation in Mesopotamia dating back to the third millennium BC. The oldest archaeobotanical evidence is from Egypt, circa 1550 BC. The Greek author Herodot reported that garlic and other alliums were the primary source of nourishment for the slaves that built the pyramids. In ancient Rome, garlic was considered a food of the peasantry, a stigma that held for a long time; it is now one of the most important vegetable crops of southeastern Europe. In Switzerland and Austria, garlic

was long grown in vineyards, as the warm, sunny locations and minimally fertilized and irrigated soils made for ideal garlic growing. Wild garlic is now naturalized in central European vineyards, along with crow garlic (*Allium vineale*).

CHIVES
Allium schoenoprasum

Chives are easy enough to grow in any garden, no matter how small. Individual varieties differ in the vigor and height of their growth, the thickness of their hollow leaves, and the color of their flowers, though descriptions of these are often missing in seed catalogs.

WHAT YOU'LL NEED
• three to five clumps for vegetative propagation
• 10 clumps to produce seed

POLLINATION NOTES Like all alliums, chives are self-infertile outcrossers, meaning that different varieties can cross-pollinate each other.

Chives seeds

PROPAGATION Chives are another of those alliums that can be propagated vegetatively by dividing plants or generatively by seed. Germination rates of chive seeds are high only in the first year, so use fresh seed. Plants are perennial and bring forth many pink or purple flowers every year. Most newer varieties do not flower and can only be propagated vegetatively. Chives do best when rejuvenated every two to three years by digging up, dividing, and replanting elsewhere in the garden where they or other alliums have not been grown recently. The more chives are cut back, the more they tiller. Drying out in the summer can kill chive plants.

For bouquets and ornamental gardens: the pink and purple flowers of chives

HARVEST Seeds ripen in mid to late summer. Cut seedheads, dry, and thresh.

SELECTION CHARACTERISTICS
- vigorous growth and frequent harvestability
- minimal or late tendency to flower
- tender or strong hollow leaves
- resistance to disease
- good, spicy aroma, no soapy aftertaste

DISEASES AND PESTS Chives are susceptible to the same diseases and pests as the common onion. The most common disease is rust (*Puccinia allii*), which mainly affects chives and leeks and can cause large reductions in yield. This fungus often shows up in late summer/early autumn in wet years and thrives best in very high humidity and temperatures in the 50–75°F (10–24°C) range. Symptoms: round or elongated orange spots with tears, the entire plant turns a lighter shade of green. Prevention: apply horsetail (*Equisetum arvense*)/clay slurry to plants in high-risk areas.

CULTIVATION HISTORY Chives were domesticated several times in several different places from various wild populations. They were first documented in Europe in Charlemagne's *Capitulare de Villis*. Wild chives retract in summer; they grow in the mountainous areas of North America, Europe, and central and eastern Asia. Alpine chives (*Allium schoenoprasum* ssp. *alpinum*) grows in the marshy meadows, bogs, and moist, steep slopes of the Limestone Alps and can be used just like common chives. Siberian chives, another variety of this species, has hollow, more thick leaves, grows vigorously, and flowers late (and not at all after cutting).

GARLIC CHIVES
Allium tuberosum

Garlic chives is an Asian crop plant that has recently taken European gardens and kitchens by storm. The name comes from the fact that it grows like common chives but tastes more like garlic. Its flat, tough leaves, about 0.25 in. (5 mm) wide and 10–12 in. (25–30 cm) long, can be used to season soups, salad, or meat dishes; their flavor is mild and does not hold as long in the mouth as that of garlic. Garlic chives are thought to have cancer-preventing properties. Flowers and flower buds are delicious when cooked in butter or pickled and make for beautiful plate ornaments.

WHAT YOU'LL NEED
• three to five healthy clumps for vegetative propagation
• 10 clumps to produce seed

POLLINATION NOTES Garlic chives is an outcrosser, like all onion family plants. Its fertile, white, star-shaped flowers are carried in a semi-spherical umbel-like flower head. Different varieties can cross-pollinate each other, though they do not cross with garlic, leeks, or other alliums.

PROPAGATION Garlic chives are perennials. Grow them just like common chives: seed in clusters from early spring to early summer (or as late as late summer) outdoors or in pots. Within three or four months, "bushes" 10–12 in. (25–30 cm) tall will have grown. Rejuvenate every three to four years by digging up clumps, dividing them, and replanting in a new spot. After the second year, garlic chive plants produce fertile, white flowers from midsummer to early autumn. Garlic chives can be grown in locations that are too cold for regular garlic. Plants are hardy

Garlic chives seeds

The flat leaves of garlic chives

to zone 4; they prefer full sun but tolerate some shade and lower average temperatures than garlic.

HARVEST As for onions.

SELECTION CHARACTERISTICS
• vigorous, uniform growth
• for use of flowers: early flowering
• for use of leaves: late flowering

DISEASES AND PESTS Garlic chives are susceptible to the same diseases and pests as onions and garlic. Plants are usually robust and healthy, however.

CULTIVATION HISTORY Garlic chives have been cultivated for thousands of years in their Asian homelands. Originally domesticated in China (around 1000 BC), plants quickly spread to neighboring countries and remain an important crop in China, Japan, Korea, and Vietnam. Wild garlic chives grow at elevations of up to 8200 ft. (2500 m) in Mongolia, Russia, Korea, and in the Himalayas. A great diversity of varieties occur in these countries of origin; companies that specialize in herbs offer additional types with, for example, round leaves or violet flowers.

Poppyseed and relatives

PAPAVERACEAE

The majority of species in the poppy family are herbaceous. Plants are characterized by their milk-like sap, an emulsion of a watery fluid and latex that usually contains toxic alkaloids. Depending upon the species, other substances may also be present, such as morphine in *Papaver somniferum* (the epithet means "sleep-inducing"). Poppy is therefore also a pharmacological and drug plant. Only very few poppies, like the California poppy (*Eschscholzia californica*), have no such sap; the sap of greater celandine or tetterwort (*Chelidonium majus*) is deep orange in color.

Poppy ovaries are superior to the stalk; the fruit usually takes the form of a seed capsule, though horned poppies (*Glaucium* spp.) produce seedpods. Flowers are usually individuals, in rare cases forming flower heads. The seeds of many poppies have a relatively high oil content.

When poppy flowers open, the calyx releases at its base but remains upon the still-enclosed petals like a cap until the pressure becomes too great, at which point it falls off. Poppies grow all over the world, though they prefer the temperate zones of the northern hemisphere and dry, low-nutrient soils.

● ●

OPIUM POPPY
Papaver somniferum

The opium poppy is a beautiful plant with nutritious seeds. Some varieties have especially attractive flowers; others have been bred for seeds with high oil content. Older varieties form capsules with holes in them that allow seeds to sprinkle out like a salt shaker. Most have closed seed capsules and in this way are true cultivated varieties: without the hand of man, such poppies would not be able to reproduce.

Names like gray, brown, blue, or white

Poppyseeds

poppy refer to the color of the seed, as the seed photos show. Gray poppy seeds have a fine, mild flavor. White poppy has a nutty flavor. The blue-gray seeds of blue poppy have a somewhat harsher flavor and more intense aroma.

WHAT YOU'LL NEED
• 10 ft.^{2} (1 m^2) of plants

POLLINATION NOTES Poppy can self- and cross-pollinate. The large flowers open early in the morning and are visited by honeybees, bumblebees, and other insects that practically bathe in them. In this way, cross-pollination can occur.

GROWING FOR SEED Sow seeds as early as possible (early to mid spring). Either plant in 12 in. (30 cm) rows or broadcast. Seed needs one to two weeks to germinate and can do so at 37°F (3°C)—"Poppies need cold feet," they say in South Tyrol, Italy. Starting poppyseeds indoors does not typically work. Plants thrive in cooler regions, like in the Alps, yielding seeds with

Poppyseeds are ripe when they rattle inside the seed capsule.

higher oil content than in warmer regions. Since plants grow slowly at first, it is ideal to plant in soil with a minimal weed seed bank, and the soil must be weeded/harrowed well when plants are young. It is often necessary to thin out plants, as it is easy to oversow its small seeds.

HARVEST Capsules are ready for harvest when the entire plant is brown and seeds rattle in the capsules when shaken. Beware of birds at this point, as they love to snack on ripe poppyseeds, to the point of clearing out small patches entirely by causing capsules to fall to the ground and breaking them open.

SELECTION CHARACTERISTICS Poppy is enjoying a resurgence in popularity in central Europe, with many new field introductions. Possible selection criteria for home gardeners:

- yield (amount of seed per capsule, number of capsules per plant)
- flower color (mark plants with flower of desired color with tape)
- tendency to produce side shoots
- shape and size of capsules
- flavor
- oil content of seeds
- color of seeds

DISEASES AND PESTS The main challenge in growing poppies are weeds, which can crowd out slow-growing young plants. Weed regularly. Downy mildew (*Peronospora* spp.) and parasitic leaf diseases can affect patches that were sown too densely or too late. When seed is sown early enough, plants have been thinned, and weeding is done often enough, these diseases do not cause any major problems. If birds are a problem, try covering the patch in bird netting.

CULTIVATION HISTORY The opium poppy is one of Europe's oldest crop plants, one of the few from the Neolithic period that is not from the Middle East (where it did not arrive until the Bronze Age). It is presumed to have been domesticated in the western Mediterranean region. The oldest finds, from Poland to Germany, Switzerland, northern France, northern Italy, and southern Spain, date from the Stone Age (4600–3800 BC).

Worldwide production of opium poppy has been sharply reduced because of the possibility of producing the drug opium from some varieties.

Poppy in the kitchen

Traditional poppy-growing areas in Europe each have their own specialty fare. In South Tyrol, Italy, it is *Mohnkrapfen* (poppy crullers), which are baked for festivals. In the Waldviertel region of Austria, where gray poppies are the most common varieties grown, *Mohnzelten* (poppy "tents") are the traditional festival food. Poppyseed is prepared in the same basic manner in all regions: it is not ground but rather mashed, which makes it into a coarse, succulent meal.

Purslane and relatives

PORTULACACEAE

The most important cultivated plants of this family are purslane (*Portulaca oleracea*), also known as pigweed, and miner's lettuce (*Claytonia perfoliata*), also known as winter purslane or Indian lettuce.

● ●

PURSLANE
Portulaca oleracea

WHAT YOU'LL NEED
• 15 to 20 healthy, well-formed plants

POLLINATION NOTES Purslane is a cleistogamous self-pollinator, meaning pollination takes place in the bud before the flower opens. The corona of the flower is often not developed. Though it is sometimes reported in green strains, there is no real danger of cross-pollination between multiple varieties.

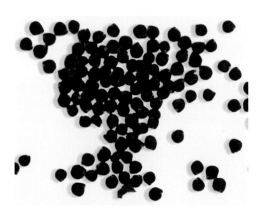

Purslane seeds

GROWING FOR SEED Sow purslane for seed in late spring, after the last frost; however, seeds can be sown until midautumn, with many gardeners sowing over and over again during this stretch for a nonstop supply of purslane for the table. Sow directly outdoors in rows or broadcast. Seeds germinate better with light, so cover only lightly with soil. Thin to one plant every 6–8 in. (15–20 cm). Leaves can be harvested three to four weeks after sowing, and plants can be harvested two or three times.

HARVEST The shiny, black seeds fall easily from seed capsules that have turned brown. Place a paper bag underneath the stalks, and tap or strip seeds into the bag. Seeds ripen over the course of two to three weeks, so harvest regularly during this period.

SELECTION CHARACTERISTICS There are no true varieties, only different strains named for their appearance—'Grüner' (green), 'Gelber Breitblättriger' (yellow wide-leaved), etc. Yellow-leaved purslanes are softer but also likelier to rot. They have a delicate flavor, whereas green varieties often taste much better, with a strong, intense flavor.

DISEASES AND PESTS Arche Noah has yet to observe any problems with diseases or pests.

CULTIVATION HISTORY Wild purslane, native to Europe, is a weed in gardens in warm regions. The cultivated form (ssp. *sativa*) differs from the species in that it grows upright rather than staying close to the ground. Its egg-shaped, fleshy leaves, along with its practically invisible flowers, are eaten raw or lightly steamed. The slightly sour flavor comes from omega-3-hepta-linoleic acid. The plant has also been described as a medicinal, with supposed anticarcinogenic, antibacterial, and antiviral effects.

MINER'S LETTUCE
Claytonia perfoliata

The wild version of miner's lettuce is found along the North American Pacific coast from Mexico to southern Canada. Miner's lettuce is grown for seed just like purslane; it is an annual plant and a strict self-pollinator. The only difference is that it is sown in mid to late summer (early autumn to midwinter in an unheated greenhouse). When growing in the summer, miner's lettuce needs shade. The ideal temperature for germination

Common purslane has thick, succulent leaves.

is 54°F (12°C), but it then grows best at 40–46°F (4–8°C). Like purslane, there are no bred varieties but rather strains. Sow in autumn when growing for seed. Flower stalks start to grow in early to mid spring. Miner's lettuce is very hardy, taking temperatures as low as −4°F (−20°C) when covered in snow. The seed harvest can be challenging because green seeds often fall out before ripening, and within a few days the entire seed yield can be gone. For this reason, cut plants at soil level when the first seeds ripen. Hang plants upside down to dry. Later, tap out seeds and winnow them with sieves. Home gardeners may find it convenient that seeds fall out on their own. Self-sown volunteer plants can then be harvested in late summer.

Miner's lettuce seeds

Miner's lettuce, also known as winter purslane or Indian lettuce

Rhubarb and relatives

POLYGONACEAE

More than 800 species are members of the knotweed family. The common family name comes from the segmented structure of their stalks with their knot-like bulges.

Two genera in this family include plants that are grown as vegetables: dock and sorrel (*Rumex*) and rhubarb (*Rheum*). The pseudocereal buckwheat is also a member of this family, as are several ornamental plants like silver lace vine (*Fallopia aubertii*). Several other knotweeds, although both edible and even ornamental, are considered noxious weeds (e.g., Japanese knotweed, *Reynoutria japonica*).

● ●

BOTANICAL CHARACTERISTICS Knotweed family plants are monoecious, and their flowers are either perfect or single-gendered. The flowers are for the most part small and sit individually on stalks.

Overview of the knotweed family

COMMON NAME	GENUS	SPECIES
buckwheat	*Fagopyrum*	*esculentum*
rhubarb	*Rheum*	*rhabarbarum, rhaponticum*
dock, sorrel	*Rumex*	spp.

BUCKWHEAT
Fagopyrum esculentum

Buckwheat has long figured in Alpine mountain farming, usually grown as a second crop after the grain harvest in early summer. In eastern Austria, buckwheat was grown as the primary crop, traditionally used for food and for fodder. In recent decades, buckwheat has been grown significantly less, though it is still popular among organic farmers and home gardeners as a green manure plant or as bee forage. Buckwheat seeds can be used just like cereal grains and are gluten-free.

Tartary buckwheat (*Fagopyrum tataricum*) was once grown for flour and livestock feed. It has all but disappeared in the intensive agriculture of western Europe but is often found in plots of local buckwheat varieties. It is a selfer with greenish white flowers that are of no interest, even to bees.

WHAT YOU'LL NEED
• 10–20 ft.² (1–2 m²) of plants or a buckwheat field

POLLINATION NOTES Buckwheat is an insect-pollinated outcrosser; its flowers are white to pinkish red. Mild weather is important for good pollination. Wind, rain, and drought can also affect pollination negatively; expect reduced yields in such conditions.

GROWING FOR SEED Broadcast or sow in rows, on poor soils, in late spring or midsummer (or whenever seed is traditionally sown in your area). Seeding rate: 20–25 seeds/ft.² (200–250 seeds/m²). Buckwheat can be sown in midsummer because it requires only three to four months to produce ripe seed; it will even germinate in relatively dry soil. On the other hand, buckwheat does not handle the intense heat of the summer well; temperatures above 77°F (25°C) can reduce seed yields by up to 40%. Buckwheat flowers about five weeks after germinating and is in bloom for about six weeks, with most seeds forming in the first two to three weeks. Summer sowings must allow time for seeds to ripen before the first autumn frosts, as buckwheat is not hardy.

HARVEST Timing the harvest can be difficult, as seeds ripen over a long period. The ideal time is when the lower leaves have fallen off and around three-quarters of the seeds have hardened and reached their final color. Harvest early, before the morning dew has evaporated, to help prevent seed from dropping to the ground. Cut entire plants and thresh and winnow right away, waiting until you have just seed to dry. Buckwheat seed can be silvery gray, brown, or black.

Common buckwheat seeds

Tartary buckwheat seeds

SELECTION CHARACTERISTICS

- yield
- seed size
- stability
- synchronous ripening
- drought tolerance

DISEASES AND PESTS Buckwheat is not particularly susceptible to disease and is even grown conventionally without plant-protection measures.

CULTIVATION HISTORY Buckwheat comes from southwest China, where it gradually spread from the Himalayas. In Bhutan and Nepal, buckwheat is, along with the potato and barley, one of the most widely grown field crops. It can even be grown at 10,000 ft. (3000 m). Many authors presume that buckwheat was brought to eastern Europe with the Mongols in the 13th century. By the 16th century, buckwheat had reached areas of Switzerland north of the Alps.

Because famines occurred time and again in Europe, the short-seasoned, easily cultivated buckwheat was eagerly welcomed there. It was cultivated in depleted soils instead of grain and also in sandy or even acidic bogs. It also did well in the silicate soils of the valleys of eastern and southern Switzerland. Buckwheat reached its peak cultivation in the 17th and 18th centuries, after which the potato slowly pushed it into the background. In Slovenia, however, cultivation, breeding, and research on buckwheat are still important industries. Since many secondary plant compounds can be extracted from the leaves and seeds of buckwheat, the international pharmaceutical industry has recently taken notice of the plant as well. Rutin, the most important of these phytochemicals, is being used to treat venous diseases.

Buckwheat plants can carry seeds and flowers simultaneously.

RHUBARB
Rheum spp.

The genus *Rheum* contains 50 or so species, two of which are grown as vegetables: garden rhubarb (*R. rhabarbarum*) and so-called false rhubarb (*R. rhaponticum*). Rhubarb is an herbaceous perennial that already has a permanent place somewhere on the border of many home gardens. Leaf stalks are harvested every spring for the table; to ensure their robust growth, remove flower stalks (unless you are growing for seed). A bonus: the large,

All knotweed family plants develop similar fruits. Seen here are rhubarb seed stalks.

still-closed flower buds of rhubarb can be steamed and eaten like broccoli (they are very sour and take some getting used to!). Rhubarb contains oxalic acid, the level of which increases as the season progresses; this has led to the tradition in Europe of ceasing to harvest rhubarb after St. John's Eve (23 June), which also helps the plant recover for the following year. Plants wilt in late summer and overwinter with underground buds.

WHAT YOU'LL NEED
• three or four healthy plants
• cool, damp site

POLLINATION NOTES Rhubarb is an outcrosser that is pollinated by wind and insects. Its perfect flowers are inconspicuous. If you have more than one variety in your garden and you wish to produce seed, allow only one variety to flower per year. *Rheum rhabarbarum* and *R. rhaponticum* can cross-pollinate each other, despite being distinct species.

PROPAGATION Varieties are easily maintained by propagating them vegetatively, which is the way rhubarb is usually propagated. Plants require nutrient-rich soil and high humidity; they thrive in half shade and do not like full sun. Rhubarb plants should be regenerated every eight to 12 years. Rhubarb often thrives in a greenhouse. In autumn, plants can either be separated and replanted, or three to four rhizomes can be taken from a two- to three-year-old mother plant. These rhizomes can be further divided, such that each part has at least one bud; then the leaves are removed, and each division is potted. After about six weeks, these new plants can be planted out. Rhubarb can be planted anytime from spring to autumn.

Propagating by seed is also possible, though we recommend this only for those who enjoy experimenting, as traits tend to compartmentalize themselves in individual offspring. Seedlings tend to be very heterogeneous and can be harvested in the second year at the earliest, but it is better to wait until the third year.

HARVEST Harvest seeds as soon as they turn brownish. Dry seeds on the seedhead, thresh or pluck off seeds, winnow with a sieve and in the wind.

SELECTION CHARACTERISTICS Individual varieties are distinguished by the inner (some are blood-red) and outer color of their leaf stalks, the thickness and length of leaf stalks, and earliness. Other selection criteria:

• late flowering
• speed of secondary growth

DISEASES AND PESTS Diseases are rarely a problem with rhubarb, though plants can

A frog's-eye view of a rhubarb plant (late spring)

be affected by some viruses and downy mildew (*Peronospora jaapiana*). Turnip mosaic virus can also affect rhubarb and is a concern for commercial rhubarb producers. Symptoms: lightly colored mosaic or bulges on young leaves, eventually leading to intense yellow discoloration. Treatment: remove affected plants (viruses cannot be cured). Downy mildew does not cause major problems. Dock rusts (*Puccinia phragmitis*) may appear occasionally in gardens sited near reeds. Symptoms: round, red-outlined leaf spots, white patches of spores on leaf undersides.

CULTIVATION HISTORY The epithet *rhabarbarum* comes from the Greek *rha* (name of the river Volga) and *barbaron* ("foreign"), literally "of the foreign Volga region." This is a puzzling name, as no *Rheum* species grows there: all are from Asia, with many coming from the mountains around the China-Tibet border, in the tall forb layer near the tree line. The first species to reach Europe was Turkey rhubarb (*R. palmatum*), which was used in traditional Chinese medicine as a purgative and is now often grown as an ornamental. Garden rhubarb was unknown in Europe until the 18th century.

DOCK, SORREL

Rumex spp.

Docks and sorrels come in various shapes, sizes, flavors, and harvest seasons. Although many are old crop plants (or plants long gathered from the wild), all *Rumex* species should be eaten in moderation due to their high oxalic acid content. Docks are an early fresh perennial vegetable; they can be harvested in early to mid spring, long before the first lettuce. To harvest greens throughout the year, cut plants back to their last few leaves, three to four times per year. French sorrel (*R. scutatus*), with a fine acidic flavor and small arrow-shaped leaves, can be harvested from early spring to late autumn. Patience dock (*R. patientia*) produces large, non-sour leaves, though only in spring; it can only be eaten cooked and makes for a good soup. Wrinkled dock (*R. rugosus*) is a cultivated form of sorrel

Dock seeds

with an acidic taste. Common or garden sorrel (*R. acetosa*) can be found wild and harvested as such, or grown in the garden. Three other species native to Europe that can be found wild or cultivated in the garden are sheep's sorrel (*R. acetosella*), wood dock (*R. sanguineus*), and Alpine dock (*R. alpinus*). Sheep's sorrel is more tender than wrinkled dock. Wood dock has beautiful blood-red veined leaves and is not sour, as dock often is. Many *Rumex* species' roots can be used as a natural dye.

WHAT YOU'LL NEED
• five to 10 healthy plants

POLLINATION NOTES All *Rumex* species are outcrossers, pollinated either by wind or by insects. Wild varieties can cross with cultivated varieties, though only with those of the same species. Docks and sorrels blossom from late spring to midsummer, with pink/white flowers affixed to reddish stalks.

PROPAGATION All species are perennial and can be propagated vegetatively in spring or autumn. Seed in rows or in clusters in late summer or early to mid spring. Seeds prefer exposure to light, so cover only lightly with soil when sowing seed. *Rumex* species are highly variable in size, and planting distances will therefore depend upon the species; smaller species like French sorrel, wood dock, wrinkled dock, and sheep's sorrel can be planted or thinned to 6 by 10 in. (15 by 25 cm), with patience dock being sown in 10–15 in. (25–40 cm) rows. All prefer wet sites and love regular watering. Leaves stay tender

Dock leaves ready for harvesting

Ripening sorrel seeds

longer and also become sourer in half shade. Transplant after three years growing in the same spot.

HARVEST Dock and sorrel seeds ripen in practically every climate. Remove seedheads by cutting (this must be done in a timely fashion to avoid seeds falling on the ground) and hang to dry. Seeds are easily plucked or threshed out and winnowed with a sieve and the wind. Since seeds are hygroscopic (they attract moisture), dry them well (silica gel may be necessary) and store them in a well-sealed container, or sow them the same year.

SELECTION CHARACTERISTICS Of all the *Rumex* species, only wrinkled dock has distinct varieties, which are often named for the place the seed was acquired ('Grossblättriger von Belleville' [large-leafed from Belleville] or 'Goldgelber von Lyon' [golden yellow from Lyon]). For all *Rumex* species, leaf size may vary by source location of seed. For French sorrel, the most important selection criterion is leaf size. Possible selection criteria for all other species:

• softness and tenderness of the leaves
• fast and early growth
• vigorous secondary growth after cutting
• late flowering

DISEASES AND PESTS A common fungal disease is leaf spot (*Cercospora* spp.). Symptoms: round spots, first grayish brown, then brown/black. Treatment: harvest no seed from and remove afflicted plants, as the disease is seed-borne.

Various aphids affect dock and sorrel, as does the green dock beetle (*Gastroidea viridula*), a small, green-gold beetle whose larvae can cause significant damage. The beetles can only fly over short distances, so infestations do not spread quickly, but they can quickly and massively reproduce themselves in a small area. Treatment: collect beetles, spray with a neem oil biopesticide.

CULTIVATION HISTORY Alpine dock grows in the very fertile soils around Alpine cottages and around manure left behind by cows in pastures. Alpine farmers and shepherds have fermented its leaves to make a sauerkraut-like product or cooked it like spinach. Leaf stems can be used like rhubarb. In Switzerland, cooked leaves are mixed in with bread dough, and dried or fermented leaves are fed to pigs. Livestock avoid the leaves while still on the plant. Indeed, all dock and sorrel species native to Europe have found use in the kitchen and were sometimes grown and bred in the garden. Michael Machatschek (1999) has documented the various uses in detail.

Spinach and relatives
CHENOPODIACEAE

Many species of the Chenopodiaceae populate the salty, nitrogenous soils of beaches. Goosefoot, the family common name, is a reference to their typical leaf shape, the silhouette of which brings to mind the webbed feet of geese.

Many chenopods have a characteristic purplish red coloring: red beets, the blazing red leaf stalks of some Swiss chard varieties ('Ruby Red'), or the red leaves of red orache. Few vegetables outside of the goosefoot family have this deep purple color (rhubarb of the knotweed family and a few amaranths), making chenopods relatively easy to identify. Another secondary metabolite that many chenopods produce is somewhat less desirable: oxalic acid. Oxalic acid binds with calcium and magnesium, and overconsumption can "steal" calcium from the bones. Calcium oxalates, which are thereby produced, are tiny, pointy crystals that can lead to kidney stones in higher concentrations. Many goosefoot family vegetables tend to accumulate nitrate salts. Harvest these plants in the afternoon on sunny days (especially where soils are highly fertile) for vegetables with lower nitrate concentrations.

● ●

GENERAL PROPAGATION CHARACTERISTICS
All chenopods are wind-pollinated, as their small, inconspicuous flowers would indicate (that is, they have no need to attract insects). It is rare that insects play any significant role in pollination. Some family members (spinach, orache, quinoa) flower in the first year; others, not until the second (beets, Swiss chard, good King Henry). Multiple varieties of one species must be either mechanically isolated with row cover or spatially separated with sufficient isolation distances. In home plots, where buildings, hedges, and other plants

A chenopod in flower

An eye-catching chenopod: tree spinach, *Chenopodium giganteum*

The purplish red typical of many chenopods. This is a stalk of tree spinach, *Chenopodium giganteum*.

hinder the movement of pollen in the air, 300–1000 ft. (100–300 m) should suffice, depending upon the species. For large-scale growing of seed in fields, isolation distances of over 4 miles (7 km) are used.

Overview of the goosefoot family

COMMON NAME	GENUS	SPECIES
spinach	*Spinacia*	*oleracea*
beets	*Beta*	*vulgaris* ssp. *vulgaris* convar. *vulgaris* var. *vulgaris*
spinach beet	*Beta*	*vulgaris* ssp. *vulgaris* convar. *cicla* var. *cicla*
Swiss chard	*Beta*	*vulgaris* ssp. *vulgaris* convar. *cicla* var. *flavescens*
orache	*Atriplex*	*hortensis*
good King Henry	*Chenopodium*	*bonus-henricus*
quinoa	*Chenopodium*	*quinoa*
strawberry spinach	*Chenopodium*	*foliosum*

SPINACH
Spinacia oleracea

Spinach is a popular leaf vegetable and an excellent green manure plant. It produces leaves prolifically in cool, moist weather, but as days get longer and hotter, plants quickly bolt. (Try growing heat-tolerant New Zealand spinach or orache in high summer to harvest spinach-like leaves throughout the growing season.) The high iron content of spinach is, by the way, a myth! Apparently, a typographical error in an early analysis of its nutritional value increased the iron content tenfold. It does, however, contain a considerable amount of oxalic acid, which binds with calcium, which is needed for bone growth; so, kids that don't like spinach should not be swayed by any parent or educator touting its health benefits.

WHAT YOU'LL NEED
- 25 to 30 plants
- trellis
- gloves for sharp-seeded varieties

POLLINATION NOTES Spinach is a wind-pollinated outcrosser. It is also dioecious, meaning that each plant is either male or female; because both sexes are necessary for fertilization and seed is harvested only from female plants, it is especially important to have enough plants. Male plants can be recognized by the fact that they blossom just before female plants do; their conspicuous stamens distribute pollen over the course of two to three weeks. Female plants bloom inconspicuously, with small yellow-green flowers in the leaf axils. The occasional plant may have perfect flowers; the latest breeds all do, which allows for a more regular harvest.

Spinach seeds

Different varieties can be isolated by time (see next paragraph), space (at least 650 ft. [200 m] from the next flowering variety), or mechanically, with row covers.

GROWING FOR SEED Spinach is an annual. Plant spinach in late summer or early spring. In zones 6 and above, late summer plantings will overwinter outdoors and bloom in midspring, for a seed harvest in late spring. Spinach sown in midspring will blossom in early summer and produce seed in midsummer. With a delayed second sowing in the spring, two varieties can be grown for seed in one season. Some varieties are not quite hardy enough for zone 6 and can be grown only in late summer in zones 7 and above.

Spinach is a long-day plant, the critical day length being between 10 and 14 hours. As the days grow longer, spinach is increasingly likely to bolt. Different varieties are more or less bolt resistant. Male plants are less useful to vegetable growers, as they bolt earlier than female plants and therefore produce fewer spinach leaves for harvest. Keep the harvesting of leaves from plants selected for seed production to a minimum.

HARVEST Remove male plants, which die before the seeds of female plants are ripe. Wait until all seeds are ripe before beginning with the harvest. Cut seedheads, briefly allow them to dry completely, then thresh and clean with a sieve. Wet fruits are tough and do not thresh well. Most varieties from recent breeding are derived from var. *inermis* and have round seeds. Many older breeds are of var. *oleracea* and have pointy seeds that are unpleasant to handle during harvest and cleaning. Gloves can be of help.

SELECTION CHARACTERISTICS
- true-to-type leaf form and size
- robust development of leaf rosette
- winter spinach: winter hardiness
- spring spinach: earliness
- resistance to downy mildew
- bolt resistance

DISEASES AND PESTS The most common disease of spinach is downy mildew (fungus: *Peronospora farinosa* ssp. *spinaciae*). It typically appears with wet weather or in greenhouses. Overwintering plants are at highest risk. This fungus affects only spinach. Symptoms: lightly colored bulges on top side of leaf, gray/violet patches of fungal growth on bottom of leaf. This disease is not seed-borne. Remedies: crop rotation (waiting at least three years to grow spinach in the same spot again), sufficient plant separation, removal of diseased plants, and proper composting.

CULTIVATION HISTORY The wild ancestor of cultivated spinach is unknown. It was presumably domesticated in Iran and spread through Asia via India. In the 12th century, Arabs brought spinach to Spain, where it then spread to other countries. It was first documented in central Europe

Spinach is dioecious, and the male flowers bloom just before the female flowers do. Female flowers are found in the leaf axils (right).

by Albertus Magnus but was not widely grown there until the end of the Middle Ages. Since it could be grown in a wide variety of soils, had high yields, and delicious leaves that grew rapidly, spinach has been historically more popular than sorrel, orache, good King Henry, Swiss chard, and other leaf vegetables; indeed, it has become the favored leaf vegetable in many areas.

BEETS

Beta vulgaris ssp. *vulgaris* convar. *vulgaris* var. *vulgaris*

The species *Beta vulgaris* is another fascinating example of the diversity that people have teased out of one original form. Not only beets but also Swiss chard, mangelwurzel, and sugar beet (which is itself a cross of mangelwurzel and the white Silesian fodder beet) are all derived from it. People found different parts of the plant useful and bred for improvement in those parts. Fodder and sugar beets are propagated in the same way as common beets.

Beet seeds

WHAT YOU'LL NEED
• 10 healthy plants
• overwintering strategy
• four stakes and string
• row cover for isolation in second year

POLLINATION NOTES All plants of the genus *Beta* flower inconspicuously and over a long period; their fine-grained pollen can be carried by the wind for miles. Beets (and Swiss chard) are wind-pollinated outcrossers, and beets will cross with Swiss chard, mangelwurzel, and sugar beet. Plants grown for seed must be isolated, either mechanically (with row cover or isolation cage) or spatially: at least 1000 ft. (300 m) for diverse home gardens, over 4 miles (7 km) for commercial production.

GROWING FOR SEED Wait until at least early summer to sow beets to grow for seed; this produces beets of sufficient size for selection in autumn and yet helps minimize their size for storage. Early sowing can also lead to bolting in storage. So that individual beets can develop well, take special care with planting distances; this is also important when replanting the following spring. Direct-sown seed must be thinned, as more than one plant can come out of each pellet. Plants that bolt the first year and those whose form is not true-to-type (leaf shape, leaf color, etc.) should be removed.

Select at least 10 plants for seed production in autumn. This will yield far more seed than is needed in the average home garden, but it is important to maintain genetic diversity. Store selected plants, ideally in a root cellar at 33–40°F (0–5°C) in total darkness.

Select plants again (for storage life and health) when planting out in the spring. Plant out second-year beets in the spring on an overcast day up to the base of the leaves. Water well. Wait until the risk of a killing frost has past before planting out in the spring.

Beets can be overwintered outdoors in zones 8 and above. In this case, sow in mid to late summer. Plants can be selected in the spring before they bolt.

HARVEST Ripe seed pellets typically contain two to five seeds. Ripe seeds, that is, the brown pellets the seeds are contained in, do not fall easily from the plant, so they can and should remain there until fully ripe. Place entire plants in a warm place with good air circulation to dry completely, then thresh in a bag and winnow with a sieve. Seeds remain in the pellets.

SELECTION CHARACTERISTICS Like all chenopods, beets tend to accumulate nitrate salts. Varieties with a minimal tendency to accumulate nitrates are a focus of organic breeding.

Varieties differ from each other primarily in size, shape, and color of root and leaves. There are varieties with light to dark red roots but also varieties with yellow or white or white-and-red striped roots. Uniformity of color is what is typically sought. Lighter colored varieties are particularly good for pickling with other

Beet seed stalks in the foreground, beet leaves in the background

vegetables, as these beets will not stain them like red beets would. Beets with spherical roots grow faster than those with long, cylindrical roots. Potential selection criteria:

- whole plant: true-to-type (as much as possible, remove non-true-to-type and diseased plants during the first year)
- health of stored beets: do not propagate plants afflicted with cercospora (seed-borne), look for resistance to powdery and downy mildew
- leaf: good foliation, dense nodality
- external traits of the root: size, firmness, shape, smoothness, lack of side roots
- internal traits of the root: best determined by taking a core sample (up to 0.25 in. [5 mm] in diameter). Otherwise cut out small pieces of the root with a knife. Disinfect wounds on the beet with wood ash or animal charcoal and allow to dry. Select for: color, uniformity of color or clear zoning of color, taste, storage life.

DISEASES AND PESTS In areas where beets have been grown historically, a multitude of diseases can present problems. Your local agricultural extension office or gardening association may be able to tell you which diseases are the most common or present the biggest challenges. Away from large-scale beet growing areas, disease pressure is much lower. Leaf spot disease of beets and chard (fungus: *Cercospora beticola*) is seed-borne or transmitted from afflicted plants. It appears in beet-growing areas in warm, dry summers. Symptoms: round, gray/brown spots with reddish border. The spots are spread irregularly on the leaves and can kill them. Remedy: crop rotation (growing chenopods not more than once every four years).

Different species of downy mildew (fungus: *Peronospora farinosa* f. sp. *betae* and f. sp. *spinacea*) can afflict beets and chard during cold, wet periods. Symptoms: carpet of spores on leaf bottoms, heart leaves curl up. Remedies: avoid growing in moist areas or near fodder and sugar beet fields,

Various shapes of beet roots

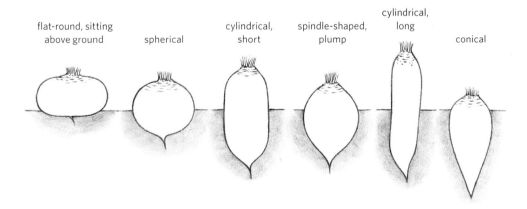

flat-round, sitting above ground

spherical

cylindrical, short

spindle-shaped, plump

cylindrical, long

conical

increase plant spacing, raised beds, preventive spray of horsetail compost tea.

The silvering disease of red beet (bacteria: *Corynebacterium betae*) can affect beets going to seed. This is a seed-borne disease. Symptoms: silvery, shiny leaf parts. Remedy: remove infected plants.

Beet mosaic virus is not seed-borne but rather is transmitted by aphids. Symptoms: leaves (especially the inner, not yet fully developed leaves) are checked in a mosaic pattern, older leaves wilt and die early. Infections often do not affect yield. Remedies: carefully battle aphids, do not plant out near overwintering spinach. Root rot (fungus: *Phoma betae*) is another beet disease. This fungus causes spots on all parts of the plant and can be a problem in storage. It overwinters on dead plant debris and in the soil.

Aphids can thrive on plants being isolated under row cover. Check beets under row cover regularly and react quickly with beneficial insects or a soft soap spray.

CULTIVATION HISTORY Wild beets (*Beta vulgaris* ssp. *maritima*) can be found from the Mediterranean coast to the Atlantic coast of Europe. The wild beet is a perennial beach-loving plant with branched shoots. Presumably uses were found for wild beets and thus began its domestication. Romans brought these plants from the Mediterranean region and into the cooler north, where Germanic peoples and Celts were growing turnips. The words "beta" and "cicla" can be found in literature dating back to the Middle Ages. It has not been possible to clearly differentiate between these two forms, however.

Crescentius noted the beet as a typical garden plant in 13th-century Bologna, Italy. Since the 16th and 17th centuries, the beet has only grown in importance.

SWISS CHARD, SPINACH BEET
Beta vulgaris ssp. *vulgaris* convar. *cicla*

There are two different groups of cultivars: Swiss chard (var. *cicla*) and spinach beets (var. *flavescens*). Swiss chard develops large, shiny or crimped leaves; spinach beet develops ribbed stalks up to 4 in. (10 cm) wide. Practical differentiation between the two is more a matter of use, as the stalks of Swiss chard can be eaten just like the leaves of spinach beet can be eaten. And, of course, there are in-between forms. Many varieties of chard were developed in Switzerland, hence the English common name Swiss chard. Leaf stalks can come in any number of colors and combinations thereof. 'Ruby Red' Swiss chard has deep red stalks, 'Fordhook Giant' has almost silvery stalks, and 'Five Color Silverbeet' is a colorful mix. Such beautiful selections can also serve as ornamentals.

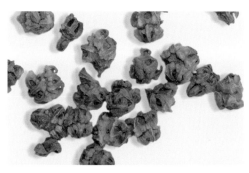

Swiss chard seeds

WHAT YOU'LL NEED
- 10 healthy plants
- overwintering strategy
- four stakes and string
- row cover

POLLINATION NOTES As for beets.

GROWING FOR SEED Swiss chard and spinach beets are grown for seed just as they are grown for food. Dig up plants as late as possible (late autumn/early winter, depending upon climate—in any case, before a killing frost). Place in a container with, for example, coco-peat or wood shavings (medium should be moist but not wet), and place in a root cellar. Cut off leaves, taking care not to damage root and to leave leaves emerging from the heart of the crown intact. Continually observe

One recognizes by the flowers and seeds that beets and Swiss chard are of the same species.

The fire-red stalks of spinach beet 'Roter Vulkan' (red volcano)

plants in storage throughout the winter to make sure mold and rot do not get out of control. If plants start to bolt before the ground is clear of snow, plant them in pots and wait for an overcast day after the ground clears to plant them out. Water well when planting.

Red, orange, pink, and yellow varieties of Swiss chard are not as winter hardy as those with green and white stalks, the latter in some cases overwintering in zone 5. Swiss chard is otherwise considered to be hardy to zone 6, where it can be overwintered outdoors.

HARVEST As for beets.

SELECTION CHARACTERISTICS
- Swiss chard: shape and size of leaves, consistent leaf color (light green, yellow-green, green, dark green, silver-green, orange, red, purple, violet), crimped or shiny-smooth leaf surface
- spinach beet: length and thickness of stalk; the development of large, tender individual stalks or of a compact plant that is harvested all at once; stalk color (white, silvery white, yellow, orange, red, purple)
- do not harvest seed from plants with cercospora leaf spot disease
- do not harvest seed from plants that bolt in the first year (Swiss chard and red spinach beets especially tend to bolt as the weather gets colder in autumn)

DISEASES AND PESTS As for beets.

CULTIVATION HISTORY Chard is a very old crop plant that has been grown since at least the second century BC, presumably domesticated around the Mediterranean. It made its way to Syria and Babylonia, where it was known as *silq*. It was also grown by the Greeks and Romans and, as the Roman Empire expanded north, came to central Europe, where it was a popular garden plant up through the 16th century. Colorful varieties were described in ornamental plant literature until around 1930, but since then the ornamental qualities of Swiss chard and spinach beets have been all but forgotten. They remain popular vegetables in Italy and the Balkans.

ORACHE
Atriplex hortensis

This is an old European plant whose smoother, milder-tasting leaves are usually eaten like spinach. Orache comes in yellow (var. *lutea*), green (var. *hortensis*), and red (var. *rubra*). In general, green oraches have more succulent leaves, and red and yellow oraches are more interesting for culinary purposes, adding color to entrees, salads, and the like. Younger leaves can be eaten raw. Orache is easy to cultivate at home, quickly developing a huge mass of leaves, but it is hardly found at market, for its leaves wilt and become unsightly just as swiftly.

WHAT YOU'LL NEED
- five to 10 plants
- stakes and string or a trellis

POLLINATION NOTES Orache is a wind-pollinated outcrosser. When multiple varieties are grown near each other, see to it that they do not flower at the same time; red, yellow, and green varieties can cross with one another and lose their true-to-type color. It is possible to isolate mechanically with row cover, but it is more difficult with orache because flowering stems can be over 6 ft. (2 m) tall. Isolation distance: at least 300 ft. (100 m).

GROWING FOR SEED The first seeding should be done as early as possible, as soon as the ground has cleared of snow (late winter to early spring). Seed can be broadcast or sown in rows. When a plant is cut in early summer above the lowest leaf axil, it enters a second phase of vegetative growth, and a second leaf harvest is possible about four weeks later. To have fresh leaves all season long, sow more seed every month until late summer.

Orache prefers full sun but can tolerate half shade and can be sown along the edges of beds to provide shade or as an in-between crop. When growing for seed, thin to 8 in. (20 cm) within the row, 10 in. (25 cm) between rows. Do not harvest leaves from plants selected for seed production. Leaves become bitter as soon as the plant flowers.

Self-sowing makes for easy gardening: seeds quickly distribute themselves in the garden and the plants that spring from them can be left where there is space. Seedlings of red varieties are easy to identify, though the trained eye can also differentiate green and yellow varieties from the many related weed species (such as lamb's quarters). Plants that grow from self-seeding are often the prettiest and most vigorous. Orache can turn into a weed in the garden; whether this is

Orache seeds

The translucent fruits of garden orache reveal their hidden treasure in sunlight.

A leaf of red orache

welcome or annoying depends on the individual gardener.

HARVEST The first seeds typically ripen in midsummer. As soon as the membranes, which surround individual seeds, are dry, quickly harvest seed stalks to avoid losing seed. Allow seeds to dry completely, then thresh in a bag and winnow with a sieve. Leave the membranes intact, as their removal negatively affects germination rates.

SELECTION CHARACTERISTICS
- leaf: size, juiciness, crispiness, true-to-type color (some red varieties tend to become more green in time)
- plant: vigorous secondary growth

DISEASES AND PESTS Although the diseases affecting spinach can theoretically affect orache, this hardly ever happens. The black bean aphid (*Aphis fabae*) can, however, sharply reduce seed yields. Remedies: spray aphids with cold water, remove affected shoots.

CULTIVATION HISTORY Orache cultivation is documented in ancient Greece by Theophrast (3rd century BC) and in ancient Rome by Palladius (5th century AD). The Romans brought orache to central Europe, where it was widely grown; it is mentioned in the *Capitulare de Villis* (9th century) as well as in the writings of St. Hildegard of Bingen (11th century). It is, however, seldom mentioned in vegetable books of the 16th and 17th centuries, likely due to the increasing diversity of leafy vegetables around this time, which perhaps pushed orache into the background.

GOOD KING HENRY
Chenopodium bonus-henricus

Good King Henry is yet another leafy vegetable that was pushed aside when spinach was introduced to the gardens of central Europe in the Middle Ages. But it remained at other locations: it is an old "village plant" that follows in the footsteps of people. It self-sows and loves nitrogen-rich soils, which it finds along paths all the way up into the doorsteps of Alpine dairies and cottages. Young leaves, which have a flour-like powder on their undersides, make for a tasty, spinach-like vegetable with a vitamin C content comparable to peppers and parsley. Other uses are not as well known: the young shoots of early spring can be prepared and eaten like asparagus; young, unripe flower heads can be used like cauliflower.

Good King Henry seeds

WHAT YOU'LL NEED
• five to 10 healthy plants

POLLINATION NOTES Good King Henry is a wind-pollinated outcrosser. Its inconspicuous flowers develop into a branched flower cluster, or panicle.

GROWING FOR SEED An herbaceous perennial, good King Henry is hardy to zone 3 and produces seed after the second year. Seed can be direct sown early in the growing season (mid to late spring) or late (late summer to early autumn). Autumn plantings germinate at a reliably higher rate. Thin plots that are too dense. In humid areas, such as in the Alps, it can grow to 28 in. (70 cm) tall, though in drier climates it likely will not grow past 16 in. (40 cm). It can also be propagated vegetatively with cuttings.

HARVEST Good King Henry seed is harvested just like corn salad. Dry harvested seeds thoroughly.

SELECTION CHARACTERISTICS To date, little breeding work has been done on good King Henry, and there are no known true varieties. Potential selection criteria:

• vigorous growth
• mild flavor
• earliness, to fill the early-season fresh produce gap

DISEASES AND PESTS Good King Henry is a robust plant; no diseases or pests have affected our plots at Arche Noah.

Good King Henry blossoms in some areas in mid to late spring.

In central Europe, Alpine herders who like to have good King Henry growing at their doorstep are the only ones who need to pay special attention to their plots to make sure they are not eaten away by stray goats or sheep. Root voles also like good King Henry.

CULTIVATION HISTORY Good King Henry is thought to have originated in the eastern Mediterranean region; wild plants that grew near settlements were first gathered and then cultivated. It has a long history as a medicinal plant, being used as a dressing for swelling and open wounds or as a salve for infections; and before spinach showed up, it was one of the most popular leafy vegetables in Europe, remaining in high demand in English markets until the turn of the 20th century. Today good King Henry is seldom grown in home gardens or found in markets.

How good King Henry got its name

Its common name shows that the plant has long been held in high regard. According to linguist Jakob Grimm, Henry (German: Heinrich) comes from the Germanic *haganrich* (literally, "king of the hedge"), which in turn is a name for a gremlin with goose's feet (definitely a member of this family!) who helps out around the house and puts things where they belong. Its counterpart is Böser Heinrich (Bad Henry), or dog's mercury, which is highly poisonous (though actually unrelated to good King Henry).

QUINOA
Chenopodium quinoa

Quinoa (an Indian name for the plant) was an important part of indigenous agriculture. It is a pseudocereal: not a cereal botanically but with a nutritional value and usefulness similar to cereal grains. Because it contains no gluten, it cannot be made into bread in the way gluten-containing grains can. It is, however, highly interesting to people with celiac (UK: coeliac) disease or gluten allergies for this very reason. Quinoa is a fairly nutrient-dense food: it is relatively high in essential amino acids (especially lysine), unsaturated fat, magnesium, calcium, and iron. Young leaves and shoots can be eaten like spinach.

WHAT YOU'LL NEED
• 16 ft.² (1.5 m²) of plants or a quinoa field

POLLINATION NOTES Quinoa is a self-fertile outcrosser. Its flowers have no petals and bloom in panicles. There are contradictory claims to be found in the literature, but the likelihood of crossing seems to depend on location (temperature, wind patterns, barriers) and variety. Observe an isolation distance of at least 300 ft. (100 m). Use row covers for mechanical isolation.

GROWING FOR SEED Quinoa thrives even in poor soils and, though it is generally heat-loving, it can be grown most anywhere in zones 5 to 10 (almost all continental Europe). Sow midspring as soon as the ground is warm enough. Weed often when plants are still young, as they develop more slowly than most weeds. Spacing if seeding in rows: 10–12 in. (25–30 cm) between rows, 6 in. (15 cm) within the

Quinoa

row. Quinoa can also be started indoors: thin when plants have two true leaves, plant out when 4–6 in. (10–15 cm) tall.

HARVEST In late summer, directly after flowering, the first quinoa seeds start to ripen. They ripen over a long period of time but hold on to the plant well. A dry late summer is ideal for seed ripening; the ideal seed harvest time is when seeds fall out when rubbed, usually early autumn. Thresh well-dried seedheads in a bag and winnow with a sieve.

SELECTION CHARACTERISTICS Selection criteria are very dependent on the variety. The most important criterium is probably a low level of saponin, which is toxic and causes a bitter taste. (Skim off foam when cooking to help reduce saponin content of cooked quinoa.)

DISEASES AND PESTS Wet weather in the summer can drastically reduce yields by encouraging a fungus, which is not visible on the outside of the plant, that inhibits seed production. Birds like to eat the seeds, so bird netting can be helpful.

CULTIVATION HISTORY The cultivated form is the only known form of quinoa; it has been grown in Bolivia and Peru for thousands of years. Known to Incas as the "mother of all grains," it was, along with potatoes and corn (maize), a most important foodstuff and considered holy to boot. After Spanish colonization, the plant disappeared along with those who grew it (Spaniards didn't know what to do with quinoa, as it could not be used to bake bread, the staff of life for Europeans), and isolated indigenous communities maintained quinoa's existence since that time. Today, they and other cooperatives grow quinoa in the highlands of Peru and Bolivia at elevations of up to 13,800 ft. (4200 m). In Europe, quinoa was grown here and there as a fodder plant until the early 20th century. Since the 1970s, quinoa has enjoyed a resurgence of popularity thanks to the "discovery" of its high protein and amino acid contents. More recently, both quinoa and amaranth are increasingly grown as cereal replacements, and new varieties are beginning to be bred.

Quinoa in the kitchen

The naturally occurring toxin saponin is found on the seed coat of quinoa. It causes foam to develop on the surface of the water when cooking and has a blood-thinning effect in the body. Soak overnight, then wash quinoa thoroughly with hot water before cooking, and skim off any foam that forms. The amount of saponin varies from variety to variety.

Quinoa seedheads in early autumn

STRAWBERRY SPINACH
Chenopodium foliosum

The catchy name of this chenopod comes from its round, strawberry-like fruits. While the berries do not have much to offer in the way of flavor, they are edible and make excellent garnishes. This flashy plant is also choice as an ornamental in the garden or as a container plant. The leaves of strawberry spinach can be used like spinach, raw or cooked; they are triangular, much smaller than those of spinach, and must be individually plucked. The young rosettes can be harvested in the spring. In strawberry spinach, fruits are mixed with leaves; in its close relative, strawberry blite (*Chenopodium capitatum*), fruits and leaves are found on separate areas of the stem.

WHAT YOU'LL NEED
• 10 ft.² (1 m²) of healthy plants

Strawberry spinach seeds

POLLINATION NOTES Strawberry spinach is a wind-pollinated outcrosser with inconspicuous flowers. Isolate multiple varieties by at least 300 ft. (100 m). The round fruits develop after flowering.

GROWING FOR SEED Strawberry spinach is a light feeder that can be grown in practically every soil. Seeds need 15 to 20 days to germinate. Spring seedings (one to two months before last anticipated spring frost) bolt relatively quickly. Late summer/early autumn seedings develop robust rosettes the following year before flowering. Strawberry spinach leaves can be harvested for the table three months after planting. Do not harvest leaves from plants intended for seed production.

HARVEST Leave the red fruits on the plant until they begin to wilt. Seeds must be freed from the fruits for storage. Place fruits in a bowl of water and carefully puree with a hand mixer, or press fruits through a fine sieve. Then wash and dry seeds. Or mash fruits and let soak in water for one to two days (see "Wet Processing Without Fermentation") and then wash.

SELECTION CHARACTERISTICS Little breeding work has been accomplished, and there are no varieties of strawberry spinach per se, only different origins. Potential selection criteria:

• development of a robust leaf rosette
• bolt resistance
• good flavor
• abundant fruit set

The red fruits of strawberry spinach are great for garnishing entrees.

DISEASES AND PESTS No problems are known to us. Still, there remains the potential that anything that affects other chenopods could affect strawberry spinach.

CULTIVATION HISTORY Strawberry spinach originally comes from southern Europe and central Asia. It has been cultivated over the centuries in European gardens, as an ornamental and as a vegetable, and is sometimes found naturalized near dumps and along paths. Yet another of the leafy vegetables that lost popularity in favor of spinach in the Middle Ages, the strawberry spinach is even now rarely grown but enjoying a resurgence, thanks to its brilliantly colored fruits.

Squash

CUCURBITACEAE

Cucumbers are among the most popular vegetables in Europe, and squash is becoming more popular all the time, yet these are just the tip of the iceberg in a family full of interesting vegetables. The 850 species of cucurbits (as gourd family plants are called) hail from every continent. All are sensitive to frost and love warmth, and for this reason they thrive in tropical climates; many are climbing vines that grow spiraling tendrils, though the tendril-forming trait has been bred out of zucchini and other varieties. Among the native European cucurbit species are the squirting cucumber (*Ecballium elaterium*), white bryony (*Bryonia alba*), and red bryony (*B. dioica*). Several species are used in floristry, such as the horned melon (*Cucumis metuliferus*) and the lollipop climber or marble vine (*Diplocyclos palmatus*).

● ●

GENERAL PROPAGATION CHARACTERISTICS
Cucurbits can produce fruits which are large or small, round or elongated, and smooth or prickled. The biggest cucurbit fruits are among the largest of any in the plant kingdom. Botanically, their fruits are considered to be berries. Many cucurbits are dioecious, but common crop species like cucumbers, squash, and melons are monoecious: each plant produces male flowers and female flowers. The gourd family also has perennial species, such as chayote or mirliton (*Sechium edule*), a feature in Louisiana's Cajun cuisine and a delicacy in Central America and India.

The exploding cucumber (*Cyclanthera brachystachya*) is a climbing cucurbit species.

Overview of the gourd family

COMMON NAME	GENUS	SPECIES
squash, pepo squash, summer squash, zucchini (courgette), pumpkin	Cucurbita	pepo
squash, maxima squash, winter squash, giant squash, buttercup squash	Cucurbita	maxima
squash, moschata squash, butternut squash	Cucurbita	moschata
squash, fig-leaf gourd, chilacayote	Cucurbita	ficifolia
squash, mixta squash, silver-seed gourd, cushaw, ayote, pipián	Cucurbita	argyrosperma
winter melon, wax gourd	Benincasa	hispida
calabash, bottle gourd	Lagenaria	siceraria
cucumber	Cucumis	sativus
melon, cantaloupe, honeydew	Cucumis	melo
watermelon	Citrullus	lanatus

Cucurbita spp.

The genus *Cucurbita*, which comes from the Americas, consists of 30 species, five of which have been domesticated and whose fruits we call "squash": *C. pepo*, *C. maxima*, *C. moschata*, *C. ficifolia*, and *C. argyrosperma*. Most squash grown in gardens and found in markets belong to the first three species. Zucchini (UK: courgette), for example, a *C. pepo* type, is found in most any vegetable plot, but lately it is joined more and more by other, tendriled representatives of the genus. Indeed, in the last few years there has been a veritable squash boom in kitchens and kitchen gardens. Whether as an autumnal decoration or as a healthy vegetable with complex flavors, squash has become a popular garden crop. People the world over enjoy growing, looking at, and eating these colorful, diversely shaped fruits.

Types and representative varieties of the three most popular squash species

BOTANICAL NAME	COMMON NAME
Cucurbita pepo	
var. *turbinata*, 'Ebony Acorn'	acorn
var. *longa*, 'Cocozelle von Tripolis'	cocozelle
var. *torticollis*, 'Summer Crookneck'	crookneck
var. *pepo*, 'Jack o' Lantern'	pumpkin
var. *clypeata*, 'Sunburst'	scallop
var. *fastigata*, 'Orangetti'	spaghetti squash, vegetable marrow
var. *recticollis*, 'Early Prolific Straightneck'	straightneck
var. *cylindrica*, 'Black Beauty'	zucchini
Cucurbita maxima	
'Sun Spot'	buttercup squash
'Blue Hubbard'	hubbard squash
'Boston Marrow'	marrow squash
'Hokkaido'	red kuri squash
'Turk's Turban'	turban squash
Cucurbita moschata	
'Cobnut'	butternut squash
'Pennsylvania Dutch Crookneck'	neck pumpkin

A TANGLE OF TERMS The term "squash," an indigenous American word meaning "young, unripe, and raw," is the general umbrella term for the edible fruits of *Cucurbita pepo*, *C. maxima*, *C. moschata*, *C. ficifolia*, and *C. argyrosperma*. The term "gourd" is loosely reserved for inedible fruits of the cucurbit *Lagenaria* *siceraria* (bottle gourd, birdhouse), which see. Yet this distinction is not so clear, as there are, for example, *C. ficifolia* fruits that are called gourds and deliciously edible *L. siceraria* fruits called squashes (opo squash).

Further confusion arises with the terms "pumpkin," "summer squash," and "winter squash." Pumpkin is not a botanical but rather a physiological term; it is applied freely to any squash that looks like a pumpkin. The word itself is an alteration of the Old English *pumpion*, itself a twist on the French *pompon*, which is derived from the Greek *pepon*. Pumpkins are usually varieties of *Cucurbita pepo*—but not always: the giant pumpkins of pumpkin-growing contests are usually *C. maxima*, and there are also *C. moschata* and *C. ficifolia* pumpkins. Some pumpkins are considered edible; others are not, due to their high cucurbitacin content.

Female (left) and male squash flowers

Summer squashes are certain *Cucurbita pepo* squash varieties grown for their soft, immature fruits for eating over the summer; zucchini is the best known. Winter squash, often reserved for *C. maxima*, can equally refer to squashes of any species that are grown to maturity and thus store longer than summer squashes. The storage life of winter squash varieties ranges widely, from several weeks under ideal conditions for some, to several months for others.

KNOW WHAT YOU GROW The ability to tell the species apart is vital when growing squash for seed. Squash plants, which are outcrossers, cross readily with others of the same species but only rarely with others of a different species. So, for example, a pumpkin can cross with a zucchini (both are *Cucurbita pepo*) but not with a buttercup squash (*C. maxima*). Cross-pollination has its advantages and disadvantages: characteristics and traits that have been selected for over generations can quickly disappear through cross-pollinating, yet interesting new varieties are also developed in just this way.

In order to be clear about what varieties will cross with what other varieties, you will need to know to which *Cucurbita* species each squash you are growing belongs. If you are not using labeled original seed from a reliable source, you will have to determine the species yourself. One method is to observe the seeds; *C. ficifolia* seeds are black or gray; *C. moschata* seeds have a characteristic silvery golden sheen and a rough surface, and so on. A much more reliable method for determining the species is to observe the stem of the fruit:

- pepo squash: stems have five primary longitudinal ribs, sometimes with more secondary ribs in between, and are somewhat prickly
- maxima squash: stems are woody, round, and 0.5–2.5 in. (1–6 cm) thick; fruits often slip (separate from the vine on their own) when ripe
- moschata squash: stems are edged, sometimes starkly so, may be somewhat rough, and may have small knobs; the base of the stem is either protruding or appears to rest atop the fruit

POLLINATION NOTES Squash plants are monoecious; each plant produces male flowers and female flowers. All squashes are insect-pollinated outcrossers, with honeybees and bumblebees being the most important pollinators. Male and female flowers are each open for only one day. Female flowers are easily identified by the large ovary, which often looks like a small version of the fruit, even before pollination. Male flowers have much longer stems than female flowers; their stamens grow together to form a single column, and they have on their surface an oily substance that helps their pollen grains stick to visiting insects. Male flowers have pollen and nectar, female flowers only nectar; honeybees appear to bathe in the base of yellow squash flowers, whether male or female, spending large amounts of time there.

Since all squashes that belong to the same species can cross with one another,

great isolation distances must be used between varieties of the same species (see previous table). Even in an ideal garden, with diverse flowers and physical barriers like bushes, houses, and tall plants, varieties of the same species should be grown at least 800 ft. (250 m) apart. (Remember to consider neighbors' gardens as well.)

Squash can be kept from cross-pollinating by growing in an isolation cage or hoop house, though this can be a challenge for large-growing varieties. Ideally, grow 12 (or at least six) plants, and use pollinator insects like honeybees, mason bees, or bumblebees. Flies can be used as a last resort, but they do not pollinate as well.

HAND POLLINATION Hand pollinating squash plants is time-consuming but fun—and a fairly certain way of ensuring that cross-pollination does not occur. This method can also be used to intentionally cross two varieties. Here is how it is done, and here is what you'll need before you start:

- six to 12 healthy plants
- at least two plants flowering at the same time
- at least one female flower
- at least three male flowers from another plant
- tape or plastic clothespins
- labels
- time the evening before pollination and time the morning of pollination

Preparation. To avoid inbreeding and to increase the chances of a successful pollination, prepare flowers from several plants: at least one female flower and three male flowers from another plant. It is necessary to pollinate one plant with the pollen from another plant: though a female flower can be pollinated by a male flower of the same plant, this usually results in sterile and/or poorly developed seed. The fruit that develops after self-pollination may also be deformed. It is important to prevent insects from accessing flowers before they can be hand pollinated. Ripe flower buds will have just begun to turn yellow and can be further recognized by their swollen size; they are set to open in the early morning hours. Prepare by taping ripe flower buds shut

the night before they open, therefore, to keep insects out. Take special care to tape female flowers in such a way that they can be reopened the next day without damaging the flower (which could result in insects having access to the flower); Lukas Heilingsetzer recommends using plastic clothespins instead of tape.

Implementation. The next morning, select one of the female flowers you taped shut the previous night and pluck three taped male flowers of the same variety but not from the same plant as the female flower. Make sure the flowers are dry and that they look as if they will burst open on their own. Remove the petals from the

For hand pollination, the flower bud on the right is too young and the bud on the left too old. The bud in the middle has just turned yellow and is to be taped shut in the evening for the next day's hand pollination.

male flower, thus exposing the pollen-carrying anthers. Now remove the tape from the female flower, which should then open on its own, in slow motion. Be careful at this point that no insects suddenly fly by and in, pollinating the flower before you do! Tap the stigma of the female flower with the anthers of the male flower, then quickly re-tape the female flower (again, to keep insects out). Flowers close naturally at midday, so pollination should take place before then, and on hot days in the very early morning hours.

Further hand-pollinating tips:
- Remember to label all pollinated flowers with a tag or ribbon. Without a label, there is no way to recognize which fruits come from hand pollination and which do not. Attach tags loosely, allowing for stems to grow up to 2.5 in. (6 cm) thick.
- When planting out in the spring, use wide spacing between squash plants to make it easier to determine what flower belongs to what plant.
- Hand pollination works best with the first few flowers. It works best with later flowers if all fruits have first been removed with a sharp knife.
- The chances of success are higher in the early morning hours; pollen loses its capacity to fertilize when temperatures are too high.
- Check on hand-pollinated flowers after a few days to confirm success. As soon as fertilization takes place, the fruit begins to grow. Each fertilized egg cell yields one seed.
- The number of fruits that should be left on each plant depends on the length of

the growing season and the individual variety. Leave only one or two fruits on varieties that produce very large fruits, two to four for medium fruits, all for small fruits. In any case, the plant, fruit, and seed require sufficient nourishment. When nourishment is sufficient, seeds develop well. Seed size is also dependent on species and variety.

HARVEST Seeds are harvested from fully ripe fruits, which have a hard skin that can no longer be scratched with a fingernail and a dried stem. Store ripe fruits at low room temperature (54–63°F [12–17°C]). Cellars are often too cold and too moist. Remove seeds after one to two months of storage, which allows seeds more time to ripen and improves their viability (except for *Cucurbita pepo*). Seeds can also be taken from fruits stored for even longer. Depending on the variety, seeds that have been removed from the fruit may be difficult to separate from the flesh. In this case, soak in room-temperature water for 24 hours, then rub seeds against one another in the water. Place in a sieve or on paper towels to gently finish drying seeds. Temperatures of 72–77°F (22–25°C) are ideal; avoid temperatures above 86°F (30°C), which can cause the hull to crack. Test a few squash seeds for dryness and integrity by pinching, bending, or breaking; light brown *C. maxima* seeds especially can be very hard when dry but also empty (that is, not viable).

SELECTION CHARACTERISTICS
- growth habit: bush or vining
- individual shape, color, and size of leaves

- early flowering with a good balance of male and female flowers (varieties that are not yet adapted to long summer days in northern latitudes do not produce female flowers until late summer; varieties that come directly from Central America are adapted to 12-hour days and need to be bred to adapt to longer days)
- good fruit set
- early and/or full fruit ripening
- uniform, true-to-type fruit shape and color of skin and flesh
- flavor (raw, steamed, roasted) and consistency of flesh, not bitter (= low in cucurbitacin)
- hard or soft skin
- storage life
- resistance to disease (powdery mildew, viruses)

DISEASES AND PESTS For the most part, the diseases that affect squash grown for food also affect squash grown for seed. The main difference is in dealing with viral diseases. Zucchini yellow mosaic virus can afflict all cucurbits and, though usually spread by aphids or mechanically (via garden tools and the like), it can also be seed-borne. Well-defined, dark green blisters develop on the leaves; growth of new shoots is stunted; warts and boils form on infected fruits. Do not save seed from these plants, and remove them as soon as possible, though their fruits can still be eaten. Another virus that can pop up is the cucumber mosaic virus, though it is not yet clear whether it can be seed-borne. The virus overwinters on ornamental plants and weeds and is spread to young cucurbits in spring by aphids.

Hand pollinating squash

Tape male and female flowers the evening before pollination is to take place. Take special care when taping female flowers so that they can be open and shut the next day without injuring the flower.

The following day in the morning, open and remove petals of male flowers. Carefully remove tape from female flowers.

Tap and rub the stigma of the female flower with the male "pollen brush." Repeat with two more male flowers.

Re-tape the female flower and label with date and (if crossing two varieties) the name of the "pollen father."

A light and dark green checkered pattern appears on infected leaves, especially younger leaves. Older leaves may get light and dark yellow spots as well as become deformed. Fruits stay small, with the skin becoming bumpy and developing yellow rings. Row cover or fine-meshed netting can help protect plants from aphids. Spraying a soapy solution can help get rid of aphids.

The most important fungal disease, especially for zucchini, is powdery mildew, caused by the fungus *Erysiphe cichoracearum*. It appears first as powdery spots on leaf tops, spreading then to become a whitish gray layer on the tops and bottoms of leaves, then ultimately covering stems and fruits. Powdery mildew mainly affects older plants in cool weather in late summer, when dew forms overnight and plants do not dry well in the cool days. If such a cool period is then followed by a return of sunny, warm weather, the fungus thrives and spreads. Serious cases can interfere with seed ripening. Powdery mildew is not seed-borne but can be spread by infected plant material in compost or mulch. The fungus *Rhizopus stolonifer* can cause rhizopus soft rot in stored fruits.

CULTIVATION HISTORY All *Cucurbita* species originated in the New World. The fruits of most wild squash species, bitter and inedible, were originally gathered for their nutrient-rich seeds and durable rinds. Squash is still grown along with corn (maize) and beans in the *milpa* crop-growing system of Mesoamerica.

Cucurbita pepo comes from the Mexican squash *C. fraterna* and the Texan squash *C. pepo* ssp. *microcarpina* var. *texana*, both of which wild forms have bitter fruits and stringy flesh. Presumably, they were first grown for their highly nutritious (though small, compared to present-day pepe squash) seeds; earliest evidence of domestication is between 7500 and 5500 BC in northeastern Mexico. *Cucurbita maxima* derives from the South American species *C. andreana*; the original form of maxima squash is found in Argentina and Bolivia. First evidence of cultivation comes from coastal areas of Peru between 2500 and 1500 BC; dissemination to the north began in the post-Columbian era. Moschata squash has no known wild ancestors; it is presumed to have been domesticated around 5000 BC in southern Mexico and Central America. Nor has the wild ancestor of *C. ficifolia* been traced, though we do know it was first cultivated in the mountainous regions of Peru (oldest evidence is circa 3000 BC). *Cucurbita argyrosperma* is from Mexico and Guatemala.

PEPO SQUASH
Cucurbita pepo

The name "pepo squash" is not commonly encountered outside of seed-saving circles, but we have no hesitation in using it here, for our audience, to avoid confusion. Plants have rough, prickly leaves, ribbed shoots, and hard stems with prickly hairs and five to nine ribs. Leaves are often distinctly five-lobed, sometimes cut away deeply, and mottled. Zucchini and scallop squash are classic summer squashes. Though some forms like pumpkins, acorn squashes, and varieties like 'Sweet Dumpling' and 'Delicata' are eaten ripe, practically all other pepo squashes are eaten unripe. Pepo squash flesh is more (spaghetti squash) or less "noodle-y" and maintains its integrity even when cooked. When growing summer squash for seed, do not harvest when normally harvested for eating, as the seeds have not yet ripened. Fruits should remain on the plant until the skin can no longer be scratched with a fingernail and the stems begin to dry. At this point they can be removed from the plant and set in a cool place to finish ripening. Fruits must then be broken into to remove the seeds. This is made easier for zucchini after a light frost, which makes seeds easier to separate from flesh. If you live in an area where

seed ripening coincides with the first autumn frost, simply leave fruits in the garden until the first autumn frost. The seeds themselves should not be allowed to freeze. Do not use this method if, for example, seeds are ripe in late summer and the first frost is not expected until late autumn, as the seeds may germinate when left in the fruit for so long. The fruits of most varieties cannot be stored for more than four months.

Warning: many inedible gourds containing the bitter-tasting compound cucurbitacin also belong to this species. Cucurbitacin is toxic and can cause digestive problems. Since these gourds can cross with squashes in this species and pass the cucurbitacin-producing trait on to them, do not eat fruits that taste bitter and do not save seed from such fruits.

Pepo squash seeds

Pepo squash varieties, including 'Custard White', 'Sweet Dumpling', 'Delicata', and 'Orangetti'

MAXIMA SQUASH
Cucurbita maxima

Maxima squash is also called winter squash and giant squash. Vines are soft (not prickly), round, and usually have minimal hair. Leaves on the other hand are soft, hairy, large, and round; the leaf border is often wavy. The fruit stem is round, soft when still green and finally woody. There are many delicious winter squash varieties of *Cucurbita maxima*, some of which can be stored for up to a year. The flesh comes apart when cooked and purees well.

Maxima squash seeds

Maxima squash varieties, including 'Blue Banana', 'Turk's Turban', 'Hokkaido', and 'Blue Ballet'

MOSCHATA SQUASH
Cucurbita moschata

Moschata squash needs lots of heat and cannot be grown outdoors for seed in cooler regions. Moschata squash fruits have sweet, usually orange, non-stringy, gelatinous flesh and taste sweet and often nutty. Vines develop felt-like hairy tendrils, and their growth projects out. Leaves are rounded, lobes are often not well defined. The fruit stem is somewhat angled; its base is much wider than the rest and often looks as if it is sitting atop the fruit.

Moschata squash seeds

Moschata squash varieties, including butternut squash and 'Muscade de Provence'

FIG-LEAF GOURD
Cucurbita ficifolia

Fig-leaf gourds are the most cold-tolerant of the cucurbits: in Mexico, chilacayote (as it is known there) is grown at elevations of up to 8500 ft. (2600 m). Fruits store well, for up to two years; they are reminiscent of watermelons in shape and color, being light to dark green with white spots and stripes. They are also used similarly to the watermelon: in Mexico, Asia, and in some European countries, the flesh is made into candy. Seeds too are eaten, roasted. Fig-leaf gourds are often described as being perennial, but they produce fruit only once. They are sometimes grown in the understory of cucumbers because of their resistance to fusarium fungi.

Fig-leaf gourd seeds

Fig-leaf gourd leaves really do look like fig leaves.

MIXTA SQUASH, SILVER-SEED GOURD

Cucurbita argyrosperma

Mixta squashes are relatively uncommon in Europe. They need more heat than most other squashes and usually require a long season; they cannot be grown outdoors for seed in cool regions. Plants grow to be very large and have large, hairy leaves, which are lighter colored than those of moschata squash. The fruit stem is hard, ribbed (often reminiscent of pepo squash), and the base is somewhat enlarged. Seeds are white or beige; those of some varieties have a well-defined border and cracks in the surface, and are covered in a thin, cellophane-like layer. Silver-seed gourds

can cross with moschata and pepo squash, one of the few *Cucurbita* species that can cross-pollinate other species in the genus. Some varieties: all cushaws (except 'Golden Cushaw'), 'Mixta Gold', and 'Pepita'.

Mixta squash seeds

The green-striped cushaw is listed on Slow Food's US Ark of Taste, "a catalog of over 200 delicious foods in danger of extinction."

WINTER MELON, WAX GOURD
Benincasa hispida

Though it is not of the genus *Cucurbita*, winter melon is grown just like squash. Fully ripe fruits weigh up to 110 lb. (50 kg) and can be spherical, egg-shaped, or oblong. Their dark green rind is thin, hard, and waxy. The epithet *hispida* (Lat. *hispidus*, "rough") reflects the fact that the entire plant, including young fruits,

Winter melon seeds

A wax layer develops on the rind of winter melon as the fruit ripens, hence the alternative common name.

is covered in small, white, brush-like hairs. Unripe fruits are eaten raw in salads; steamed, sautéed, or pickled; or made into soups and stews. Young leaves, flowers, and young shoots can also be eaten. Winter melon is common in China and India but is less known in the West, perhaps because of the long growing season required; plants need at least 85 days to ripen, often longer. Because it also needs heat in the summer, we recommend growing in a greenhouse in temperate climates. Young plants require lots of water; older plants prefer dry heat. Leave only one fruit per plant when growing for seed. If you try to grow for seed but the season ends up being too short, try one of the many delicious recipes for unripe fruits.

CALABASH, BOTTLE GOURD
Lagenaria siceraria

The calabash is one of the oldest crop plants in the world. The unripe fruits, leaves, and shoots of varieties with minimal bitter cucurbitacin content are prepared as vegetables. In Pakistan, leaves are removed of their veins and eaten like spinach. Its dried shells are valued decoratively, in arts and crafts, and for many utilitarian items: bowls, ladles, spoons, drinking vessels, pipes, musical instruments, and much more. Different varieties produce wildly varying fruit shapes whose hardened rind can serve a multitude of purposes; for example, one cultivar ('Weinheberkürbis') was used in the wine-growing regions of Austria and Hungary to siphon wine out of casks.

POLLINATION NOTES Flowers are white, smaller than those of *Cucurbita* species, and as thin as tissue paper. Calabash plants are monoecious, producing long-stemmed male flowers and short-stemmed female flowers. Male and female flowers open in the evening. Over night, various night-active insects carry pollen to female flowers; during the day, hoverflies take over. Bumblebees and honeybees can also pollinate calabash. Flowers wilt the day after blossoming and lose their petals a few days later. When growing indoors or when it is too windy for insects to pollinate effectively, hand pollination is necessary.

GROWING FOR SEED Plants need to climb. Certain varieties with long fruits need their fruits to hang so they can grow straight. In this way it is also easier to select for long, true-to-type fruits. Calabash fruits should stay on the plant until the first frost. As long as the growing season is not very short in your area, even large-fruited varieties should be able to produce ripe seed.

HARVEST When stems turn yellow/brown, fruits are ready to harvest. They should then be stored in a temperate (but not too warm) and well-ventilated place for further ripening and drying. Seeds can germinate or rot when fruits are stored in temperatures that are too high. Calabashes with ripe seed are lightweight, and their seeds rattle inside. Fruits must be dry before seeds are removed. Make a small hole in the rind to remove seeds, so the rind can be used thereafter. Scrape out

Male calabash flower

Calabash seeds

A diverse array of bottle gourds (from bottom left): 'Mini Bottle', 'Weinheberkürbis' (wine dispenser squash), 'Speckled Swan', and 'Dinosaurierkeule' (dinosaur leg)

seeds with a small spoon. Some people are allergic to the dried, dusty fruit flesh; wear a dust mask if no one else is available to remove seeds for you. Bendable seeds are too wet for storage and should be further dried until they are hard and have the typical brown color. Though some varieties do produce white seed, usually white seed is a sign of unripeness (test: ripe seeds can be broken with a fingernail). Some calabash seeds become hard, yet are not viable; break a few to see if the endosperm has indeed developed.

DISEASES AND PESTS Calabash plants rarely succumb to disease. Protection seems to come from the strong smell of the plant and its fuzzy leaves.

CULTIVATION HISTORY Bottle gourds are known only in their cultivated form. Because they can be made into so many useful things, they were important parts of many cultures before ceramics were adopted. They originated in southern and eastern Asia, from which latter region comes the earliest evidence of their cultivation (5000–3000 BC). They arrived in Egypt in 3500 BC as commodities, and the oldest written documentation concerning them dates from 6th-century northern China. Yet the oldest finds are from the New World (7200 BC): calabash seeds remain viable even after drifting in oceanic saltwater for many months, which is presumably how they traveled from the Old World to the New. Wild populations can now be found in southern and eastern Africa.

CUCUMBER
Cucumis sativus

Cucumbers, the most-grown cucurbit in Europe, are cultivated on all continents. These annual plants start out upright, then creep across the ground or up trellises. In common with all *Cucumis* species, vines are unbranched and separate. Cucumbers are of several types, for example:

- English cucumbers: non-prickly, long, often greenhouse-grown cucumbers; often 16 in. (40 cm) long or longer
- garden cucumbers: with white or black prickles
- gherkin cucumbers: small cukes with several fruits per leaf axil
- Sikkim cucumbers: with red-orange rind
- lemon cucumbers: spherical, look like lemons

WHAT YOU'LL NEED
- six to 12 healthy plants
- overripe (yellow-orange) fruits with true-to-type shape
- large glass jar or plastic bucket
- coffee filter

Cucumber seeds

POLLINATION NOTES Cucumbers are self-fertile outcrossers, primarily pollinated by bumblebees and honeybees, though other insects occasionally participate. They do not cross with squashes or melons. Cucumbers are monoecious: female flowers are easily recognized by their cucumber-shaped ovary; male flowers have a simple, straight stem. There are also some dioecious varieties. A female flower can be pollinated by a male flower of the same plant (selfing), though the variety will quickly show signs of inbreeding depression this way. Out-crossing is much more common and guarantees the passing on of genetic diversity. Younger cucumber plants generally have more male flowers, with female flowers coming later, depending on weather and day length. Short days and low temperatures encourage the formation of female flowers.

Spatially isolate multiple varieties grown in the same year by at least 500 ft. (150 m) or use isolation cages. The isolation distance depends on garden configuration, with the danger of cross-pollination decreasing when varieties are separated by tall plants like corn (maize) or pole beans. Such tall plants additionally function as wind protection, which is appreciated by cucumbers (cukes love heat and calm air). Otherwise, cucumbers (like squash) can be pollinated by hand. Closing flowers with tape can be a greater

Various shapes of cucumbers

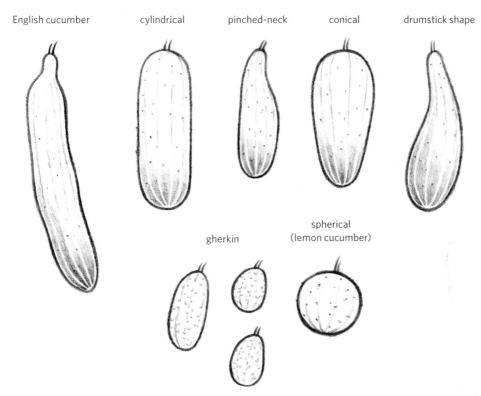

English cucumber   cylindrical   pinched-neck   conical   drumstick shape

gherkin

spherical
(lemon cucumber)

challenge for cucumbers than for squash, since cucumber flowers are much smaller. You may find it easier to use small bags or tea filters closed tightly with clothespins. Pollinate with a small brush.

Newer commercial varieties are mostly parthenocarpic (genetically purely female) varieties. These produce high fruit yields without pollination. Seeds normally do not form, making these varieties not particularly useful for home seed propagation. Parthenocarpic varieties will develop seeds when grown together with an open-pollinated cucumber variety, which may be problematic if you were expecting seedless cucumbers.

Garden cucumbers will climb when given the opportunity.

GROWING FOR SEED Leave the first one or two cucumbers on the plant until seeds are ripe. Do not leave cucumbers on the main vine to go to seed, as this will reduce overall yield, especially for English cucumbers. One cucumber can yield 100 to 500 ripe seeds. Seeds do not ripen until the cucumber fruit has gone far beyond eating ripeness; the rind is hard and usually yellow-orange, though sometimes brown. White-rinded cucumbers turn more of a light yellow color when seeds are ripe. Remove fruits at this point and store them on a dry surface protected from the weather. The riper the fruits, the higher the quality of the seed. The flesh of non-rotting fruits, if there are any, can be used to make pickles. Different cucumber varieties vary in their propensity to climb; enthusiastic climbers can be given a trellis of some sort to climb up. Allowing cucumbers to climb can result in sun-burned fruits in hot regions, but this method also helps reduce the risk of fungal infections, especially in wetter regions. Those that tend not to climb can be grown on the ground; landscaping fabric can be laid between rows to help prevent rotting fruits.

HARVEST Cut fruits with ripe seed in half the long way and scrape out seeds with a spoon or finger. The seeds are surrounded with a gelatinous substance that helps prevent seeds from germinating in the moist environment of the fruit upon ripening. This layer can be dissolved by fermenting the seeds (for particulars, see "Wet Processing with Fermentation"). Add water to the mass of seed and pulp. The fermentation process is complete when the gelatinous layer has dissolved, usually after 24 hours, at which point the seeds should quickly be washed and dried. Nonviable seed usually floats at the top, heavy viable seed sinks to the bottom. Nonviable seed can also be winnowed with the wind, once all seeds are dried.

SELECTION CHARACTERISTICS
- earliness and/or long harvesting period
- disease resistance (especially against powdery mildew when growing outdoors)
- fruits free of bitter compounds
- number of fruits per plant
- portion of fruit that is fleshy and not part of the seed-bearing core (cross-section)
- prickly/smooth rind
- shape of neck
- overall shape (snake-like, horn-like, etc.), size, color
- drought tolerance

DISEASES AND PESTS A frequent disease pathogen is the cucumber mosaic virus, which may affect yield. The virus causes a light and dark green checkered pattern on leaves, especially young ones. It can also infect fruits, causing light spots to appear on their surface. It has yet to be determined if the virus is seed-borne. Another mosaic virus affecting cucumbers is the zucchini yellow mosaic virus, which can cause extensive crop damage. Well-defined, dark green blisters on leaves and fruits are the classic symptoms, with fruits completely withering

Different cucumber varieties, all overripe and ready to have their seed harvested

away in extreme cases. It is almost always spread by aphids, though about 1% of the time it is spread by seed. Remove plants suspected to be infected, and do not grow cucurbits in that bed the following year. Fusarium stem rot, caused by *Fusarium solani*, is a seed-borne disease that mainly occurs in greenhouses and not in outdoor gardens. Afflicted plants suddenly wilt and die. Fusarium fungi can live in the soil for years, so wait four or five years before growing in the same bed after an infection. Bacterial leaf spot disease (*Pseudomonas lachrymans*) is seed-borne and also enters the plant through injuries on leaves and stems. Angled, yellowish brown spots appear, which may be slimy or crusty on the underside. Rain, wind, and garden maintenance can help

spread this disease. Other seed-borne diseases include cucumber scab and anthracnose (for symptoms and treatment, see melon). Powdery mildew (*Erysiphe cichoracearum* and *Sphaerotheca fuliginea*) is not seed-borne and is mostly seen on the tops of leaves; in wetter locations, powdery mildew can cause crop failure, especially in mid to late summer. Seedborne downy mildew (*Peronospora* spp.) often appears when dew forms nightly for prolonged periods.

CULTIVATION HISTORY The cucumber originally comes from India. Its bitter-tasting wild ancestor can be found in the subtropical valleys of the Himalayas. This bitterness is still found in some cultivated varieties, especially in the portion near

Cucumber seeds—the older, the better?

Classic German-language seed literature suggests that cucumber seed quality increases with age: "It is not the case for all vegetables that the most recently harvested seeds are best; some crops, like cucumbers and melons, produce fruits earlier when grown from three- to six-year-old seed than when grown from one- or two-year-old seed. This is an exceptional case, however, as otherwise the freshest, most robust seeds yield the most vigorous plants" (Lucas 1905).

And from another source: "Many gardeners, especially older ones, claim that five- to six-year-old seed is best. Others believe further that they get the best results when the seeds are first carried around in their pants pockets for several days. . . . My experiments have shown that two- to three-year-old seeds are indeed best [, and others have] confirmed that fresh cucumber seeds yield little more than leaves and vines" (Barfuss 1894).

the stem. Cucumber cultivation in India appears to be a very old practice, having likely begun by 2000 BC or earlier. From there it spread west (Iraq by 700 BC) and east to China, where mainly long-fruited varieties were bred. Europe and the USA are now the most important breeding centers, and the development of hybrid cucumbers, many parthenocarpic, is well advanced.

MELON

Cucumis melo

Melons are a diverse lot of tropical annual vines, and all appreciate lots of heat. The many types of melon come from two distinct subspecies, *agrestis* and *melo*. Most varieties grown in China and India are agrestis melons; these generally have white flesh that is not sweet and either hard and crunchy or mealy. They are often eaten raw like cucumbers or harvested young and cooked. Melo melons are much more common in the West. Some ssp. *melo* types:

- cantaloupe, muskmelon: fruits are ribbed, mid-sized, with a hard, scaly or raw surface; flesh is sweet, aromatic, and usually orange; muskmelon types have netted (not ribbed) rinds
- Inodorus Group (honeydew, casaba): fruits are usually larger, later-ripening, and better-storing than cantaloupes and muskmelons; rinds are smooth or wrinkled, but not netted; flesh is white or green; ripe fruits do not slip (separate on their own) from stems

- Flexuosus Group (Armenian cucumber, snake melon): cucumber-shaped fruits, non-aromatic; used unripe like cucumbers
- Dudaim Group (Queen Anne's pocket melon): small fruits with a strong, characteristic aroma, carried about in earlier days for their perfume

WHAT YOU'LL NEED
- six to 12 healthy plants
- fruits at eating-ripeness stage

POLLINATION NOTES Melons are monoecious—each plant produces separate male and female flowers. Although female flowers can be pollinated by male flowers of the same plant, cross-pollination via bees and small flies is more typical. For this reason, crossing of multiple varieties of the same species grown too near each other is not only possible but likely. Melons do not cross with watermelons, cucumbers, or squash, however. Hand pollination is possible (follow the instructions given for squash) but more difficult

Melon seeds

than for either cucumber or squash, as a high percentage of hand-pollinated flowers fall off. Hand pollination is time-consuming and requires a steady hand. The first few female flowers are the most likely to take. Remove non-hand-pollinated flowers and fruits so the plant can produce more flowers for hand pollination. At Arche Noah we have achieved high pollination rates growing melons in isolation cages with introduced pollinators.

GROWING FOR SEED For a successful hand pollination, prune the plant to make it easier to work with and focus on the flowers you want to use. Shorten the main vine on young plants back to three flower buds and the main side vines to two. Flower buds are found in the leaf axils and are stimulated to bloom when the vine is cut. Melon seeds are ripe as soon as the fruits are edible. Overripe fruits are no longer so tasty, but seed yield in overripe fruits can be up to 10% higher than in fruits of eating ripeness. For this reason, allow fruits from successful hand pollination to go overripe to increase seed yield.

HARVEST As for cucumber, except it is not necessary to ferment melon seeds: they are not surrounded by a germination-inhibiting gel.

SELECTION CHARACTERISTICS
- earliness
- plant health
- number of fruits per plant
- suitability for storage
- adaptation to local climate
- flavor (especially sweetness) of fruit

Various melon varieties

DISEASES AND PESTS Cucumber scab, caused by the fungus *Cladiosporum cucumerinum*, can be seed-borne. Symptoms include black, sunken-in spots on fruits and sometimes leaves. A jelly-like substance also appears with the spots on the fruits. Fungus on the leaves eventually eats through the tissue, leaving behind holes. The fungus grows ideally at 72–73°F (22–23°C), so where temperatures can be brought far above this, as in a greenhouse, the fungus can be effectively kept under control.

The pathogen causing anthracnose, the fungus *Colletotrichum orbiculare*, can also be seed-borne. Symptoms: seedlings from infected seed develop "burn spots" and then die. On the leaves of mature plants, small yellow spots that then turn brown appear. Round, brown or black spots form in depressions on the surface of the fruit. Remedies: thorough destruction of plant material, disinfection of tools and hands, crop rotation of at least three years.

CULTIVATION HISTORY The melon is an Old World plant. Wild forms of ssp. *melo* are found in subtropical central Asia and in the Middle East, whereas wild forms of ssp. *agrestis* are found in the tropical areas of the Old World. The melon was domesticated several times in several different places, leading to the diversity we know today. The oldest finds of seeds are from Egypt (3800–3500 BC) and China (circa 3000 BC). The oldest finds in Europe come from Greece (1400–900 BC).

WATERMELON
Citrullus lanatus

The deliciously refreshing watermelon is the most widely traded cucurbit in the world, with many hybrid varieties offering few seeds and thin rinds. Fruits often have red flesh, but there are also yellow-, green-, and white-fleshed varieties. Plants are usually covered with small hairs and have pinnate leaves, making them easy

Hami melon

From ssp. *agrestis* comes this special variety. Under ideal conditions, the snow melon (as it is also known) can produce large fruits (8 by 12 in. [20 by 30 cm]). What makes this variety so unique is that ripe fruits burst at their tips. The snow-white flesh has a foamy consistency and a strong melon aroma. In South America, Hami melons are made into a delicious beverage by pureeing them and mixing them with honey.

Watermelon seeds

to distinguish from muskmelon vines, with which they are sometimes confused. In some countries, like China, varieties with high-oil-content seeds are grown; the seeds are then roasted and eaten as a snack. Other varieties are grown specifically as livestock feed.

WHAT YOU'LL NEED
- six to 12 healthy plants
- fruits at eating-ripeness stage

POLLINATION NOTES Watermelons are monoecious, but, as with cucumbers, some more recent varieties are dioecious. All varieties, including the citron melon, can cross with one another. To avoid cross-pollination by insects, especially bees, observe an isolation distance of at least 500 ft. (150 m) between different watermelon varieties. Otherwise, hand pollination is necessary (follow advice given for squash). Under ideal weather conditions, where plants are not under stress, hand pollination of watermelon is 50–75% successful. Use the first available flowers for pollination. The exception is late-ripening varieties, which cast off 90% of their first flowers; use the next flowers in that case. It can often be difficult to determine which flowers will open the next day, so use insect-proof bags instead of tape to close flowers or even to cover entire vines.

GROWING FOR SEED As typical subtropical plants, watermelons need lots of heat, more so than melons. They are sensitive to low (nighttime) temperatures and need a long, warm, mostly dry growing season. Watermelons are heavy feeders and are not to be pruned. In temperate climates, only one to three fruits per plant should be left to ripen.

HARVEST Seeds are usually ripe before the fruit is completely ripe for eating, even when the seeds are still white or light brown. Ripeness is best determined by checking the tendril on the fruit on the opposite end of the stem; the fruit is ripe when this tendril has become brown and dry. Clean and dry the seeds. The ripe seeds spat out from eaten watermelons can also be saved and used. It is not necessary to ferment watermelon seeds. Citron

The unmistakable fruit and leaves of the watermelon

melon seeds (see sidebar) must be pulled out individually from the hard flesh of the fruit. Seeds often do not darken until put into storage.

SELECTION CHARACTERISTICS Watermelon varieties differ in the color of the flesh, the size and shape of the fruit, and the color and pattern of the rind. Seeds are, again depending on the variety, black, brown, red, green, or white. Potential selection criteria:

- earliness
- plant health
- number of fruits per plant
- flavor (especially sweetness) of fruit

DISEASES AND PESTS Watermelons are grown with relative ease only in hot climates and are more susceptible to fungal diseases in wetter climates. Fusarium rot (*Fusarium roseum*) is not seed-borne

but is often found in the soil and on plant debris. Yellowish brown spots are usually seen on ripe or near-ripe fruits. Prevention: keeping fruits off of wet soil, crop rotation of at least three years. Bacterial speck disease is caused by the bacteria *Pseudomonas syringae* and can be seed- or soil-borne. This is the main bacterial disease where watermelons are grown on a large scale. Use at least a four-year crop rotation to help prevent bacterial speck. Viral diseases can also be a problem in watermelon cultivation, causing spots and checkered patterns on young leaves and stunted growth. Remove plants with viral infections.

CULTIVATION HISTORY Wild forms of watermelon are densely hairy vines with small, bitter fruits; they grow in the Kalahari Desert of Namibia and in southern Africa. The watermelon was an important fruit in ancient Egypt, with the earliest evidence from around 2000 BC. It quickly spread to India and China, where the desert watermelon was bred. The desert watermelon was then brought back west by Arabs. In Africa, the oil- and protein-rich seeds are eaten raw; in India, seeds are ground and baked into a kind of bread; in the Far East, the seeds are roasted. Large-seeded varieties have been bred in China for just this purpose (roasting); hybridizers in Japan have been working in the other direction, breeding varieties with small seeds, so as not to interfere with consumption of the fruit's flesh. Seedless hybrids first started appearing in the 1950s.

Citrons, melon and otherwise

A lesser-known member of the species is the citron melon (*Citrullus lanatus* var. *citroides*). Citron melon is not eaten fresh like the watermelon but rather is pickled, candied, or made into jams and jellies. The citron is a citrus crop (*Citrus medica* var. *medica*).

Tomato and relatives

SOLANACEAE

Except for the potato (which is a tuber, not a fruit), the crop plants of the nightshade family produce fruits (peppers, tomatoes) that we consider culinarily to be vegetables. Most of the family's cultivated vegetables come from the New World and were unknown in Europe until the 16th century; their wild ancestors are found in Central and South America. The exception is the eggplant (aubergine), which is native to India and was brought to Spain by Arabs in the 10th century.

There are more than just food plants in this family, however. Several members are ornamentals (tobacco, petunias), and many species are loaded with toxic alkaloids. Various thornapples (*Datura* spp.), bittersweet nightshade (*Solanum dulcamara*), and deadly nightshade (*Atropa* spp.) are poisonous but nevertheless valuable pharmacologically.

● ●

BOTANICAL CHARACTERISTICS Botanically speaking, nightshade flowers are perfect, with five petals and five sepals conjoined; the ovary is superior, and the fruit is either a capsule (thornapple) or a berry (pepper, tomato, eggplant).

GENERAL PROPAGATION CHARACTERISTICS Most nightshade family plants are annual or perennial herbaceous plants. In either case, fruits and seeds are produced in the first growing season. (Every rule has an exception: the tree tomato, *Cyphomandra betacea*, does not set fruit until the

The fiery colors of jalapeño and chili peppers

second or third year.) Pollination behavior is less straightforward. Cultivated nightshade family plants mostly self-pollinate in the short days of the northern latitudes of North America and Europe, but the possibility of cross-pollination cannot be ruled out. More precise information is found in the individual entries.

Overview of the nightshade family

COMMON NAME	GENUS	SPECIES
tomato	*Solanum*	*lycopersicum*
pepper	*Capsicum*	*annuum, baccatum, chinense, frutescens, pubescens*
eggplant (aubergine)	*Solanum*	*melongena*
groundcherry	*Physalis*	*peruviana*
tomatillo	*Physalis*	*ixocarpa*
potato	*Solanum*	*tuberosum*

The fruits change color when seeds are ready to harvest.

The many looks of the Solanaceae

TOMATO

Solanum lycopersicum

WHAT YOU'LL NEED
- six to 12 healthy plants
- diverse array of flowers in garden to distract potentially cross-pollinating insects
- poles or trellis and string (except for determinate varieties)
- glass jar
- coffee filter

POLLINATION NOTES Tomatoes are predominantly self-pollinators, but cross-pollination by insects, mainly bumblebees, can occur; there are conflicting reports as to its frequency in the literature and in the claims of growers. Ancient forms of tomatoes were actually reliant on insects for cross-pollination, and tomatoes did not become self-fertile until they were domesticated. Some authors are of the opinion that the length of the style determines how great the risk of cross-pollination is. When the style is longer than the stamen, it is easier for the stigma to be pollinated by an insect than by the flower's own anthers. The length that the style grows to is likely determined by day length, as varieties that grow long styles in the southern USA do not grow long styles in Europe. Gardeners growing tomato seed in Virginia reported that bumblebees and honeybees cross-pollinated 10–15% of the varieties they were propagating. Gardeners at Arche Noah have yet to find any significant evidence of crossing. Perhaps the preferences of insects in the USA differ from the preferences of European bees? Tomato flowers are not generally considered to be among the favorites of bumblebees; they only visit them when there are no other flowers available. If cross-pollination does occur, simply do not propagate non-true-to-type fruits further. Crossing can also be reduced by shaking trellis-bound plants at midday or several times a day, thereby helping pollen fall from the anthers onto the stigmas.

Beefsteak tomatoes often produce double flowers on terminal panicles, which then fuse together, forming the seams typically seen, to make one fruit. Such fruits are not a symptom of cross-pollination, nor are they malformations; the double flowers that produced them are, however, more susceptible to cross-pollination.

GROWING FOR SEED Tomatoes are grown for seed just as they are grown for food, even to pruning suckers, which will maximize the size, number, and flavor of your tomatoes. To protect your favorite variety

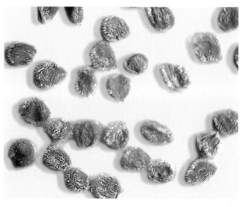

Tomato seeds

from cross-pollination, take the following precautions:

- isolation distance of at least 10 ft. (3 m) for varieties whose styles are shorter than the stamens
- isolation distance of 30–40 ft. (10–12 m) for varieties whose styles are longer than the stamens
- harvest seed from fruits from the middle of the patch, developed from flowers buried deep in the foliage

HARVEST Harvest seed from at least six to 12 plants to maximize the genetic diversity passed along to the next generation. Ideally, you will observe the plant over the entire growing season and identify fruits from which you will harvest seed while they are still on the plant. If seeds are instead saved by just putting a few off to the side when processing tomatoes, you will no longer be selecting for certain growth traits of the plant itself.

Harvest fruits from the first or second panicles from the plants you have selected. Taste them and save seeds from the best-tasting ones. Plants may look slightly different from one another due to crossing and (much rarer) mutations. You may find it fun and exciting to save seed from unexpected-looking plants and fruits and develop a new variety.

Generally speaking, do not harvest seed from any sick plant (lest the trait "prone to disease" be selected for), but exceptions can and should be made when, for example, the variety is otherwise unavailable or has long since proven itself in the garden.

Fruits harvested for seed must be of full eating ripeness but not moldy. If the growing season is too short to fully ripen tomatoes (as is sometimes the case at high altitudes or in maritime climates), harvest fruits and put them in a warm place like a windowsill or greenhouse. Tomato seeds are processed wet by fermenting them. Seeds in the fruit are surrounded by a gelatinous sac, which helps prevent ripe seeds from germinating in watery fruits. Fermentation dissolves this germination-inhibiting layer (for details, see "Wet Processing with Fermentation"):

- small quantities: slice fruits in half and scoop out seeds with a spoon or squeeze into a glass jar; add some water and a pinch of sugar
- large quantities and cocktail or wild tomatoes: slice fruits in half and place in a bucket or large glass jar; puree with a hand-held blender and add some water

Not all tomato varieties yield red fruits. These fruits are ripe, even though they are white ('White Beauty') and greenish yellow ('Green Zebra').

SELECTION CHARACTERISTICS

- plant: healthy, early ripening (or, for better-storing varieties, late ripening), uniform, compact, floriferous, true-to-type growth habit (determinate: plants reach a fixed height; indeterminate: no limits to growth), minimal tendency to form suckers
- fruits: flavor, burst-resistant skin, true-to-type shape, true-to-type traits (flesh color, skin color)

DISEASES AND PESTS The most common disease of outdoor-grown tomatoes is late blight, *Phytophthora infestans*. This fungal disease, which affects fruits and leaves, can turn into a real plague in hot, humid years, causing complete crop failure in a matter of days. It often starts as grayish green spots on older leaves; leaves wither and dry up in dry weather, rot in wet weather. Late blight is rarely a problem in greenhouse culture, and it is not seed-borne, so seeds may be harvested as long as the fruits themselves are not diseased.

Various viral diseases can also affect tomatoes. Symptoms: young leaves curling up at the tip, light streaks along leaf veins. Remove afflicted plants to help prevent viruses from spreading. Curled leaves may also be caused by physiological factors. New leaf growth in diseased plants often appears normal at first.

Blossom end rot is not really a disease but rather the result of a calcium deficiency. It occurs in hot, dry weather followed by rain (or watering). Symptoms: fruits are brown and sunken-in opposite the stem end. Some varieties ('Black Plum', for example) or individual plants are especially susceptible. Do not save seed from plants prone to blossom end rot.

CULTIVATION HISTORY Tomatoes come from the wild currant tomato (*Solanum pimpinellifolium*), a native of northwestern South America (Ecuador, Peru) which likely spread north in pre-Columbian times, as a weed. Indian communities in present-day Mexico domesticated it and integrated it into their irrigated agricultural practices. The cherry tomato (var. *cerasiforme*) is the likely archetype of the wide array of large-fruited cultivars that

Cross-sections of different tomatoes

bilocular (cocktail tomatoes)

trilocular

quadrilocular

multilocular (beefsteak tomatoes)

Europeans met when they arrived in the New World.

After Columbus, the cultivated form of the tomato traveled back to South America and on to Europe, where it received a mixed reaction upon its arrival. Italians were the first to truly embrace it, whereas in central Europe it was not even eaten by the peasantry. The tomato was all over Spain and Portugal by 1600 and was grown in practically every garden and offered in restaurants by the 18th century. The Turks brought it to the Balkans (and thence to eastern Europe). Central and western Europeans held on to the idea that tomatoes were poisonous the longest, though they adopted them early as an ornamental curiosity. Tomatoes were not commercially available in Switzerland until the second half of the 19th century. Widespread hunger during World War I turned the tomato into a food for the people there, while in western Austria and South Tyrol, Italy, tomatoes were not grown widely until the 1920s.

Although the tomato has been widely grown in Europe for over a century now, the plant still needs lots of warmth and remains sensitive to cold and wet weather. The wild original forms of tomato are receiving renewed attention from contemporary plant breeders because of their resistance to diseases that plague commercial growers. Many new varieties have these resistance traits bred into them. Wild forms of tomatoes can be grown in the garden in the same way cultivated varieties are grown.

PEPPER
Capsicum spp.

The genus *Capsicum* comprises 25 species, all native to Central and South America, with the greatest diversity in the Andes of southern Brazil and Bolivia. Most cultivated peppers belong to *C. annuum*, the rest to *C. chinense*, *C. frutescens*, *C. baccatum*, and *C. pubescens*. Except for *C. pubescens*, these species can all cross with one another. Because of this, many varieties do not obviously belong to a particular species.

The bushy plants of this genus are grown as annuals or perennials. Perennial varieties are not at all hardy but can be overwintered indoors when vegetation is cut back in the fall. Fruits come in all shapes and sizes, including pointy, bell-shaped, round, cubical, and elongated. The range of colors is also very large, with unripe fruits appearing green, violet, or light yellow, and ripe fruits becoming red, orange, yellow, or brown. You will need to acquaint yourself with each variety to know when they are ripe and if the seed was crossed.

Pepper seeds

WHAT YOU'LL NEED
- six to 12 healthy plants
- diverse array of flowers in garden to distract potentially cross-pollinating insects
- a greenhouse, or a climate that allows fruits to ripen
- support poles
- for hot peppers: rubber gloves and goggles for seed harvest

POLLINATION NOTES Peppers are primarily selfers, but all species can be cross-pollinated by insects, especially honeybees and bumblebees. When bees are desperate, pepper flowers will do just fine, and they often visit before flowers have a chance to pollinate themselves. For this reason, it may be best to propagate only one variety at a time in the greenhouse. Interspecies cross-pollination is also possible. Flowers are white, yellowish, or light or dark violet.

The risk of cross-pollination is generally lower when growing outdoors. For the first few years at Arche Noah, we had no problem growing pepper varieties right next to each other; slowly and increasingly, however, cross-pollination occurred. *Capsicum baccatum* and *C. frutescens* in particular will certainly be visited by bees; isolation is essential.

When crossing happens (for example, when a spicy pepper has crossed with a sweet pepper), it is best to start over with fresh seed, unless you like the new combination. To avoid crossing:

- Keep varieties at least 100 ft. (30 m) away from each other.
- For extra protection, enclose individual flowers or stalks in insect-proof sacks; do not enclose entire plants in bags, as the reduced light may hinder fruit production.
- Gently shake flowers, whether bagged or not, on a regular basis to encourage self-pollination.

GROWING FOR SEED Though in some regions they are grown on a very large scale, peppers are primarily garden plants, started indoors and set out in late spring, when all danger of frost is past. Cultivation works best where summers are hot; in central Europe, that means wine- and

The flowers of *Capsicum baccatum* var. *pendulum* 'Bishop's Crown' have yellow or brown spots at the base of the individual petals.

corn-growing regions. Certain more robust, less cold-sensitive varieties can be grown for seed in cooler areas. Where growing for seed outdoors truly is not an option, row cover, hoop houses, or greenhouses can provide the necessary warmth and season extension.

Growing for seed is easily combined with growing peppers for the table: fully ripe fruits are harvested when growing for seed, and the flesh can be eaten. When fruits are harvested too early, seed viability drops dramatically. Seed ripening can be sped up and seed quality improved by allowing only three or four fruits to grow per plant and removing all other flowers (fewer fruits = larger seeds = better seed viability). Removing the very first flower of the pepper plant helps speed vegetative growth and further fruit development.

HARVEST Harvest only the first few fruits the plant produces, as seed from later fruits often has germination rates of only around 60%. Fruits (and, by extension, seeds) are ripe when the final color change has fully occurred (from green to red/yellow; light yellow to dark yellow/orange/red, etc.). Seeds are then no longer white but rather a golden yellow. Seed can be harvested from ripe fruits or from fruits that have dried on the stalk; never harvest seed from moldy fruits, however. Remove seeds from the flesh of the fruit by hand or with a spoon, and remove plant debris. Take great care when working with hot spicy peppers! Wear rubber gloves (the "hot" chemicals, capsaicinoids, slowly build up on the fingers and cause a burning sensation that is

difficult to get rid of) and goggles to avoid burning yourself. Bell peppers often yield around 200 seeds, hot peppers less. Separate nonviable seeds from viable seeds in a container of water right after harvesting. Nonviable seeds float and can be poured off the top, while viable seeds sink to the bottom. Spread seeds out on a clean surface (a window screen, for example) and allow to dry in a warm place. Seeds dry enough for storage make a cracking sound when broken.

SELECTION CHARACTERISTICS Seed should be harvested only from healthy, well-nourished plants. General selection criteria

Visits from bumblebees and other insects can result in individual varieties crossing with one another.

include vigorous growth and tolerance of weather extremes (drought, wet and/or cool climates). Other selection criteria:

- plant: uniform, rapid growth; true-to-type growth (tall and vertical to flat and expansive); non-brittle branches; number of fruits per plant
- fruit: thick walls for bell peppers; true-to-type shape (pointy, blocky, round); degree of heat; rapid ripening; flavor (it is worth it to taste all harvested fruits, as individual fruits from the same plant can taste slightly different)

DISEASES AND PESTS Home gardeners rarely have any pest-related problems with peppers; plants grown outdoors are

Various shapes of peppers

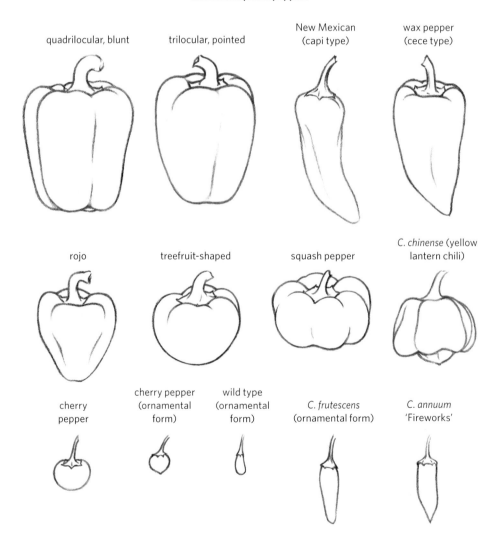

quadrilocular, blunt

trilocular, pointed

New Mexican (capi type)

wax pepper (cece type)

rojo

treefruit-shaped

squash pepper

C. chinense (yellow lantern chili)

cherry pepper

cherry pepper (ornamental form)

wild type (ornamental form)

C. frutescens (ornamental form)

C. annuum 'Fireworks'

attacked only rarely, and fruits are not damaged directly (exceptions: bright-line brown-eye moth, European corn borer). But a variety of diseases affect pepper plants. Typical symptoms: young leaves are curled and get blisters or spots; plant growth is stunted. Viruses express themselves more frequently when growth stagnates (e.g., during cold periods) and may seem to disappear in the next generation of leaves on the plant. A latent viral infection is still present, however. Since viruses can bc transmitted by seed, do not save seed from virally infected plants unless the variety is endangered. Gardeners who smoke must take special care to avoid spreading the tobacco mosaic virus from cigarettes to pepper plants. Wash

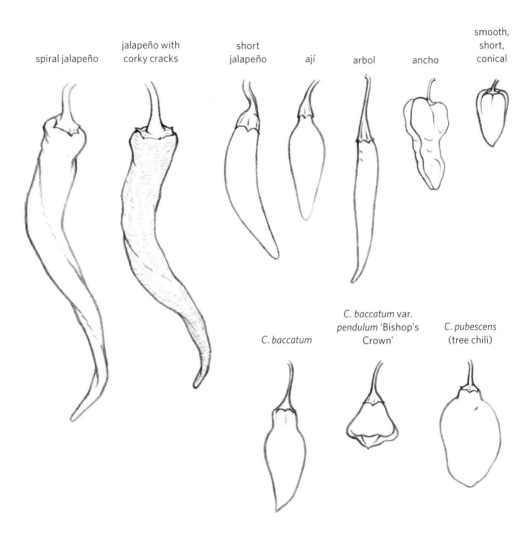

spiral jalapeño

jalapeño with corky cracks

short jalapeño

ají

arbol

ancho

smooth, short, conical

C. baccatum

C. baccatum var. pendulum 'Bishop's Crown'

C. pubescens (tree chili)

hands well after smoking (or, simpler but probably not easier, stop smoking).

Verticillium wilt is a fungal disease that can be a problem in greenhouses, especially in commercial growing, where crop rotation is neglected. Symptoms: first a few individual leaves, then the entire plant wilts. The fungus clogs nutrient pathways, and the plant becomes unable to take up water. The disease is easily diagnosed: cut a cross section at a node below a wilted leaf. Tissue infected with verticillium wilt has a brown discoloration. Treatment: remove infected plants. Prevention: do not grow peppers for four years at this location.

CULTIVATION HISTORY Wild peppers are native from Central America to the warm, temperate regions of southern South America. Most wild forms produce small, red fruits that stand vertically on the plant; the fruits are attractive to birds, who eat them and spread their seed. Since birds have no sensory receptors for spiciness, they do not feel the heat of these extremely hot fruits. Indigenous Americans domesticated these plants in at least three separate events. Domestication changed the plants: fruits now hang below the leaves and stay attached to their stems. Peppers are among the oldest crop plants of the western hemisphere. Archaeobotanical finds show that *Capsicum chinense* has been gathered since 8000 BC (cultivated since 2000 BC in Peru and 1500 BC in Chile), *C. annuum* gathered since 5000 BC (cultivated since 3500 BC in Mexico), and *C. baccatum* and *C. pubescens* gathered since 2500 BC in Bolivia.

Europeans took to the pepper quickly. In 1493, Columbus carried peppers (*Capsicum frutescens*) back with him to Spain; Spaniards brought *C. annuum* back with them 30 years later. In the 16th century, peppers arrived in eastern and central Europe from the Iberian peninsula. By about the middle of that century, the pepper had reached Italy and Hungary, and a multitude of pepper-based local dishes came into being. The extensive use of the pepper in these two countries led to the development of many new varieties, in particular, thick-fleshed varieties used for their raw flesh. Capsaicin-free varieties were bred in the 19th century, and mildly hot varieties came to be around the turn of the 20th century, through the accidental crossing of hot and sweet varieties.

Trade routes from Portugal brought

Capsicum baccatum var. *pendulum* 'Bishop's Crown' is also grown as an ornamental.

peppers to Asia; from there, the Turks carried it to the Balkans, and vegetable gardeners from the Balkans introduced the pepper to Austria. Eastern Austria sits in the Pannonian Plain, an area of rich loamy loess soil that makes for good pepper growing; 'Neusiedler Ideal', 'Wiener Calvill', and several other local varieties were developed here. In Hungary, peppers were grown as a cheap alternative to black pepper. A typically Hungarian use of the pepper plant is to dry and pulverize its fruits; indeed, the name for this spice in English, paprika, comes from the Hungarian word for pepper. The most important areas of pepper cultivation in Hungary are near Szeged on the Tisza river and around Kalosca on the Danube river.

EGGPLANT, AUBERGINE
Solanum melongena

Eggplants (UK: aubergines) are perennial plants from tropical India, but they are normally cultivated as annuals in temperate climates. Botanically speaking, the fruit is a berry, which is enjoyed broiled, roasted, steamed, or sautéed. Older varieties have prickly stems and sepals, traits that have been slowly bred away; newer varieties produce fruits weighing over 2 lb. (1 kg), though cold tolerance tends to be the main emphasis of modern breeding. Eggplants are medium-heavy feeders and need lots of water and warmth; they do not like cool nights. The leading producers of eggplant are China, Turkey, Japan, and Egypt.

WHAT YOU'LL NEED
- six to 12 healthy plants
- support poles and string
- overly ripe fruits that have fully changed color and may be mushy

POLLINATION NOTES Eggplants are self-fertile outcrossers. Honeybees and bumblebees are their primary pollinators. To secure an early fruit set, shake plants often as soon as they flower. Multiple varieties will more than likely cross when grown near each other. Isolation distances depend upon location. In temperate central Europe, 330 ft. (100 m) is sufficient, but ⅓ mile (500 m) is recommended in the tropics. As with peppers, mechanically isolating individual flowers can also be effective. Always keep some original seed in storage, to be safe. Perhaps an interesting new variety will come into being through accidental cross-pollination, but if the result is unwelcome (or the variety is rare), it is best to have that backup.

GROWING FOR SEED Except for allowing fruits to progress beyond eating ripeness,

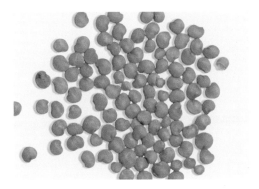

Eggplant seeds

growing eggplant for seed is the same as growing for food; and cultivation is the same as for the tomato, except that it is not necessary to prune suckers. As for peppers, removing the first flower encourages vegetative growth and fruit development. For a fast fruit set and bushier growth habit, shorten shoots; otherwise the plant will need support poles. In cooler climates, the best fruits may be produced by cutting back to two or three main branches and allowing only two fruits per branch.

HARVEST Seeds are not ripe until the fruit has completely changed color. White-fruited varieties turn golden yellow, purple varieties turn dark brown, green varieties turn yellowish green. The seeds themselves are light brown. If the growing season is too short to ripen seeds, plants can be brought to a heated indoor space to finish ripening, or whole plants can be uprooted and hung upside down indoors. Separating ripe seeds from the flesh of the fruit can be tedious and time-consuming. Seeds are easiest to remove from fruits that have become soft and mushy. Fruits can be cut into thin strips the long way and seeds can be pressed out with a rolling pin or scraped out with a spoon. Clean seeds in a sieve with water. Dry in coffee or tea filters; no more than a teaspoon of seed per filter. Some seed propagators have had success with fermenting seeds (see "Wet Processing with Fermentation").

The large flowers of the eggplant attract many insects.

SELECTION CHARACTERISTICS Eggplant varieties are extremely diverse, from small and round to large and elongated or pear-shaped. Fruits can be white, yellow, green, red, purple, light or dark violet, or black. Some varieties are even striped or marbled. Potential selection criteria:

- true-to-type fruit shape
- uniform color and pattern for all fruits

'Green Apple' eggplant is green when eating ripe, yellow when seeds ripen.

- plentiful fruit set
- fruit retains eating ripeness for a long time
- tender skin of fruit
- absence of bitter compounds
- earliness
- cold tolerance
- lack of thorns on sepals and/or stems

DISEASES AND PESTS There are no known seed-borne diseases. Spider mites are a problem in organic eggplant cultivation, the eggplant apparently being the spider mite's favorite food. Young plants become infested indoors and then follow the plants when they are planted out. The best preventative measures: anything that encourages rapid, vigorous growth of seedlings and introducing beneficial insects (mesostigmata: parasitic mites). Potato beetles and aphids like to munch on the leaves of eggplants grown outdoors. Greenhouse whiteflies (*Trialeurodes vaporariorum*) can cause problems in greenhouse culture. Again, parasitic mites can be used.

CULTIVATION HISTORY The eggplant comes from tropical India. The exact wild form is unknown, but a certain small, prickly bush in northern India is believed by many to be it. Occasionally one reads that the eggplant is from Africa, which is untrue. The likely wild form carries its bitter green fruits upright at the ends of stalks; they turn yellow when ripe. It is not known when exactly the eggplant was domesticated, but there is a name for it in Sanskrit. It reached China in the 5th century AD, the Arabic world by sea in the 7th century, and Persia by the 8th century. Arabs brought it to Spain in the 10th century; it was in Italy by the 15th century and in the rest of Europe by the 17th century. The first eggplants to be grown in central Europe and England had white, egg-shaped fruits (hence one common name); these are still the most widespread varieties in tropical Africa and southeast Asia. "Aubergine" is the French version of the Spanish *berenjena*, which itself is derived from the Arabic *bâdhingân*. Most eggplants available in supermarkets are hybrids.

Various shapes of eggplants

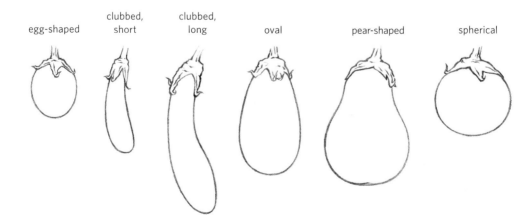

egg-shaped   clubbed, short   clubbed, long   oval   pear-shaped   spherical

GROUNDCHERRY
Physalis peruviana

The fruits of the groundcherry are orange-yellow and about the size of a cocktail tomato. Fruits grow in a papery husk until maturity, at which point they often break through. When stored with the husk, they keep for weeks. Fruits have a sweet-sour taste and lots of pectin; they are eaten raw, in jellies and compotes, and dried. The plant is a highly branched bush that grows to be about 3 ft. (1 m) tall when grown outdoors, 6 ft. (2 m) when grown indoors. Another species, the strawberry ground-cherry (*Physalis pruinosa*), is grown like any other groundcherry; it is smaller, and its brown berries ripen early and have a unique flavor. Chinese lantern (*P. alke-kengi*), another close relative, is often grown as an ornamental.

WHAT YOU'LL NEED
- six to 12 healthy plants
- support poles or trellis

POLLINATION NOTES The flower is perfect and self-pollinates. Cross-pollination can occur, according to the literature, but we have never observed it at Arche Noah.

GROWING FOR SEED The groundcherry is a perennial in warm, frost-free regions but is grown as an annual where it freezes in the winter. Plants can withstand temperatures as low as 23°F (–5°C) when the root ball is dry. The time of ripening of the fruit is highly dependent on location, anywhere from late summer to early fall. Growing under glass or plastic can speed ripening by several weeks, though with lower yield as plants put more energy into growing leaves.

Grow like tomatoes, though sucker removal is not necessary. Pruning makes for an easier harvest. Plants are very drought tolerant, though yield is better when they are watered well in hot weather.

Groundcherry seeds

The fruit of the groundcherry grows inside a lantern-like husk.

HARVEST To clean seeds, put fruits in a container with some water and mix with a hand mixer. Seeds separate best from the flesh of overripe fruits. For eating-ripe fruits, crush them in a container with water and let them soak for a day before cleaning. Add lots of water to the fruit-seed puree and stir. Good seeds sink to the bottom. Carefully pour off the pulp and nonviable seeds from the top, then repeat two or three times until water is clear. Seeds should be completely free of pulp. Wash seeds in a very fine-meshed sieve and lay out or hang in a coffee filter to dry.

SELECTION CHARACTERISTICS
- size and aroma of fruit
- husk
- earliness
- reduced vegetative growth (perhaps also small size of bush), yet no reduction in yield

DISEASES AND PESTS No diseases or pests have caused any crop damage at Arche Noah.

CULTIVATION HISTORY As the epithet suggests, the species presumably comes from the Peruvian Andes, but the wild form is found all over South America. Cultivated varieties were first bred in southern Africa. Seafarers brought the plant there over 200 years ago; they carried it on ships to prevent scurvy. Groundcherries are now cultivated in Central and South America, southeast Asia, and Australia.

TOMATILLO
Physalis ixocarpa

Like the groundcherry, the tomatillo grows inside a papery husk until it is ripe, when it usually bursts through. Fruits can be eaten raw, ripe or unripe, but it is the taste of unripe fruits that most people prefer. Depending on the variety, plants can grow to be 1–3 ft. (30–100 cm) tall. Ripe fruits range in color from yellowish green to yellow or white.

WHAT YOU'LL NEED
- six to 12 healthy plants

POLLINATION NOTES Tomatillos are self-infertile, making them obligate crossers. At least two plants must be grown together for fruit set to occur. Use an isolation distance of at least 500 ft. (150 m) between multiple varieties grown at the same time.

Ripening tomatillos burst through the husk and may turn purple with exposure to light.

GROWING FOR SEED Grow like tomatoes; pruning suckers is not necessary. Growing for seed is the same as growing for food.

HARVEST Seeds have ripened when the fruit is fully grown. With very ripe or overripe fruits, seed extraction and cleaning can be accomplished with water in a bowl. For hard fruits, use a hand mixer (see groundcherry for more details).

SELECTION CHARACTERISTICS Different varieties produce different-sized fruits. Potential selection criteria:

- vigorous growth
- fruit size
- color of fruit
- yield
- earliness
- resistance to splitting (the fruits of flatter-shaped varieties split far more often than globose varieties)

DISEASES AND PESTS Though tomatillos rarely have problems with pests, they are subject to the various viral diseases that affect nightshades. Growers in cooler regions have reported fruits contracting a tough, black, as yet unidentified fungus. Since this can likely be spread by seeds, destroy infected fruits.

CULTIVATION HISTORY The wild form grows in Mexico and Guatemala. The tomatillo was domesticated in southwest Mexico, where it is called *miltomatl* or *tomate verde* and used as the basis for salsa verde, a green, usually hot, sauce.

POTATO
Solanum tuberosum

The potato, introduced from the New World to the Old less than 500 years ago, is an important food staple around the world. Potatoes come in every imaginable shape, size, color, and texture; for example, those who have made or tasted Austrian dumplings or Swiss scrambled potatoes, both made from potato dough, know that these dishes can only be made with fluffy, dry-textured "floury" potatoes. Yet the diversity remaining within this one crop plant pales in comparison to the spectrum of varieties originally brought to and developed in Europe, not to mention the diversity found in the potato's areas of origin.

WHAT YOU'LL NEED
- 25 to 30 potatoes

POLLINATION NOTES Potatoes are selfers, for the most part. They are propagated by seed only for breeding purposes. Vegetative propagation is the standard method for maintaining varieties.

PROPAGATION We recommend presprouting potatoes to get a head start on growth (up to four weeks!) compared to non-sprouted potatoes, as well as to help fight diseases like potato blight (*Phytophthora infestans*). Place tubers in flats at 50–60°F (10–15°C) about four weeks before planting out. Tubers should get light but no direct sunlight. Ideally the tubers will produce shoots 0.5 in. (1 cm) in length from every eye with well-defined root bumps. Harden off sprouted tubers before planting out to avoid damage from the cold.

Potatoes like well-manured soils, though the manure should be applied the previous autumn. At the same time, one of the potato's great strengths is that it also grows in meager soils.

Plant potatoes out in mid to late spring. If you are unsure about the best planting date in your area, ask area farmers and gardeners. Planting distances: 20–28 in. (50–70 cm) rows, 12 in. (30 cm) apart within the row. Plant potatoes 3–4 in. (8–10 cm) deep. Plant into hilled rows: hill soil up about 8 in. (20 cm) high with a plow or hoe, so the soil can warm up faster and to improve drainage. Plant tubers with sprouts facing up in small holes made in the hilled rows. When above-ground foliage has grown to about 8 in. (20 cm) high, hill up soil again. This helps increase yield, as new tubers are formed by shoots covered with soil.

Cultivate potatoes as early in the year as possible to help avoid aphid attacks and viral infections. Viruses cause tubers to get smaller from year to year, which reduces overall yield. Viruses are spread by aphids. When the first generation of aphids appears and one aphid infects one potato, it takes three weeks for the virus to travel from leaf to tuber. The virus is then planted out again the following year unless new virus-free seed potatoes are acquired. For these reasons, we

'Arran Pilot' is a favorite heirloom potato in the United Kingdom, prized by gardeners for its taste, scorned by commercial growers for its lack of uniformity.

recommend the following two-step preventative measure during cultivation:

1. Set out insect monitor cards. Start checking regularly in early summer to see if any aphids are stuck to the cards. Three weeks after the first aphid is found, it's time for step 2:

2. Pull up the green, above-ground shoots of potato plants. Simply rip out the entire above-ground portion of the plant. It may be easiest to stand directly on the hill plants are growing in, to hold tubers underground with your feet while you pull the bushes out. The tubers of these plants will be smaller, but they will have ideally been kept virus-free and can be used as seed potatoes the next year. Allow tubers to ripen in the ground for two weeks, so their skin can harden. Do not cut stems! The resultant wound would be an ideal place for aphids to suck the juices of the potato plant.

A fully fledged plant can grow from each eye of a potato. Yet for each potato, half the eyes are better developed than the other half. To encourage all eyes to develop their full potential, cut tubers in half (except for a small "bridge" connecting the two) two weeks before planting out.

If you have very few seed potatoes of a given variety, production can be maximized by cutting down tubers to one eye per piece. Simply cut each eye out, along with a cylindrical portion of potato flesh; an apple corer works well for this. In this way, you can get up to about 10 seed potato pieces from one tuber. Wait until the wounds have dried before planting in pots. When new roots have established themselves, plant out in the garden more densely than you would otherwise plant potatoes.

HARVEST Harvest tubers to be used as seed potatoes the following year by pulling the bushes early, as described in step 2. Otherwise, wait until the above-ground foliage dies off, usually in early autumn. Leave tubers in the ground for two weeks after the foliage dies before harvesting, to harden their skin.

Store potatoes in dark, well-ventilated conditions at low temperatures (35–39°F [2–4°C]). Sprouting should be inhibited until late winter, so that sprouting can take place with maximum vigor in spring. Cellars with dirt floors are ideal, but only

A Swiss potato specialty

Maluns is a typical dish of scrambled or long-fried potatoes from the Swiss canton Graubünden. It is made with 'Parli', a traditional "floury" potato variety with sunken eyes. This cultivar is unusually high in starch and remains relatively dry when boiled, yet does not crumble. Parboiled potatoes are quickly skinned in one "yank," then mashed and sautéed for a long time in butter with wheat flour and salt—a hearty meal for hard-working farmers.

if freezing is an impossibility in all corners, as this can kill the tubers. Potatoes should not be kept with apples, which emit ethylene gas, thus shortening the life of any vegetable stored with them.

SELECTION CHARACTERISTICS Selection should not be based merely on shape, size, and health of the tubers but also on the vigor and health of the foliage. Mark the best-looking and most vigorous bushes with a pole, and harvest seed potatoes only from these plants. Ideal seed potatoes are mid-sized. Further selection criteria may include:

• shape and color of tuber (inner and outer)
• good skin development
• earliness
• storage life

DISEASES AND PESTS The biggest problem in potato cultivation regardless of the region is potato blight (*Phytophthora infestans*). Symptoms: starting in early summer, foliage first turns brown, then a silvery white fungal layer forms on the undersides of leaves, leading to an early death of plants. The disease can spread further on tubers in storage. Prevention: plant with sufficient spacing for good air circulation in the foliage; plant only in areas with good air circulation; do not grow potatoes directly following tomatoes or near tomatoes in the same year; apply stinging nettle and horsetail slurry. Treatment: remove and destroy (burn or hot compost) afflicted foliage (tubers can be eaten). Tubers from infected plants can be used as seed potatoes only when the foliage was removed early enough; otherwise, the tubers themselves are also infected, and the disease will likely spread in storage and in the following crop. Early potato varieties are at lower risk of potato blight than late varieties.

Various viruses pose an additional threat and cause a reduction in yield from year to year. Symptoms vary. A mild infection may go undetected. In more serious cases, leaves may turn yellow and curl up and/or be stunted. Tubers do not grow to be very large. We recommend pulling the greens of plants that appear to have a virus; do not further propagate such plants. Prevention: find a so-called field-resistant variety that yields well despite infection. Such varieties can be hard to find. If you come across a variety that is grown year after year in a garden or field and yields never go down and plants never appear sick, this is likely a field-resistant variety.

The Colorado potato beetle (*Leptinotarsa decemlineata*) can cause significant crop damage in some years. The beetle crawls out of its winter quarters around the time dandelions start to bloom. It feeds on the foliage of potato plants and leaves eggs behind on leaf undersides. Two weeks later, red larvae with black spots on their sides emerge. In severe cases, the beetles can defoliate an entire crop. Treatment: early and regular collection and removal of beetles, eggs, and larvae. In rare cases, apply a Bt (*Bacillus thuringiensis*) solution. This should truly be the exception and not the rule, as regular use of this organic pesticide can quickly lead to a buildup of resistance in the potato beetle. Another unwelcome pest is the wireworm (the larvae of various beetles of the family Elateridae). They often appear after grasslands are plowed and gnaw on roots, thereby killing plants, and chew holes and tunnels into tubers. Prevention: not using fresh manure in amending soil, encouraging natural enemies like hedgehogs and birds. Treatment: cut potatoes into slices and bury as a decoy; dig up after a few days, and collect and destroy wireworms. Slugs may also appear after plowing up grasslands and cause even larger holes in tubers than wireworms. Nematodes (*Globodera rostochiensis* and *G. pallida*), or roundworms, also affect potatoes. Pinpoint-sized cysts are found on roots in early to mid summer; these contain roundworm eggs. Symptoms: stunted growth, wilted leaves. Prevention: not growing any crops in this garden for three to four years, especially nightshades, chenopods, and sorrel.

CULTIVATION HISTORY Eight thousand years ago, the potato was already an important crop plant for the indigenous peoples of South America, and in the Peruvian and Bolivian Andes, it remains, along with corn (maize) and beans, a staple food to this day. Potatoes thrive at altitudes that are too cool for corn. Andean farmers plant many potato varieties together, but certain dishes are each prepared with only one variety.

The potato appears to have been brought independently and separately to Ireland, England, and Spain. It took around 200 years for it to really take off in the Old World. The first Europeans to have potatoes were royal families and their gardeners: Clusius, the gardener at the Imperial Botanical Gardens in Vienna, provided the first botanical description of the "Papas Peruvianum"; the first European to grow potatoes on a field scale was the Prussian Great Elector Friedrich Wilhelm in 1651.

Sources of Seed and Equipment

ORGANIZATIONS FOR MAINTAINING CROP DIVERSITY

Austria
Arche Noah
arche-noah.at/etomite

Canada
Seeds of Diversity Canada
seeds.ca

France
Association Kokopelli
kokopelli-semences.fr

Germany
Agro Coordination
agrarkoordination.de

Dreschflegel
dreschflegel-verein.de

Kiekeberg Open-air Museum
kiekeberg-museum.de

Kultursaat
kultursaat.org

VEN
nutzpflanzenvielfalt.de

Italy

Heirloom Gardening Association, South Tyrol
sortengarten-suedtirol.it

Laimburg Research Center for Agriculture and Forestry
laimburg.it

Seed Savers Italy
civiltacontadina.it

Spain

GRAIN (Genetic Resources Action International)
grain.org

Sweden

SESAM
foreningensesam.se

Switzerland

Alpine Crop Association
berggetreide.ch

Berne Declaration
evb.ch/en

Pro Specie Rara
prospecierara.ch

United Kingdom

Garden Organic
gardenorganic.org.uk

Millennium Seed Bank Partnership
kew.org/science-conservation/
save-seed-prosper/millennium-seed-bank

Plants For A Future
pfaf.org

Seedy Sunday
seedysunday.org

USA

Native Seeds/SEARCH
nativeseeds.org

Seed Savers Exchange
seedsavers.org

Veganic Agriculture Network
goveganic.net

International organizations

Bioversity International
bioversityinternational.org

Global Crop Diversity Trust
croptrust.org

SAVE (Safeguard for Agricultural Varieties in Europe) Foundation
save-foundation.net

Save Our Seeds
saveourseeds.org

Slow Food
slowfood.com

ORGANIC SEED: BREEDING, PRODUCTION, SALES, AND SUPPLIES

Austria

ReinSaat
reinsaat.at

Canada

Annapolis Seeds
annapolisseeds.com

Greta's Organic Gardens
seeds-organic.com

Heritage Harvest Seed
heritageharvestseed.com

Hope Seed
hopeseed.com

Salt Spring Seeds
saltspringseeds.com

Terra Edibles
terraedibles.ca

Tourne-Sol Co-operative Farm
fermetournesol.qc.ca

William Dam Seeds
damseeds.com

France

Baumaux Samen
graines-baumaux.fr

Germany

Bingenheimer Saatgut
oekoseeds.de

Bio-Saatgut
bio-saatgut.de

Dreschflegel
dreschflegel-saatgut.de

Grüner Tiger
gruenertiger.de

Munich Environmental Institute
umweltinstitut.org

Italy
Arcoiris
arcoiris.it

Netherlands
De Bolster
bolster.nl

Switzerland
Biosem
biosem.ch

Research Institute of Organic Agriculture
organicxseeds.com

Samengärtnerei Zollinger
zollinger-samen.ch

Sativa
sativa-rheinau.ch

United Kingdom
Chiltern Seeds
chilternseeds.co.uk

Edwin Tucker
edwintucker.com

Harrod Horticultural
harrodhorticultural.com

Jekka's Herb Farm
jekkasherbfarm.com

Laura's Organics
laurasorganics.co.uk

Nicky's Nursery
nickys-nursery.co.uk

Organic Gardening Catalogue
organiccatalogue.com

Organic Growers Alliance
organicgrowersalliance.co.uk

Otter Farm
shop.otterfarm.co.uk

Real Seed Catalogue
realseeds.co.uk

Sea Spring Seeds
seaspringseeds.co.uk

Secret Seeds
secretseeds.com

Seed to Plate
seedtoplate.co.uk

Stormy Hall Seeds
stormy-hall-seeds.co.uk

Terwins Seeds
terwinseeds.co.uk

USA
Abundant Life Seeds
abundantlifeseeds.com

Albert Lea Seed
alseed.com

Arbico Organics
arbico-organics.com

Baker Creek Heirloom Seeds
rareseeds.com

Bountiful Gardens
bountifulgardens.org

Deep Diversity Seed
onegarden.org/deep.htm

Fedco Seeds
fedcoseeds.com

Johnny's Selected Seeds
johnnyseeds.com

Peaceful Valley
groworganic.com

Sand Hill Preservation Center
sandhillpreservation.com

Scatterseed Project
gardeningplaces.com/scatterseed.htm

Seed Savers Exchange
seedsavers.org

Seeds of Change
seedsofchange.com

Southern Exposure Seed Exchange
southernexposure.com

Territorial Seed Company
territorialseed.com

DISPLAY GARDENS

Austria
Arche Noah
arche-noah.at/etomite

Germany
Dreschflegel
schaugarten.kuhmuhne.de

VEN
vern.de/schaugarten/lehr-und-
schaugarten-greiffenberg-uckermark-
vern-e-v

Switzerland
Erschmatt Botanic Garden
sortengarten.ch

Pro Specie Rara Berry Garden
prospecierara.ch

Wildegg Castle
musee-suisse.ch

United Kingdom
Ryton Gardens
rytongardens.co.uk

USA
Seed Savers Exchange
seedsavers.org

INFORMATION ON BIODYNAMICS

Germany
Zentrale Präparateversorgungsstelle
praeparatezentrale.de

Switzerland
Rainer Sax
demeter.ch

United Kingdom
Biodynamic Association
biodynamic.org.uk

USA
Biodynamic Farming and Gardening
  Association
biodynamics.com

Demeter Association
demeter-usa.org

International organizations
Demeter International
demeter.net

BIBLIOGRAPHY

Arche Noah. 2001. *Gemüse Inkognito. Verges-sene Kulturpflanzen vergangener Jahrhun-derte.* Arche Noah, Schiltern.

————. 2002. *Ursprung und Verwandlung.* The story of the emergence of cultivated varieties using the examples of carrots, tur-nips, wheat, plums, and lettuce. Arche Noah, Schiltern.

————. *Sortenhandbuch.* Annually published yearbook. Arche Noah, Schiltern.

Ashworth, Suzanne. 2002. *Seed to Seed.* Seed Savers Exchange, Decorah, Iowa.

Barfuss, Josef. 1894. *Die Gurke. Ihre Kultur im freien Lande und unter Glas.* The cucumber: growing outdoors and in the greenhouse. Neudamm.

Bartha-Pichler, Brigitte, and Markus Zuber. 2002. *Haferwurzel und Feuerbohne. Alte Gemüsesorten—neu entdeckt.* Aarau.

Becker-Dillingen, Josef. 1938. *Handbuch des Gesamten Gemüsebaus einschliesslich des Gemüsesamenbaues, der Gewürz- und Küchenkräuter.* Berlin.

Brancucci, Michael, and Erica Bänzinger. 2000. *Das grosse Buch vom Kürbis.* Küttigen.

Crüger, Gerd. 1991. *Pflanzenschutz im Gemüsebau.* A handbook for commercial growers. Stuttgart.

Dreschflegel e.V. (ed.). 2001. *Saatgut und Phlanzenzüchtung für den ökologischen Gemüsebau in Deutschland, Dreschflegel.* Witzenhausen.

Forschungsinstitut für biologischen Landbau, FiBL (ed.). 1999. *Krankheits- und Schädlings-regulierung im Biogemüsebau.* Frick.

————. 2002. *Hilfstoffliste.* List of allowed and recommended materials for organic agricul-ture. Frick.

Franke, Wolfgang. 1989. *Nutzpflanzenkunde.* Stuttgart.

Fritz, Dietrich, and Werner Stolz. 1989. *Gemüsebau.* A handbook for commercial growers. Stuttgart.

Geier, Bernward. 1982. *Biologisches Saatgut aus dem eigenen Garten.* Essen.

Gladis, Thomas. 1989. Die Nutzung einhei-mischer Insekten (Hymenopteren und Dip-teren) zur Bestäubung von Kulturpflanzen in der Genbank Gatersleben. *Die Kulturpflanze* 37:79–126. Berlin.

————. 1994. Aufbau und Nutzung einer Mas-senzucht von Eristalis tenax (Diptera, Syr-phidae) in der Genbank Gatersleben. *Insecta*: 92–99. Berlin.

Gladis, Thomas, Karl Hammer, and Martina Hethke. 2002. *Kürbis, Kiwano & Co.* Cata-log to the exhibition of the same name.

Guillet, Dominique. 2002. *The Seeds of Koko-pelli: A Manual for the Production of Seeds in the Family Garden: A Directory of Heri-tage Seeds.* Avignon.

Heistinger, Andrea. 2001. *Die Saat der Bäuerin nen.* The seeds of peasant women. Innsbruck.

Helm, Johannes. 1954. *Lactuca sativa* aus morphologischer Sicht. *Die Kulturpflanze* 2. Berlin.

Heynitz, Krafft, and Georg von Merckens. 1983. *Das biologische Gartenbuch: Gemüse, Obst, Blumen Rasen auf biologisch-dyna-mischer Grundlage.* Stuttgart.

Horneburg, Bernd. 2003. *Frischer Wind für eine alte Kulturpflanze!* Dreschflegel, Witzenhausen.

Ingruber, Daniela, and Martina Kaller-Dietrich (eds.). 2001. *Mais. Geschichte und Nutzung einer Kulturpflanze.* Frankfurt.

Islek ohne Grenzen. 1999. *Das Buchweizenbuch.* The buckwheat book. Arzfeld.

Jahn, Marga. 2003. Saatgutbehandlung im ökologischen Landbau. verbraucherministerium.de/forschungsreport/rep1-02/kap03.htm.

Keller, Fritz, Jürg Lüthi, and Kurt Röthlisberger. 1986. *100 Gemüse.* Zollikofen.

Köchlin, Florianne. 2005. *Zellgeflüster. Streifzüge durch wissenschaftliches Neuland.* Basel.

Körber-Grohne, Udelgard. 1995. *Nutzpflanzen in Deutschland.* Stuttgart.

Kreuter, Marie-Luise. 1991. *Pflanzenschutz im Biogarten.* Munich.

———. 1996. *Der Biogarten.* Munich.

Kunert (ed.). 1902. *Hampel's Gartenbuch für Jedermann.* Hampel's gardening for all. Berlin.

Kunz, Peter. 2002. *Gesunde Kulturpflanzen - eine Herausforderung.* Self-published, Hornbrechtikon (getreidezuechtung.ch).

Küster et al. 1999. *Korn. Kulturgeschichte des Getreides.* Corn: the history of the cultivation of grain. Salzburg.

Larkom, Joy. 1991. *Oriental Vegetables: The Complete Guide for the Gardening Cook.* London.

Lorey, Heidi. 2002. *Tartuffli. Alte Kartoffelsorten neu entdeckt.* Münster.

Lucas, Eduard. 1905. *Der Gemüsebau. Anleitung der Kultur der Gemüse im Mistbeet, Garten und Feld für Gärtner, Gartenfreunde und Landwirte.* Growing vegetables: a guide to growing vegetables in hotbed, garden and field for home gardeners, market gardeners and farmers. Stuttgart.

Machatschek, Michael. 1999. *Nahrhafte Landschaft: Ampfer, Kümmel, Wildspargel, Rapunzelgemüse, Speiselaub und andere weiderentdeckte Nutz-und Heilpflanzen.* Vienna.

Mansfeld's World Database of Agricultural and Horticultural Crops. http://mansfeld.ipk-gatersleben.de/mansfeld.

Paris, Harry. 1989. Historical Records, Origins and Development of the Edible Cultivar Groups of *Cucurbita pepo* (Cucurbitaceae). *Economic Botany Band* 43(4). New York.

Phillips, Roger, and Martin Rix. 1993. *Vegetables.* London.

Reiter, Curt. 1926. *Samenkunde gärtnerischer Kulturpflanzen und die Grundzüge des Samenbaus.* Berlin.

Riegler-Fabianek, Daniela. 1997. *Niederösterreichische Bäuerinnen kochen.* The cooking of lower-Austrian farm women. Innsbruck.

Robinson, Raoul. 1996. *Return to Resistance: Breeding Crops to Reduce Pesticide Dependence.* Davis, California.

Roger, Peter. 1996. *Wie die Kartoffel im Kanton Zürich zum Heiland der Armen wurde.* Zurich.

Sattler, Friedrich, and Eckard v. Wistinghusen. 1989. *Der landwirtschaftliche Betrieb. Biologisch-Dynamisch.* Stuttgart.

Storl, Wolf-Dieter, and Paul Silas Pfyl. 2002. *Bekannte und vergessene Gemüse. Heilkunde, Ethnobotanik, Rezepte.* Aarau.

Strobl, Heidi. 2001. *Der Kürbis. Rund und g'sund.* St. Pölten.

VEN. *Samensurium.* Annually published yearbook. Schandelah.

Vogel, Georg. 1996. *Handbuch des speziellen Gemüsebaus.* Stuttgart.

Zander, Robert. 1993. *Handwörterbuch der Pflanzennamen.* 14th ed. Stuttgart.

GLOSSARY

AWN Needle-shaped lamina. Awns are the extensions of husks for many cereal grains (rye, barley, bearded wheat varieties). They can be several centimeters long.

BERRY A fruit that is still soft and juicy when ripe. The most common berries in the vegetable world are squash, tomatoes, and peppers.

BIODYNAMIC AGRICULTURE A way of practicing organic agriculture based on the anthroposophy of Rudolf Steiner. Biodynamic farmers and gardeners seek to harness the energies and rhythms of nature to strengthen crops and livestock and to enhance soil fertility by producing and using so-called biodynamic preparations.

BOLTING The act of a plant sending up a flower stalk. The term is often used to describe plants that flower early, which is usually an indication of stress due to drought, heat, too much moisture, or soil compaction. For fennel and other plants that are sensitive to it, it can be a reaction to day length. For most crops, varieties differ widely in their resistance to bolting, but differences can also occur within a variety. Do not save seed from plants that bolt in the first year when they are not supposed to produce seed until the second year (root vegetables, Swiss chard, onions, leeks, etc.).

CAPSULE A type of fruit made of two or more carpels, or female reproductive organs. They sometimes have holes for ripe seed to fall out, or explode when ripe to spread seed.

COMMERCIAL VARIETY A variety that is professionally bred and sold in stores.

CROSS-POLLINATION This may refer to the "normal" transfer of pollen from one flower to the stigma of another or the (undesired unless done intentionally) transfer of pollen from one variety of species to the stigma of a flower of another variety of the same species.

CULTIVAR A cultivated variety, as opposed to a wild variety.

DAY LENGTH For some annual plants, the length of day (the amount of time between sunrise and sunset) determines when plants blossom. There are short-day, long-day, and day-neutral plants. Long days are days over 12 hours. Long-day plants flower in the summer, when days are longest. Most vegetables are day neutral (e.g., cucumber, tomato).

ETIOLATION When flowering plants are grown in the absence of light, they produce long, weak, pale stems.

HAND POLLINATION Pollen from the flower of one plant is manually transferred to the stigma of the flower of another plant. This is done to maintain varietal purity of a variety or to intentionally cross one variety with another. Free, open pollination is prevented.

HEIRLOOM VARIETY A variety that has been slowly selected and bred in a region by the farmers and gardeners of that region and is thus well adapted to local conditions. Self-pollinating varieties tend to form pure, distinct types; with outcrossers, lines between different types blur.

HERBIVORY The consumption of plants by animals.

HULL, HULLED The seeds of some cereal grains (most wheats, naked barley, rye) are not enclosed in hulls and can be easily threshed. Other, hulled grains (barley, spelt) are tightly enclosed in tough hulls; these grains must be hulled (that is, the hulls are to be removed) before eating.

INSECT MONITOR CARDS These cards are hung in the garden; they are colored yellow to attract a wide variety of insects and covered with a non-toxic adhesive to catch said insects. Whiteflies, leafminer fleas, winged aphids, fungus gnats, flea beetles, and more are attracted to these cards and stick to them, thus allowing gardeners to monitor what kinds of insect pests are inhabiting their gardens. Caution: beneficial insects can also be trapped by these cards.

LAMINA The usually flat, upper part of a leaf. It is also called the blade and is connected to the rest of the plant by the leaf stem.

MILPA A kind of agriculture from Central America involving growing corn (maize), beans, and squash together in a polyculture.

MYCELIUM A web of fungal hyphae (the vegetative growth of certain fungi).

NEEM INSECTICIDE An organic insecticide made from extracts of the crushed seeds of neem trees, which are native to India. Use of neem insecticides must be specifically approved on certified-organic farms.

NEW WORLD See Old World.

OLD WORLD Name for Asia, Africa, and Europe, as opposed to the Americas, which make up the New World.

OPEN-POLLINATED The genetic traits of open-pollinated plants are passed on in a continuous flow from parent plants to their offspring (not the case for hybrid varieties). Local, heirloom and most organic varieties are open-pollinated.

ORGANIC AGRICULTURE Organic agriculture is a way of farming that involves working with natural cycles and processes as much as possible. This approach can also be applied to gardening. The main goal is handling natural resources (water, air quality, soil fertility) in the most sustainable way possible. Organic farmers and gardeners seek to maximize production within the general framework of organic agriculture. They forgo the use of chemical fertilizers, drugs for livestock, synthetic pesticides, and the like in favor of environmentally friendly principles and methods. Maintaining soil fertility is at the heart of an organic farm. "Organic" is a regulated term that can be used only by growers and processors that meet certification standards.

OUTCROSSER A plant whose flowers are self-infertile, meaning they require pollen from a different plant.

POLYCULTURE The growing of different crops close together (whether in neighboring rows, mixed within rows, or mixed within a patch) for mutual benefit: one crop may repel a pest of another crop, another crop may benefit from chemicals exuded by the roots of its neighbor (allelopathy), space may simply be more efficiently used, etc.

PRECULTURE The process of germinating seeds indoors under controlled conditions. This is done so that relatively large plants can be planted outdoors after the last spring frost (which would have otherwise killed seedlings). This is also a method by which the growing season can be extended to give plants enough time to produce ripe seed. Precultured plants need to be "hardened off" before being planted out, that is, be slowly acclimated to outdoor conditions (direct sun, wind, etc.).

PRUNING SUCKERS The removal of new shoots growing in the axils between branches and the main stalk. This is usually done by hand. The purpose is to encourage the plant to put less energy into leaf development and more energy into fruit development.

RAISED BEDS A style of vegetable bed that is hilled up 8–12 in. (20–30 cm) above grade, or ground level.

SEEDPOD The fruit type characteristic of brassicas and legumes. Pods are dry and full of seeds when ripe. They may dehisce (explode) when ripe.

SELFER A plant whose flowers can accept pollen from other flowers of the same plant.

STRAIN Crops whose name, origin, or identity are not known for certain. The term is often used instead of the term "variety," and strains are often named after people or places.

SUBTERRANEAN CLOVER (*Trifolium subterraneum*). A clover species that, thanks to its low, spreading growth habit, makes for an ideal natural mulch when undersown with cabbage and carrots. It winterkills below zone 7. Studies have shown that sub clover, as it is often called, repels carrot flies and cabbage leaf beetles.

THRESHING The manual or mechanical separation of seed from the stalk of a plant.

TILLER A shoot that grows after the main shoot emerges from a seed. This is a desirable trait in cereal grains, for example, in that multiple stems and, ultimately, multiple ears form from each seed.

TRUE-TO-TYPE A specimen that displays representative attributes of a variety is considered to be true-to-type. In practical terms, that means that a true-to-type plant is growing from seed that was not crossed and shows no unusual traits. To maintain a variety as true-to-type, save seed only from true-to-type plants.

UNDERSOWING Sowing seed of another crop with or slightly later than the main crop such that the undersown crop grows in the understory. This is done to benefit the main crop by suppressing weed growth, repelling pests, etc. The main crop may have a dual function by acting as a nurse crop for the undersown crop, as when cereal grains are undersown with a grass/alfalfa mixture for hay.

VARIETY A variety is a type within a species that is uniform, consistent, and can be differentiated from others.

INDEX

ABOUT THE AUTHORS

Andrea Heistinger

Andrea Heistinger works professionally as an agronomist, author, and educator, focusing on the fields of plant breeding for organic agriculture, the practical knowledge of farmers and gardeners, and women in agriculture. She studied agriculture at BOKU, the University of Natural Resources and Life Sciences, Vienna; her publications include *Die Saat der Bäuerinnen*, *Handbuch Bio-Gemüse*, *Handbuch Bio-Balkongarten*, and numerous articles. She lives and works in the Waldviertel region of Austria and in South Tyrol, Italy.

Arche Noah

Arche Noah—Society for the Maintenance and Promotion of Crop Diversity was founded in 1990; by 2012, its membership had grown to more than 10,000. About 150 members propagate and offer seed through Arche Noah's yearbook, which is free to all members (there is a modest shipping fee for non-members). The collection focuses on central and eastern European cultivars; saplings and scion wood from fruit trees are also offered.

The society maintains a display garden at Austria's Schiltern Castle, where hundreds of cultivars from the Arche Noah collection are grown out annually. The plant and seedling market, held every 1 May in Schiltern, has become an annual tradition; at it, Arche Noah and many of its members offer seedlings and seeds of heirloom varieties for sale or trade. Arche Noah members organize many such markets around Austria. Arche Noah also publishes its own magazine (three times per year), does extensive public outreach (exhibitions, tastings) and lobbying in the field of crop diversity, and provides members with information about rare varieties and seed-saving techniques. A large database of cultivars and other information can be found on Arche Noah's website, arche-noah.at.

Pro Specie Rara

The foundation **Pro Specie Rara** was founded in 1982 in St. Gallen, Switzerland. Pro Specie Rara was thinking globally and acting locally before that catch phrase existed, through its work in preserving the genetic and cultural heritage of livestock and plants. Pro Specie Rara sees crops and livestock as living cultural artifacts that characterize regional landscapes, the loss of which would also mean the loss of cultural identity. A further purpose of the foundation is to curate knowledge of old varieties and breeds. For example, the Rätisches Grauvieh, a relatively undemanding, robust cattle breed, had at the time of Pro Specie Rara's founding almost disappeared through crossing with Brown Swiss cattle. Thus began the adventure of rounding up the last individuals that could be found from remote Alpine valleys to establish a new herd. Enthusiasts formed breeding organizations, and the breed has been successfully maintained ever since.

Multiple display gardens, orchards, and farms are at the heart of Pro Specie Rara. Enthusiasts can draw from the foundation's "seed library" through its yearbook, published each January. Those who order are asked to produce seed and return some to Pro Specie Rara to help maintain the variety. About 100 varieties from Pro Specie Rara's collection are now being sold commercially with the help of some business partnerships. A cooperative has also been established that has engaged in such projects as marketing wooly pig breeds and fruit trees and educating the public about diversity. More information at prospecierara.ch.

About the translator

Ian Miller was born in Dubuque, Iowa, and graduated from the University of California, Santa Cruz, with a degree in environmental studies, emphasis agroecology. He worked on biodynamic farms in the Austrian province of Carinthia for two years, was the garden crew leader at Seed Savers Exchange in Decorah, Iowa, for two years, and is a certified scything instructor with the Sensenverein Österreich (Austrian Scything Association). He and his wife and daughter currently split their time between Vienna, Austria, and Decorah, Iowa, where they have a small homestead and offer workshops on various aspects of low-capital farming.